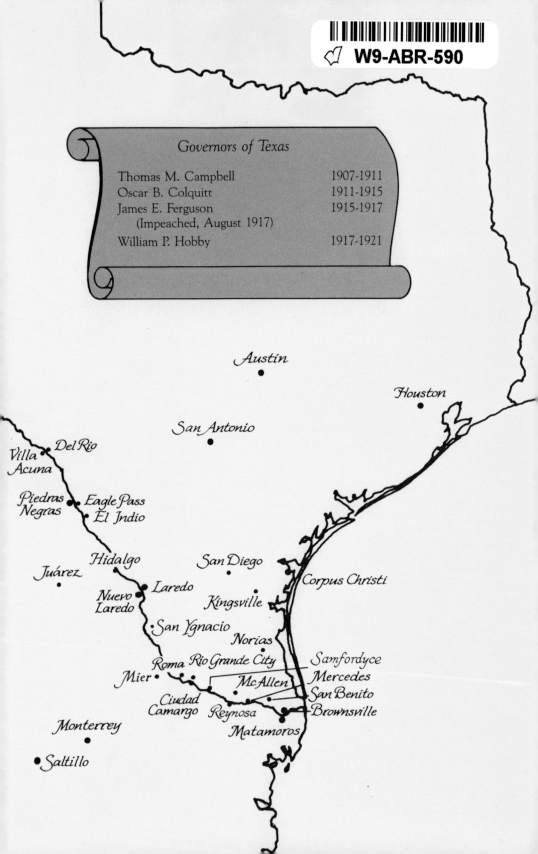

Governors of Texas

Thomas M. Campbell	1907-1911
Oscar B. Colquitt	1911-1915
James E. Ferguson	1915-1917
(Impeached, August 1917)	
William P. Hobby	1917-1921

Austin

Houston

San Antonio

Del Rio

Villa Acuna

Piedras Negras

Eagle Pass
El Indio

Hidalgo

Juárez

San Diego

Nuevo Laredo

Laredo

Kingsville

Corpus Christi

San Ygnacio

Norias

Roma

Rio Grande City

Samfordyce

Mier

McAllen

Mercedes

Ciudad Camargo

San Benito

Reynosa

Brownsville

Monterrey

Matamoros

Saltillo

Texas and the Mexican Revolution:

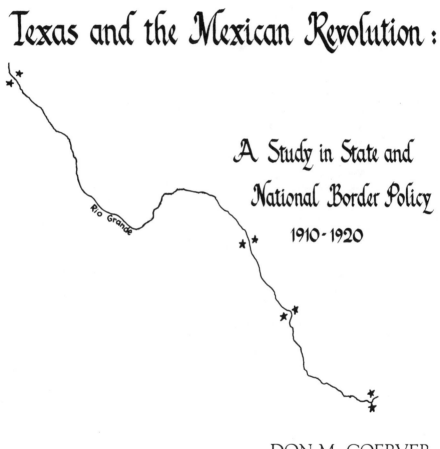

A Study in State and National Border Policy 1910-1920

Rio Grande

DON M. COERVER
LINDA B. HALL

TRINITY UNIVERSITY PRESS

Library of Congress Cataloging in Publication Data

Coerver, Don M., 1943-
  Texas and the Mexican Revolution.

  Bibliography: p.157
  Includes index.
  1. United States–Boundaries–Mexico. 2. Mexico–
Boundaries–United States. 3. Texas–History–1846-1950.
4. Mexico–History–Revolution, 1910-1920. 5. United
States–Foreign relations–1910-1913. 6. United States–
Foreign relations–1913-1921. I. Hall, Linda B. (Linda
Biesele), 1939-   . II. Title.
F786.C653 1984   976.4'4   84-2510
ISBN 0-939980-05-3
ISBN 0-939980-06-1 (pbk.)

The following have generously given permission to use the photographs in
this book: The Barker Texas History Center; the Harry Ransom Humanities
Research Center, The University of Texas at Austin; the Historical Museum,
Fort Huachuca; the Arizona Historical Society.

Portions of this book appeared in slightly different form in *Revolution on the
Rio Grande: Governor Colquitt of Texas and the Mexican Revolution, 1911-1915*
(Occasional Papers Series of the Border Research Institute), Trinity Univer-
sity, 1981.

Art and calligraphy by Keith and Toni Cheshire

Printed in the United States of America

Printed by Best Printing Company
Bound by Custom Bookbinders

Trinity University Press, San Antonio, Texas 78284

For Marie Louise, Leslie, and Douglas

Acknowledgments

The authors would like to thank the staff of the Library of Congress who greatly facilitated the use of the Hugh Lennox Scott Papers. Special appreciation goes to Dr. David B. Gracy II, director of the Texas State Archives, and his research assistants for their guidance in coping with the extensive correspondence associated with the governor's office and other state agencies. Donald E. Everett of Trinity University shared with us his extensive knowledge of San Antonio history and pointed us toward new sources of information. Donald E. Worcester of Texas Christian University provided his usual valuable editorial insights. We extend our thanks to Darlene Gladders and Ruth Ver Duin for their typing of the various versions of the manuscript and to Jennifer Jenks and David Robertson for their help in preparing the index. Finally, we would like to acknowledge the support of the late Señora Marie Therese G. de Díaz; keeper and protector of the personal archives of Porfirio Díaz, she was present at the beginning of this project but unfortunately did not live to see its completion.

Contents

List of Illustrations

Texas and the Mexican Revolution

Introduction:
A Decade of Revolution on the Rio Grande

In 1910 few persons in Texas or in Mexico would have forecast that the Rio Grande region was about to enter into the most violent period of an area with a considerable history of conflict. Having long been a place of turmoil and confrontation, the border zone seemed to have achieved a permanent degree of political stability by the early twentieth century; the Rio Grande Valley also appeared to be entering a new phase of economic development. The outbreak of revolution in Mexico, however, demonstrated the fragility of the political and economic advances that had taken place during the previous three decades. Once revolution developed on a significant scale in northern Mexico, it was impossible to keep it from spilling over the border into South Texas. Officials on both sides of the river and on all levels of government were unprepared for the extent and the duration of the violence and dislocation which were to follow.

The governors of Texas during this revolutionary decade—Oscar B. Colquitt, James E. Ferguson, and William P. Hobby—were in a particularly difficult situation both politically and militarily. With the Rio Grande comprising approximately one-half of the United States-Mexican boundary, Texas found itself on "the firing line"—as Governor Colquitt liked to characterize it—far more than any other state. A central feature of the revolutionary turmoil between 1910-1920 was the number of "twin cities" along the river, several of which were important targets for revolutionary factions. The most important of these paired cities was El Paso-Ciudad Juárez. A bewildering array of revolutionary groups contested for Juárez, with control of the city actually shifting on seven different occasions between 1911 and 1919. Each time the city changed hands or threatened to change hands, there was another "crisis at Juárez" with attendant problems for local officials in El Paso and state officials in Austin. The ongoing crisis at Juárez was the most persistent and most dangerous of the twin-city problems, but major difficulties occurred at other locations along the river, such as Brownsville-Matamoros and Laredo-Nuevo Laredo. Even smaller communities such as Presidio-Ojinaga and Eagle Pass-Piedras Negras often found themselves caught up in the revolutionary turbulence of the period.

The internal development of the Revolution of 1910 also placed major importance on the Rio Grande region. Two Mexican states which played leading roles throughout the military phase of the Revolution were on the Texas border: Coahuila and Chihuahua. The original leader of the Revolution, Francisco Madero, came from Coahuila; the first chief, Venustiano Carranza, also hailed from that state. Chihuahua was the power base for revolutionary figures such as Pascual Orozco and Pancho Villa. Both states were the scenes of heavy fighting throughout the revolutionary decade, and the northern location of the hostilities encouraged a brisk trade in arms and other military supplies across the Rio Grande. The illegality of such trade during much of the period made additional demands on state and federal authorities on the Texas side.

In the U.S., local, state, and federal officials all influenced – and were influenced by – the border situation and the search for a border policy. Efforts to coordinate the activities and harmonize the attitudes of officials at various levels led to friction, professional jealousy, misunderstanding, and jurisdictional disputes. Local and state officials normally worked in harmony, but there were frequent problems between state and federal authorities. Much of the problem lay in the fact that the state was trying to formulate a border policy while the federal government was attempting to implement a foreign policy. The governors of Texas, especially Colquitt, thought in terms of a border policy with little attention as to how it might conflict with or promote the broader "Mexican policy" being pursued by Presidents William Howard Taft and Woodrow Wilson. This tension was worsened by the approaches to the Mexican situation being taken at the federal level. Taft's cautious policy and Wilson's "watchful waiting" had the appearance on the Texas border of no policy at all. When Wilson did abandon his "watchful waiting" in 1914 over an incident in the Gulf port of Tampico, it seemed inconsistent and disproportionate to border observers familiar with the loss of life and property along the Rio Grande.

The number of federal agencies involved in the formulation and implementation of border policy also added to the growing friction in federal-state relations. The White House often failed to keep other departments of the executive branch adequately informed of its actions. Taft formed a Maneuver Division of the army in Texas without consulting or notifying in advance his own secretary of state. Wilson's personal approach to diplomacy frequently left the War Department and even the State Department uninformed about Mexican planning. A variety of federal agencies had jurisdictional concerns relating to border policy. The Department of State had overall responsibility for U.S.-Mexican relations, of which border policy was a part. The War Department had to deal with all aspects of border security as well as aid other agencies in enforcement of various federal laws. The Department of Justice and its Bureau of Investigation dealt with violations of federal law along the border and also conducted intelligence operations. The Treasury Department handled international trade matters but also was an important source of military and diplomatic information. The Department of Commerce and Labor was responsible for immigration matters. With so many agencies pursuing so many overlapping functions, there were frequent jurisdictional disputes and lapses in communication.

Compounding the problem was the involvement of the state government in federal activities. Throughout the revolutionary decade, the state aided in the enforcement of various federal laws. This arrangement was generally informal, but during the Taft-Colquitt era it became a formal relationship, with the federal government paying for expenses incurred by the state in the enforcement of federal laws. While both federal and state officials could see the advantage in such a format, it was of doubtful legality and further confused the already unclear jurisdictional boundaries. When state administrators attempted to enlist federal aid in enforcing Texas laws, the fusion and confusion of authority and responsibility was complete. Adjutant General Henry Hutchings unintentionally summarized the federal-state situation with a remark that appeared in the *San Antonio Express* of November 19, 1911, concerning enforcement of the federal neutrality laws: "I don't know anything, and I am not positive about that."

Bureaucratic problems of a different sort on the Mexican side also complicated border relations. From 1911 to 1915 it was difficult for any revolutionary faction to claim with accuracy that it governed Mexico. Even when one group controlled Mexico City, there might be two or more groups that controlled various parts of the Mexican states along the Rio Grande. The murder of U.S. citizen Clemente Vergara highlighted the problem of having more than one faction attempting to pass itself off as governing one of the border states; in early 1914 at the time of Vergara's killing, Nuevo León had governors from two different factions. Later, officials appointed by Venustiano Carranza contested for legitimacy with supporters of Pancho Villa at both the state and local levels along the Rio Grande. During one of the periodic "crises" at Juárez in February 1912, three different persons claimed to be mayor of that city. United States policy contributed to the confusion by refusing to recognize any government between February 1913 when Madero was overthrown and October 1915 when Carranza received de facto recognition.

Much of the thrust of border policy came from the action or inaction of Woodrow Wilson. As president during most of the revolutionary decade, he was in the best position to influence U.S.-Mexican relations as well as border policy. In terms of experience, personality, and philosophy, however, Wilson was poorly equipped to deal with the border problems arising out of the Mexican Revolution. Wilson's primary concern was with domestic affairs; as champion of the progressive cause at the national level, he supported a broad range of domestic reforms of which he enjoyed considerable success implementing. In the field of foreign policy, however, Wilson was inexperienced; he compounded this problem by appointing William Jennings Bryan, who was even less suited for the conduct of foreign affairs, as secretary of state. When Bryan resigned in protest over the president's handling of the *Lusitania* incident, Wilson did appoint an able and experienced diplomat, State Department Solicitor Robert Lansing, as secretary of state. Wilson, however, frequently bypassed Lansing and his department in his handling of foreign policy. Wilson and the State Department shared a European orientation in foreign policy which made it difficult to deal with Latin American affairs in general and border problems in particular. The president also often found it hard to synchronize his foreign policy and his military policy. In late 1916 and early 1917, the United States was pursuing a foreign policy which was rapidly leading to a confrontation with Germany while militarily the Wilson administration was overwhelmingly committed to the U.S.-Mexican border. Similarly, in 1919 Wilson was moving in the direction of intervention in Mexico while simultaneously engaging in a rapid demobilization of the U.S. armed forces after the end of World War I.

Wilson's idealistic view of the conduct of foreign policy often put him at odds with more realistic—or at least, more directly affected—officials in Washington, Texas, and Mexico. Texas governors, army officers, and federal officials often found it difficult to make their immediate concerns about border security coincide with Wilson's world view of liberal capitalism, hemispheric unity, and self-determination. The president himself became caught in the inner tension between trying to teach the Mexicans to be good democratic capitalists and attempting to protect American economic interests in Mexico. Unable to harmonize the basic principles of his own foreign policy, it is not surprising that he found it difficult to harmonize his Mexican policy with border needs or Carranza's demands.

The situation on the Texas-Mexican border from 1910-1920 was not the product of any one individual's actions, whether that individual was Wilson, Carranza, Villa, or Colquitt, but was instead the culmination of almost a century of development in the region. The Rio Grande as a boundary was a legal concept; it was, in fact, an integrating factor rather than a divisive one. Social, cultural, religious, and economic relationships transcended the international frontier. The true function of the Rio Grande was to identify a region rather than to delineate a border. Even if there had been no Juárez crisis of May 1911 or Columbus raid of 1916, the Revolution of 1910 would have had a profound effect on South Texas. So closely was South Texas linked to northern Mexico that a political upheaval in one was bound to have a major impact on the other. The governors of Texas—whether they acted correctly or not—at least had some insight into the indivisibility of the region; officials in Washington, and also in Mexico City, often showed little appreciation for that fact. As a result, a decade of revolution on the Rio Grande led not only to conflict between Texas and Mexico; it also produced disagreement between Austin and Washington.

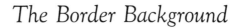

The Border Background

Long before the tumultuous decade of 1910-1920, the Rio Grande region had been a major area for friction and interaction between Texas and Mexico. The Texas Revolution of 1836 not only led to the establishment of an independent Republic of Texas; it also generated long-running disputes over the status of Texas and its boundaries. Mexico refused to recognize the independence of Texas, maintaining that it was merely a rebellious province and not a separate political entity. Even if Mexico had recognized the Republic of Texas, it was not prepared to accept the Rio Grande as its southern and western boundaries.

The ambiguous status of Texas—internationally recognized republic, rebellious Mexican province, incipient target for U.S. annexation—encouraged thrust and counterthrusts by both Texans and Mexicans. The government of Texas launched the ill-fated Santa Fe Expedition in 1841 to establish its claim to the area east of the upper Rio Grande. After an arduous march of more than 1,000 miles, the expedition arrived in New Mexico disheartened and disorganized. Mexican forces easily defeated the Texas troops, sending the survivors to Mexico as prisoners. Mexico responded to the Santa Fe Expedition with two incursions into South Texas in 1842. Both invasions resulted in brief occupations of San Antonio, a considerable amount of unease among Texans owing to their lack of a regular army, and demands for a declaration of war against Mexico which Sam Houston prudently ignored. The Texans did retaliate by launching another expedition into northern Mexico. The target on this occasion was Mier, Tamaulipas, but the outcome was similar to the one at Santa Fe. The operation was a dismal failure as well, with some of the participants even winding up in the same prison as the survivors of the Santa Fe Expedition.[1]

Border conflict continued after Texas became a state in 1845. One such clash in April 1846 served as the basis for the U.S. declaration of war against Mexico. When a Mexican cavalry detachment attacked a squadron of American dragoons north of the Rio Grande, President James K. Polk asked for and received congressional approval for a war against Mexico. The Treaty of Guadalupe Hidalgo which ended the war in 1848 also ended the lengthy dispute over the southern boundary of Texas. Mexico agreed in the treaty to recognize the Rio Grande as the line of demarcation between Texas and Mexico. The border region, however, continued to pose major problems for authorities on both sides of the boundary.

The Rio Grande not only delineated an international boundary; it also identified a frontier region, the area being at a considerable distance from the political and economic centers of Mexico. While few in number, the population was overwhelmingly Mexican in origin. Physical and legal obstacles to movement across the border were virtually nonexistent. Inhabitants of the region viewed the Rio Grande as a connecting force rather than as a line of division. Indeed, the conduct of economic activity virtually ignored the international boundary. Residents were little disposed to distinguish between commerce and smuggling, a distinction which was literally viewed as unprofitable. Cattle rustling was especially popular along the river with rustlers being willing to steal from and sell to either Mexicans or Texans. Virtually the only time in which the Rio Grande served as a barrier was when law enforcement officials—usually North Americans—found their pursuit of criminals stopped by the international boundary. Lawless elements on both sides of the border found the Rio Grande a convenient shield for their operations. South Texas also proved a congenial place for Mexican politicians who found themselves out of favor and out of office. San Antonio in particular became the unofficial capital for Mexican exiles plotting revolution; former and future presidents often used the city as headquarters for their revolutionary juntas.

While bandit raids and Indian attacks continued to trouble the border region in the 1850s, more serious political and military dislocation occurred in the 1860s. Mexico emerged from a three-year civil war between conservative and liberal forces in 1861 only to face foreign occupation by French troops who were supporting the establishment of an empire under the Austrian archduke, Maximilian. Maximilian's efforts to establish control between 1864 and 1867 led to extensive conflict that was a mixture of civil war, war of national resistance, and liberal revolution. With the liberals and the conservatives struggling for the Mexican heartland, the tenuous control exercised from Mexico City over the frontier during normal conditions virtually disappeared in many areas. Mexico had two different governments attempting to rule it: Maximilian's administration which was centered in Mexico City and a liberal regime under Benito Juárez which operated from wherever it could find a safe haven. The withdrawal of the French and the execution of Maximilian in 1867 ended this schizophrenic political situation, but the confusion of centralized authority had long-term implications for the frontier. A decade of civil war and foreign intervention had seriously undermined what little control central authorities had exercised along the Rio Grande. With state and local officials in northern Mexico often unable or unwilling to fill this jurisdictional vacuum, the situation on the border continued to deteriorate in the 1870s.

The situation was only slightly better on the Texas side of the river. Texas had seceded from the Union in February 1861 and the following month joined the Confederacy. While Texas participated actively in the war that followed and the last battle of the conflict took place near Brownsville, there was little fighting between Union and Confederate forces in most of the state.[2] With the central government of the Confederacy a distant force at best and with the state government at Austin preoccupied with waging the war, problems on the border intensified. Many supporters of the Union fled to northern Mexico while Indians, deserters, and border bandits posed major problems along the Rio Grande despite efforts by state and Confederate officials to control the area. The state government organized a special force known originally as the Frontier Regiment to maintain order on the Rio Grande. Reorganized in 1863, it retained its status as a state force throughout the war. The Confederate government also assigned a regiment to border duty under the leadership of John S. Ford, well-known Ranger and Indian fighter. Men living in frontier counties were exempt from regular conscription into the Confederate army so that they might be available for service on the frontier.

During the immediate postwar period, the political situation in Texas remained confused while the military situation on the border experienced major changes. Many Confederate soldiers, especially Texans, fled to Mexico following the defeat of the South. While President Andrew Johnson and the U.S. Congress fought over control of the readmission process for the former Confederate states, Texas found the influx of additional troops a mixed blessing. Units of the Union army introduced a military occupation of Texas, and there were major problems with black troops sent into the state. Most Texans deeply resented this northern-imposed "reconstruction" process, but there were benefits in it for the border region. Much of the occupation force served on the Rio Grande both to maintain law and order in the area and to apply pressure on the French forces in Mexico to withdraw. Mexican bandits and Indians continued to raid along the river, however, despite these additional forces.[3]

While the political situation in Texas showed improvement, peace on the border and political stability in Mexico continued to be elusive. The lawless maintained their operations along the border with little interference from Mexican officials; often state and federal authorities in northern Mexico were in league with the elements they were supposed to suppress.[4] The central government in Mexico City displayed a relative degree of stability as long as Benito Juárez, leader of the resistance against the French, occupied the presidency. The death of Juárez in 1872 set off a scramble for power that would finally see General Porfirio Díaz, another military hero of the 1860s, lead a successful revolution that would place him in the presidency in 1877.

The Border and the Recognition Question

Díaz anticipated little difficulty in obtaining diplomatic recognition from the U.S. government, especially since he had promised that Mexico would continue to pay claims owed to American citizens. This hope for early recognition encountered one major obstacle: U.S. disenchantment with the situation on the border. The government wanted to link recognition with an agreement on border problems; in particular the State Department wanted Mexican permission for U.S. forces to cross the international boundary in pursuit of bandits and Indians.[5]

The centrality of the border issue to the extension of recognition demonstrated how important the border region had become in U.S.-Mexican relations in general. In many respects the situation along the Rio Grande was little improved over the turbulent years of the 1830s and 1840s. The area continued to be lightly populated on both sides of the boundary, with most of the population Mexican in origin. There was so much interaction across the border that virtually no one distinguished between Mexicans and Mexican Americans; certainly the Anglo population rarely made such a distinction. Even the economic situation contributed to the general instability along the border. Since much of the region could not support a stable economy, especially agricultural, many turned to smuggling and cattle rustling, which were highly organized businesses by the 1870s. Profits from smuggling were so lucrative that illegal trade was seen as a major drain on financial resources that might otherwise have gone into legitimate business activities.[6]

The level of lawlessness prompted authorities on both sides of the international boundary to depend heavily upon regular army troops to maintain order. Although both Mexico and the United States concentrated their forces on the frontier, both armies often lacked adequate forces for the task of maintaining control in the region. General Edward Ord, commander of the military department of Texas, had fewer than 3,000 troops under his command, a figure which represented approximately one soldier for each 120 square miles. Ord's running feud with his immediate superior, General Philip Sheridan, further reduced the effectiveness of his already limited forces. The military situation in Mexico was even less encouraging. Several of the generals on the border also exercised a considerable amount of political power which gave them a degree of independence from central authorities and complicated the problem of enforcing law and order. In fact, many army officers were actively engaged in the very lawless activities that they were supposedly trying to suppress. Mexican forces were poorly trained and equipped, and coordination among military units along the boundary was limited.[7]

The use of South Texas as a base for launching revolutionary activities against the Mexican government also destabilized the region. Porfirio Díaz himself had used Texas to organize his successful revolution of 1876. There was rarely a shortage of exiled Mexicans or adventurous Texans ready to answer the call to revolution. One ambitious insurrectionary announced the establishment of a group with headquarters in Austin which had the goal of forming a 50,000-man army to attack Mexico. This rebel leader optimistically appointed himself "Generalissimo of the Army of Occupation of Mexico" and designated the southwestern part of the United States as the "Department of the Rio Grande." While the "Army" never materialized and the "Generalissimo" soon disappeared, Mexican officials could not afford to take lightly any exile threat no matter how improbable it appeared. One Mexican politician betrayed the uneasiness these activities caused when he denounced "the excitable Texans who are always ready for anything relating to a piratical war against a neighboring country."[8]

The Reciprocal-Crossing Treaty of 1882

One of the principal reasons for the United States withholding recognition of the Díaz regime was a desire to get some advance commitment from Díaz on a border-crossing agreement. The position of the American government generally had been that U.S. forces had the right to engage in "hot pursuit" of bandits or Indians across the international boundary. American forces would normally ask Mexican officials for permission to cross but would do so anyway if permission was not granted. This informal policy was given official status by the War Department with the issuance of the so-called Ord Order of June 1, 1877. Under the order, General Ord had authority to dispatch troops across the Rio Grande at his own discretion. The Mexican government responded by issuing an order of its own on June 18, 1877, directing military officials along the border to cooperate with American commanders but to use force to block any crossing of the border by U.S. troops. Ord literally sidestepped any potential military clash by ordering his forces to cross only when there were no Mexican troops in the area.[9]

Díaz successfully resisted efforts by the United States to obtain advance concessions as a prerequisite for recognition, and the United States recognized the Díaz regime in April 1878. Revocation of the Ord Order in February 1880 further improved the climate for negotiations on border problems. The United States continued to stress the importance of a border-crossing agreement, but the major obstacle was American reluctance to make crossing reciprocal, a point which national honor and border stability required, according to the Mexican government. Since it was apparent that most of the crossing of the international boundary would be done by American forces, the United States dropped its opposition to permitting Mexican forces to enter into U.S. territory. In July 1882, both sides agreed to a reciprocal-crossing treaty which was subsequently approved by the U.S. and Mexican senates.[10]

The restrictions placed on crossings under the treaty reflected decades of experience between the two countries. Crossings were to take place only in deserted areas at least two leagues (5.2 miles) from population centers. There were to be no crossings at all from a point fifty-two miles above Piedras Negras to the mouth of the Rio Grande. Commanders leading troops across the boundary were to inform the nearest military or civil authorities of their marching plans. The pursuing force was to return to its own territory after it had engaged the group it was following or in the event that it lost the trail. Any abuses committed by forces during a crossing would be punished by the government to which the forces belonged.[11]

These restrictions clearly were designed to avoid any clashes between military forces of the two nations and to keep to a minimum the amount of time that forces would be in pursuit on foreign soil. The agreement spared the Mexican government the embarrassment of having American forces on its soil without permission, and the reciprocal nature of the treaty also helped the Mexican government claim that the national honor had been preserved. One restriction of major significance to the Rio Grande area was the fact that the treaty covered only Indian attacks and not bandit raids. While Indian incursions from northern Mexico continued to pose major problems in New Mexico and Arizona, they were of diminishing concern along the Texas-Mexican boundary where bandit activities of various kinds became the major problem. Nevertheless, the agreement was a basic feature of border policy in the 1880s and 1890s and served as a precedent for efforts to formulate another reciprocal-crossing program during the revolutionary decade of 1910 to 1920.

The Boundary Treaty of 1884

Border problems along the Rio Grande even included the river itself. Seasonal fluctuations in the volume of water carried by the river produced changes in both the river's bank and channel. Shifts in the channel in turn created small islands in the river; the doubtful jurisdictional status of these islands soon made them centers for illegal activities such as smuggling and rustling. There had been unsuccessful efforts in the 1870s to reach an agreement which would settle these jurisdictional difficulties. A dispute over the island of Morteritos near Roma, Texas, was the occasion for a treaty which would clarify the boundary status. Following a change in the river channel in early 1884, town officials at Roma occupied the island, claiming that it was in American territory. The Mexican government denounced this "invasion of an integral part of the national territory" and maintained that Morteritos was part of the state of Tamaulipas. The United States responded by ordering troops to occupy the island so that customs officials could carry out their duties. The threat of a military clash quickly evaporated when the U.S. secretary of war revoked the order and both parties agreed to negotiate a settlement.[12]

The Treaty of Guadalupe Hidalgo which ended the Mexican War in 1848 had provided that the boundary line was to follow the middle of the river channel; in the event that there was more than one channel, the boundary was to follow the deepest one. In the decades that had followed, the United States had unofficially developed its own policy on changes in the Rio Grande's course. In the event of gradual changes, the boundary would continue to follow the river; if there was sudden change, then the boundary would not follow the new course of the river but would remain in the middle of the old channel. In November 1884, the United States and Mexico signed a treaty which essentially incorporated the principles which had served as the unofficial basis for U.S. policy since 1848. The treaty also provided that the "normal channel" of the river was the one established by the original survey made in the 1850s under the provisions of the Treaty of Guadalupe Hidalgo. In 1889 both parties established the International Boundary Commission to handle problems arising out of changes in the course of the Rio Grande.[13]

The Pax Porfiriana

While the reciprocal crossing treaty of 1882 and the boundary treaty of 1884 helped to reduce friction along the Rio Grande, other nondiplomatic developments were assisting in promoting pacification of the border. One of the most important was the growing political stability of Mexico as Porfirio Díaz consolidated his political power in the 1880s and 1890s. Having come to power on a program of "effective suffrage and no reelection," Díaz felt compelled to step down from the presidency when his term expired in 1880. His handpicked successor was his long-time personal friend and political supporter, General Manuel González. González dutifully returned the presidency to Díaz in 1884. While many assumed that an unofficial policy of rotating the presidency between Díaz and González had developed, Díaz returned to the presidency in 1884 with no intention of retiring when his second term ended in 1888. Instead Díaz conducted a clever campaign to discredit González and isolate his political supporters.[14] Díaz was to serve as president without interruption from 1884 to 1911, at which time revolutionary activity forced his resignation. This unprecedented political stability gave Díaz an opportunity to reorganize the military and extend greater central control over the border region. It also gave Díaz the opportunity to cultivate powerful allies along the border such as the Madero and the Terrazas families who had their own personal interests to protect by decreasing hostilities in the area.

Economic developments also prompted major changes in the situation along the Rio Grande. Chief among these was the extension of the railroads into southern and western Texas in the late 1870s and into northern Mexico in the early 1880s. The first railroad line reached San Antonio in 1877; San Antonio soon had rail connections east to Houston and west to El Paso. Subsequently, various companies extended rail traffic to the Rio Grande Valley. At approximately the same time, a railroad construction boom was taking place in northern Mexico. The two most important railroads under construction in Mexico were destined to link Mexico City with the Texas frontier: the northern terminus of the Mexican National Railway was at Nuevo Laredo while that of the Mexican Central Railway was at Ciudad Juárez.[15] The extension of the railroads directed population shifts toward the underpopulated Texas-Mexican frontier and permitted more settled and diversified local economies. With improved transportation and communication in the region, both the U.S. and Mexican governments found it easier and faster to exercise control in outlying areas. Finally, the new railroads helped to open up northern Mexico to even broader American economic penetration with important implications for the Rio Grande zone.

Porfirio Díaz viewed political stabilization as not only an end in itself but also as a means to an equally important end: the economic development of Mexico. Díaz and his advisors were convinced that foreign capital and technology were essential to Mexico's economic development and that Mexico must create an environment which would attract foreign investors. American investors were quick to respond to this policy and soon came to play a dominant role in Mexican railroads, mining, land, and later oil.

U.S. financiers concentrated their investments in activities that were high in profile and often geographically close to the U.S.-Mexican border. Americans assumed a prominent role in mining activities in Chihuahua with El Paso becoming a major smelting and supply center for mining activities on both sides of the border. The El Paso Smelter, owned by the ASARCO interests, had become one of the largest smelting operations in the world by the first decade of the twentieth century.[16] U.S. citizens also invested heavily in Mexican land near the frontier, and several ranchers owned property on both sides of the boundary. By the mid-1880s the United States had replaced England as Mexico's principal trading partner, with much of the trade being funneled through Texas by the railroad systems.[17] The Texas oil boom which started in 1901 with the famous Spindletop discovery soon spread down the Gulf Coast to northeastern Mexico; Texas investors, mining engineers, managers, and skilled workers were central to the rapid development of the Mexican oil industry in the first decade of the twentieth century.

By 1910 American penetration of the Mexican economy had become so extensive that it was generating additional anti-American feeling as well as growing uneasiness over the development strategy being followed by the Díaz administration. While the United States was already the dominant foreign economic influence by 1900, American involvement increased even more rapidly between 1900 and 1910, American investments more than quintupled during the decade, reaching a total of more than one billion dollars by 1911. U.S. interests controlled most of the mining industry as well as the rapidly expanding petroleum industry. The United States continued to dominate Mexican trade, accounting for approximately sixty percent of Mexico's exports and imports during the period.[18] Foreigners—mostly Americans—also owned about one-seventh of Mexico's land surface, much of it in the northern border zone.[19] By 1910 the United States in general and Texas in particular had a major stake in continued political stability and economic growth in Mexico.

Decline and Revolution

In the early years of the twentieth century, the limitations of the Mexican development pattern with its emphasis on foreign investment and the export sector were becoming increasingly obvious. There had been notable achievements in certain areas, especially transportation and communication, but other sectors of the economy failed to keep pace and even regressed. In particular the rural sector, which comprised a majority of the work force and the population, experienced a decline in its already low standard of living.[20] Emphasis on the export sector also caused major problems. As demand for Mexican imports declined, domestic opponents became increasingly critical of Díaz' policies. Such policies linked the status of the Mexican economy with international economic conditions. When a downturn occurred in the United States in 1907, it quickly spread to the Mexican economy. The 1907 recession injured those who had most benefitted from the new prosperity, especially the rising middle class which was becoming increasingly restive in the face of fiscal and political restrictions. The worsening situation called into question not only the economic advances of earlier years but also the political wisdom of continuing the system presided over by the aging Díaz and his cronies.

Although such major problems existed, there was little indication in 1910 that the system which Díaz had carefully nurtured over the decades was on the verge of collapse. In the area of U.S.-Mexican relations, especially border problems, the two decades from 1890 to 1910 had been unusually calm. Indian raids across the international boundary had long since ceased to be a problem, and the general level of lawlessness on the border had undergone a considerable decline. Revolutionary activities by Mexican exiles in South Texas were virtually nonexistent for most of the period. A few traditional problems lingered on—the treatment of Mexicans in Texas and the Rio Grande boundary questions—but did little to detract from the widespread optimism about the growing economic vitality of the border region.

The first indication of problems to come was an increase in revolutionary activity along the border beginning in 1906. The Díaz government complained frequently about the activities of such revolutionary leaders as Jesús and Ricardo Flores Magón and was particularly agitated about the growing arms trade across the border which U.S. officials seemed unwilling or unable to stop. Since local, state, and federal officials were often at odds over their relative spheres of jurisdiction in such matters, they consequently found it difficult to furnish a coordinated response. Some of the authorities also had doubts about how serious the revolutionary threats were and how much of their limited resources should be devoted to dealing with them. The Mexican government often misinterpreted this confusion and uncertainty on the part of American officials as a lack of interest in the potential exile threat.[21]

Two events scheduled for 1910—the Mexican presidential election and the centennial of Mexican independence—served as further indicators of the deteriorating situation in Mexico and along the border. The presidential election focused attention on the Díaz system and the privileged position accorded U.S. economic and political interests in it. Even supporters of Díaz held a growing conviction that American interests must be curbed, especially in economic matters. Critics of the Díaz regime questioned the elaborate ceremonies marking the centennial of Mexico's political independence from Spain in view of the growing economic dependence of Mexico upon the United States. The more violent opponents were about to take action that would not only lead to the overthrow of Díaz but would also usher in a decade of unprecedented turmoil on the Texas-Mexican border.

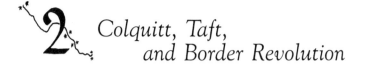

Colquitt, Taft, and Border Revolution

In 1910 elections took place in both Texas and Mexico that would have a long-range impact on U.S.-Mexican relations in general and border affairs in particular. The winner of the Texas gubernatorial election of that year was Oscar B. Colquitt. Colquitt—a lawyer and journalist with extensive political experience—had made an unsuccessful bid for the governorship in 1906 and in 1910 was a member of the powerful state railroad commission. He was considered the "conservative" candidate in the 1910 election, although this label was primarily the result of his position on the principal issue in the campaign, state-wide prohibition. Texas progressives strongly supported state-wide prohibition while Colquitt called for stricter enforcement of local-option laws. In winning the Democratic nomination and later the election, Colquitt had received important support from Mexican American voters who opposed prohibition. Prominent Mexican American political leaders in South Texas such as Francisco A. Chapa of San Antonio and Amador Sánchez of Laredo had helped turn out the "wet" votes that had produced Colquitt's narrow victory in the Democratic primary, which was tantamount to winning the governorship in heavily Democratic Texas. These political connections with Chapa and Sánchez would return to haunt Colquitt as governor when problems began to develop along the Rio Grande. Border policy was not an issue in the election since the situation along the international boundary was generally quiet. An election held in Mexico, however, would soon alter that.[1]

Election and Revolution

The Mexican presidential election of 1910 seemed to offer even less in the way of political excitement than the gubernatorial election taking place in Texas. The incumbent president, Porfirio Díaz, had originally come to power in 1877 on a program of effective suffrage and no reelection. After initially honoring his pledge by stepping down from the 1880-1884 presidential term, Díaz subsequently won reelection for every term between 1884 and 1910. There was little to indicate that substantial opposition might develop to yet another term for him in 1910. The issues in the election seemed to be the president's age—eighty—and his choice of a vice-presidential running mate, the widely unpopular Ramón Corral.[2]

The only real excitement in the campaign had been furnished by the candidacy of Francisco I. Madero, a member of a wealthy and politically connected family from the northern border state of Coahuila. Díaz was eager to showcase the prosperity and political "democracy" of his administration as the centennial of Mexico's independence approached, and he welcomed the Madero candidacy as proof that democratic processes had taken root in Mexico under his guidance. While the aging incumbent saw the public relations value of a harmless but high-profile opponent for the presidency, his reaction turned to dismay as he watched Madero generate considerable popular response. Madero's campaign came to an abrupt conclusion when he was arrested for helping one of his political supporters escape from the police. On election day in June, Madero was in jail at San Luis Potosí rather than at the polls. With the opposition in enforced retirement, Díaz and Corral moved to an easy victory in the elections. The Madero candidacy, however, set in motion a chain of events that would bring together the participants in the Mexican presidential campaign and the Texas gubernatorial campaign of 1910.

After the election, Madero posted bail with the restriction that he remain in San Luis Potosí. In October, however, Madero jumped bail and did what many other defeated Mexican political figures had done in the past; he went to Texas to plot against those who had been responsible for his defeat. Porfirio Díaz himself had used South Texas as a base for the revolution that eventually brought him to power in the 1870s. When Madero established his revolutionary headquarters in San Antonio, he continued a tradition which had been most recently exemplified in the political activities of the Mexican Liberal Party under the leadership of the Flores Magón brothers, Ricardo and Enrique. The *magonistas*, as they were called, had been active along the border between 1906 and 1910. Their "anarchist" and "socialist" tendencies had provoked a strong response from both state and federal authorities. With relations between the U.S. government and the Díaz administration on an unusually friendly basis, the federal government was especially active in pursuing political exiles; the Departments of State, Justice, War, Treasury, and Commerce and Labor mobilized their agents to deal with revolutionary activities along the border.[3]

Madero's plotting posed much greater difficulties for both state and federal authorities than had that of the Flores Magóns. Unlike the magonistas who labored with limited resources, Madero could rely upon important political and financial connections on both sides of the border. He was able to pay for the legal assistance that he needed in the United States and could finance his own intelligence network. Madero's revolution enjoyed a great deal of support among the border population, even among some officials. His political moderation also provided a marked contrast to the radical views of the magonistas. While the Flores Magón brothers agitated for a broad-based social revolution, Madero stressed political reform, emphasizing the need for effective suffrage and no presidential reelection. All of these factors required both state and federal officials to be more circumspect in their dealings with

Madero and his supporters.[4]

Texas authorities were only marginally interested in Madero's early activities, but federal authorities were closely monitoring his movements for possible violations of U.S. neutrality laws. Madero was very careful to avoid any appearance of violating these laws; he called his revolutionary pronouncement the Plan of San Luis Potosí and even backdated it to his last day in that town—October 5—to conceal the fact that it actually had been formulated later in San Antonio. Madero, however, had publicly stated that he was the head of a revolutionary junta, but in fact he had not taken any overt action from American soil to overthrow the Díaz regime.[5] State and federal authorities consequently were uncertain how to proceed against the *maderista* rebels.

Much of the government's uncertainty was due to confusion over interpretation and enforcement of federal neutrality laws, in particular the status of arms shipments. The official legal and administrative position held that it was permissible for any individual to purchase and export arms in any quantity so long as United States territory was not being used to equip an armed expedition against a government at peace with the United States. Under such an interpretation, it was completely legal for Madero to purchase arms in Texas and ship them to his supporters in Mexico, but it was illegal to organize armed bands of revolutionary exiles on U.S. soil. Federal officials in the field often did not understand this application of the neutrality laws and consequently pursued an inconsistent course in their enforcement. Contributing to the problem in general was the large number of federal agencies operating on the border. At one time or another, enforcement of the neutrality laws involved customs collectors for the Department of Justice, agents of the Bureau of Investigation, federal judges, and State Department officials. Despite this proliferation of agencies, federal officials were often short of investigative and enforcement personnel and called upon administrators of the State of Texas in implementing federal neutrality legislation. This informal cooperation in the enforcement of federal laws was of doubtful legality and often complicated enforcement procedures; when it evolved into more formal cooperation, it became the source of a series of federal-state disputes over the handling of border policy.[6]

The Revolution of 1910

Both state and federal officials were keeping Madero under close surveillance as the announced date for the beginning of the revolution—November 20, 1910—approached. Despite such precautions, Madero left San Antonio undetected and crossed into Mexico on the evening of November 19. Madero expected to find a large armed force of supporters; instead he found a small band of followers who were poorly organized and lacked weapons. After two days of fitful waiting, Madero returned to Texas to resume his plot ting against the Díaz regime. So secretive and unsuccessful was this initial effort at revolution that federal authorities were unable to produce concrete evidence that Madero had broken the neutrality laws. Nevertheless, Madero's revolution was gaining momentum along the border even though Madero's personal part in it was minimal, which led the Díaz administration to put growing pressure on the U.S. government to take action against him. More and more rebels, particularly in the northern Mexican states, were answering Madero's call to revolution and pressing the attack against the Díaz government.[7] By the time Oscar B. Colquitt assumed the governorship of Texas in January 1911, a "border problem" had developed with new and more threatening dimensions.

Governor Oscar B. Colquitt outside his home in Dallas, Texas. *Photograph courtesy of the Barker Texas History Library Collection.*

In dealing with the growing troubles along the Rio Grande, the new governor found himself in a difficult tactical and political position. Any efforts to step up law enforcement activities along the border would involve the Texas Rangers, but Colquitt had called for the reduction of the Ranger force in his 1910 campaign. Many considered the Rangers an embarrassing anachronism which had no place in modern, twentieth-century Texas. Others criticized the Rangers for their use of violence and their mistreatment of Mexican Americans, especially in the Rio Grande Valley. Since Mexican American votes in South Texas had played an important role in Colquitt's election, he assigned top priority to curbing the Ranger force which was already well under its authorized strength of eighty men. After two months of the new administration, the entire force consisted of only twelve men operating out of two posts along the Rio Grande. Another tool at the governor's disposal in dealing with the border was the Texas National Guard. While it had not fallen on such hard times as the Ranger force, it too was limited with its total strength fewer than 3,000 troops. Furthermore, Colquitt was reluctant to call out state troops because of the jurisdictional problems which such an action might produce with local officials and because of the expense involved in such a move.[8]

The increased revolutionary activity in northern Mexico led to growing problems for local, state, and federal officials. A potential crisis appeared in early February 1911, when rebel forces under Pascual Orozco threatened an attack on the major federal stronghold of Ciudad Juárez across the Rio Grande from El Paso. Any attack on Juárez brought with it the possibility of a major international incident for several reasons. For one, large numbers of Americans crossed into Juárez on a daily basis to take advantage of its entertainment facilities, most notably the horse races. Moreover, fighting in Juárez might inadvertently lead to casualties in El Paso since the revolution had passed into the realm of a spectator sport for Americans on the border. The large Mexican and Mexican American populations in El Paso added to the possibility that the revolution might spill over the international boundary, since there were many Madero sympathizers among both of these groups. Convinced that U.S. Army troops in the area were not sufficient to guarantee the security of El Paso, Sheriff Peyton Edwards of El Paso County requested that Governor Colquitt use National Guard troops to maintain order. Colquitt responded by ordering the El Paso unit of the Guard to active service with instructions to aid local officials in maintaining order and to assist federal officials in enforcing the neutrality laws.[9]

All these preparations went for naught since the rebels called off their attack when Díaz forces successfully reinforced the federal garrison at Juárez. While the expected crisis never came to pass, this incident at Juárez was a good indicator of future problems. Local, state, and federal officials were interested in cooperation but uncertain as to their relative areas of responsibility. State authorities were in an especially awkward position, caught between local officials asking assistance in maintaining order (legal and required under state law) and federal officials seeking help in enforcing the neutrality laws (a move of doubtful legality). All parties involved showed doubts early on about the competency of the other persons and agencies with which they had to cooperate. Local officials criticized National Guard officers; state officials disagreed with federal officials; federal officials of one agency feuded with federal officials of another agency; and most parties criticized the Rangers for their methods, if not their results. All in all, it was a discouraging picture, especially since much greater border crises lay ahead.

The already confused situation became even more complicated after a visit paid to the governor on February 7, 1911. On that day Joaquín Casasús, special Mexican ambassador to the United States, and Henry Clay Pierce, well-known oil man with interests in both Texas and Mexico, paid a call on Governor Colquitt in Austin. Casasús brought with him a letter from President Taft to Colquitt in which the president asked the governor's assistance in the enforcement of the neutrality laws. This request would have changed a well-established but informal practice into an official federal-state policy. While all parties involved refused public comment on the meeting, Colquitt readily assented to the new relationship but also brought up two subjects that were to be continuing problems in federal-state relations: the additional financial burden for Texas in patrolling the border and the need for federal authorities to keep state officials informed of their actions.[10]

From the beginning Colquitt showed an enthusiasm for enforcing federal legislation that would ultimately alarm federal officials. Not content with merely enforcing federal neutrality laws, the governor issued his own neutrality proclamation four days after the meeting with Casasús and Pierce. The proclamation did little more than repeat existing federal legislation, but the governor added his own special emphasis by urging all Texans to remain strictly neutral in regard to the contending factions in Mexico and by ordering all common carriers in Texas not to transport any goods considered contraband under federal laws.[11] The governor's action did not alter the legal position of revolutionary elements operating in Texas. The proclamation did not constitute state law nor did it expand upon restrictions already established by federal legislation. Instead it represented an early indication of Colquitt's strong support for law enforcement along the border and his eagerness to cooperate with federal officials. While such zeal initially pleased federal authorities, it led to major complications in federal-state relations.

The uneasy and uncertain nature of this relationship soon manifested itself in confusion over efforts to arrest Francisco Madero. After a federal warrant was issued for Madero's arrest on February 13, 1911, Colquitt directed the

Texas Rangers to arrest Madero for violation of federal neutrality laws even though no state laws had been violated. The governor immediately notified President Taft of his action; when two weeks passed with no response from Taft, Colquitt revoked the arrest order.[12] Colquitt at this time even urged Taft to take up with the Díaz administration the possibility of state troops "crossing the Rio Grande with sufficient force" to capture Madero should he reenter Mexico. The State Department declined to broach the matter with the Mexican government, feeling certain that such a request would be refused, and cautioned that federal and state officials should not "commit illegal acts by adopting measures beyond and outside of their legal powers."[13] Since standing orders from the Taft administration prohibited federal forces from crossing the border, it is not surprising that the State Department refused to enter into negotiations with Mexico aimed at securing permission for state forces to cross the international boundary.[14] What the State Department chose to ignore was that officials of the State of Texas at the urging of the federal government had already adopted "measures beyond and outside their legal powers." The events surrounding Madero's arrest were indicative of the willingness of state officials to adopt a more energetic and aggressive policy than federal authorities when it came to maintaining order along the international boundary.

In March the Taft administration took action that hinted at a more assertive border policy in which Texas was to play a central role. The president ordered the creation of the so-called "Maneuver Division" of the U.S. Army with headquarters at Fort Sam Houston in San Antonio. The official explanation for the formation of the division was that it was designed to provide "field training for officers and men"; the scale of the military movement and the secrecy surrounding it soon gave rise to reports that it would be used for intervention in northern Mexico. The U.S. Army reportedly had placed an order for 4,500 maps of Mexico with a San Antonio firm and was sending large amounts of ammunition to the border. The Taft administration later expanded its official explanation to include a role for the division in the enforcement of the neutrality laws.[15] Privately Taft acknowledged that the division was in effect being pre-positioned for possible intervention in Mexico in the event of a major threat to American lives or property. The president was counting primarily on the deterrent effect of the mobilization, since he publicly and privately expressed doubts as to whether he had the authority to order troops into Mexico; even should he have the authority, Taft had indicated that he would not send in troops without prior congressional approval.[16] The creation of the Maneuver Division meant that approximately one-fourth of the U.S. Army—about 20,000 men—would be on duty in Texas.

While the Maneuver Division was being organized, Governor Colquitt was doing some mobilizing of his own. As revolutionary activity in northern Mexico increased, the governor concentrated the Ranger force at potential trouble spots along the Rio Grande; he also called up units of the Texas National Guard for service at El Paso in response to fears of a rebel attack on neighboring Ciudad Juárez.[17] Colquitt wrote the president to express his approval of Texas as the location for the Maneuver Division and even invited him to "come to Texas for a rest if you can get Congress off your hands."[18] By the spring of 1911, however, the situation on the border was not very restful for either Taft or Colquitt.

The Battle of Juárez

Rebel strategy increasingly focused its attention on the capture of the strategic city of Ciudad Juárez. The rebels believed that the fall of Juárez would be a major psychological blow for the Díaz regime that might very well lead to the triumph of the revolution. Juárez had financial and economic importance for the contending factions, since the side controlling the city would have a significant source of income from customs duties as well as a port of entry for war materiel and other supplies. Also involved were important diplomatic implications; many rebels believed that the acquisition of Juárez might lead the United States to extend belligerent status to the Madero movement. The geographical proximity to El Paso and the many ties linking the two cities meant that any significant military action in Juárez would have an immediate impact on El Paso. With a major battle impending for Juárez in April 1911, there was a strong possibility of some international incident developing that would impose new strains on the evolving federal-state relationship.

For the U.S. government, the principal concern over such an attack was not its impact upon the political future of Mexico but rather the possibility of loss of life and property in El Paso. When rebels attacked the border town of Agua Prieta, Sonora, on April 13, two persons were killed and eleven wounded in the neighboring American town of Douglas, Arizona. Officials feared that an assault on Juárez might lead to even greater casualties and destruction of property in El Paso. This problem was exacerbated since the revolution had become a major spectator sport on the American side, with military action in any border town certain to draw a large audience. When the rebels had threatened to attack Juárez in February, both El Paso police and soldiers from nearby Fort Bliss had to be used to keep the curious away from the banks of the Rio Grande. "The disappointment of the public was something tremendous" when the battle failed to take place.[19] In offering suggestions to its readers on how to spend the coming summer vacation, the *El Paso Morning Times* recommended an excursion to the recently completed Elephant Butte Dam or a little revolution-watching since the "insurrectos are still with us in great numbers" at Juárez.[20]

State officials were worried also, particularly about the American response to the earlier Agua Prieta-Douglas incident. The number of casualties in Douglas had prompted Arizona Governor Richard Sloan to request that President Taft take "radical measures" to protect American lives and property. Taft declined to intervene militarily and instead urged Sloan to evacuate areas endangered by the fighting across the border. The president made clear his approach to such problems in his closing remarks to Governor Sloan: "I am loathe to endanger Americans in Mexico where they are necessarily exposed by taking a radical step to prevent injury to Americans on our side of the border who can avoid it by a temporary inconvenience."[21] He echoed authorities' fears that citizens of El Paso might become involved in the fighting on the Mexican side of the river. These concerns grew out of the realization that the Madero movement had significant support among the Mexican American population of El Paso, and they were buttressed by newspaper reports that various Texans were prepared to attack Juárez in the event of any casualties on the American side. The secretary of war directed army officers in the El Paso area to use force if necessary to prevent such action. The Taft administration also instructed all commanders along the U.S.-Mexican boundary that "under no circumstances" were U.S. troops to cross the border.[22] For his own planning purposes, Governor Colquitt had not received any official word from federal authorities as to what orders would be imple-

Military activities attracted audiences all along the border area, not just in the El Paso/Juárez location. Here United States soldiers and a few civilians watch a battle occurring in Nuevo Laredo. *Photograph courtesy of the Harry Ransom Humanities Research Center, The University of Texas at Austin, Falvella Collection.*

mented in the event that an attack on Juárez threatened lives and property in El Paso.

Mexican rebels likewise worried about the possible international results of an attack on Juárez. During the period of threatened attack in February, the rebel leader Pascual Orozco had notified the American consul in advance of his plans, urging him to notify Americans to seek safety. Orozco publicly stated that he would make every effort not to endanger American lives and property. By late April rebel forces under Orozco and Pancho Villa once again threatened Juárez; the rebels had seized the Mexican Central and Northwestern Railroads, effectively isolating the city. When negotiations for a peaceful settlement of the situation broke down on May 6, Madero's best forces were on the outskirts of the city, poised for a final attack.[23] With victory apparently at hand, Madero made a dramatic about-face. He ordered his troops to break off the siege and move south, a decision based on his fear that an assault on the city would lead to casualties in El Paso which in turn might provoke American intervention. As was the case with many subsequent rebel leaders in the 1910-1920 period, Madero believed that American intervention would divert and perhaps destroy the revolutionary movement.

Orozco, however, was unwilling to surrender the advantage and ordered an attack on Juárez on his own. The unauthorized assault which began on May 8 indeed quickly led to casualties on the American side; by late afternoon four were dead and nine wounded in El Paso. Although city officials and the news media warned citizens not to go near the fighting, hundreds disregarded the warnings and gathered on the banks of the Rio Grande to watch the attack. Some of the casualties, however, occurred among Americans at a considerable distance from the river who were actually trying to avoid the fighting.[24] Colonel E. Z. Steever, commander of U.S. forces at El Paso, warned the combatants in Juárez to avoid firing into U.S. territory. At the same time, General Leonard Wood, Army chief of staff, restated the official position of the United States government: "Without authority from Congress, the Army cannot cross the border no matter what happens."[25] Final casualty figures on the American side listed six killed and fifteen wounded.[26]

The fighting continued on May 9, with fewer problems on the American side since U.S. troops were being used to keep spectators at a distance from the river. This fact—that American forces were used to restrain American citizens rather than to stop the fighting in Juárez—provoked an angry response from Texas officials. Governor Colquitt strongly protested to both the U.S. and Mexican governments, but the rapid surrender of Juárez to the rebels on May 10 precluded any stronger response from the state's chief executive. Joseph W. Bailey, U.S. senator from Texas and political ally of Colquitt, hinted that Texans were prepared to take matters into their own hands if the federal government failed to take effective action. When Bailey was asked what the government's response should be if Mexican soldiers fired into El Paso, he replied, "If either [Mexican] federals or insurrectos train their guns on El Paso, the population of that city will perhaps relieve the Government of the United States from precipitating hostilities."[27]

While the events at Juárez might have led to an international incident or even a confrontation between federal and state officials, it served instead to usher in a brief period of calm along the Rio Grande. After the fall of Juárez, Porfirio Díaz agreed to resign and soon went into exile in Europe. When Madero heard of Díaz' offer of resignation, he ordered his revolutionary forces to withdraw from the frontier to avoid any possible complications with the United States.[28] The incident at Juárez-El Paso had lasted only a few days; it would, however, play a major role in shaping Governor Colquitt's response to future border crises. Colquitt was convinced that officials in Washington did not understand the situation, and he was determined to avoid a repetition of casualties on the Texas side such as had occurred in El Paso even if it meant that the State of Texas had to take military action. A federal-state confrontation had not been avoided; it had only been postponed.

A Federal-State Border Policy

The false calm that descended on the border encouraged President Taft to begin dismantling the Maneuver Division. In early July the first units left for their regular stations. Although the Division officially ceased to exist on August 7, its creation led to a long-term increase in the number of army troops in the border area, since all units of the division still at San Antonio as of that date were permanently reassigned to the Department of Texas, making it numerically the largest department in the U.S. Army. The War Department, scouting in Texas for possible sites for new army posts, was considering placing two divisions in Texas, a move which would have required a drastic relocation of army personnel in favor of the border region. The Maneuver Division experience had also furnished a good insight into the expenses of strengthening border defenses; the War Department estimated that its mobilization had cost more than two million dollars.[29] Consequently border security and finances were prime topics when President Taft and Governor Colquitt finally met in September 1911.

While Colquitt was much concerned with improving security along the Rio Grande, he also understood the financial implications of such a move for the state government. Colquitt had inherited a substantial deficit from his predecessor in the governorship, Thomas Campbell, and found it difficult to get extraordinary appropriations out of a frequently hostile legislature.[30] Although patrolling the border was basically a federal function, the governor was more than willing to have the State of Texas assume more responsibility in the area—so long as federal financing would help defray the additional expenses involved. Policing the border would require a substantial increase in the Ranger force, which had scarcely a dozen members to patrol approximately nine hundred miles of border. The answer to the state's manpower problem, so Colquitt reasoned, was for the federal government to provide the financing needed to expand the Texas Rangers.

President Taft embarked on a lengthy trip through twenty-four states in September 1911 to explain his policies. In the course of this trip, Taft met with Governor Colquitt at Hutchinson, Kansas, to discuss federal-state cooperation in dealing with the border problem. During the meeting, Colquitt assented to a major increase in the Ranger force in exchange for Taft's promise that the federal government would pay for the additional expense incurred. Taft and Colquitt further agreed that state officials would continue to aid federal authorities in enforcement of the neutrality laws.[31] In the following months, the Ranger force rapidly expanded under this new accord. State law enforcement officials were also authorized to confiscate any goods on Texas soil aimed at promoting revolutionary activities in Mexico and to arrest anyone firing into Mexico from Texas. There were specific orders that the "Texas militia should cross the border only when acting under the U.S. military."[32]

This latest agreement between Taft and Colquitt in effect continued past policies but with the additional feature of federal funding. It also demonstrated the ambiguous and legally uncertain relationship that existed between federal and state authorities. Federal funds would go to state forces to implement federal laws—the neutrality legislation—and to fulfill a federal function—protection of the border. Events would demonstrate, however, that once state officials assumed certain federal responsibilities, it became difficult for them not to become involved in or to seek others. For example, maintenance of border security involved Texas officials in such federal concerns as customs matters and immigration policy. Ironically, the augmented Ranger force was to have its first major test in a situation that proved politically embarrassing for the governor. Colquitt found himself in the middle of a controversy surrounding the activities of the Mexican exile, General Bernardo Reyes.

The Reyes Conspiracy

Prior to the Revolution of 1910, General Bernardo Reyes had been one of the most powerful military and political figures in Porfirian Mexico. Reyes had seen extensive military service in northern Mexico, demonstrating his loyalty to Díaz and a talent for political intrigue. He later served as governor of the border state of Nuevo León for more than two decades during which time he played a key role in promoting the industrialization of Monterrey. As one who combined military support with a penchant for economic development, Reyes appeared a logical successor to the aging Porfirio Díaz, and various political "clubs" began to lobby for a Reyes candidacy in the 1910 presidential elections. Díaz, however, had not become an "aging dictator" without developing a considerable talent for eliminating potential rivals and possible successors. Díaz dispatched Reyes on a meaningless military study mission to Europe in 1909, effectively exiling him and removing him as a factor in the 1910 presidential equation.[33]

Following the resignation of Díaz in May 1911, Reyes returned to Mexico, erroneously assuming that he could resume where he had left off in 1909. He found instead that revolutionary events had left him behind and that he was in a hopeless political contest with the nominal leader and hero of the Revolution, Francisco Madero. Reyes—a "popular" leader in 1909—was unable to make the necessary adjustments and aroused only moderate enthusiasm for his presidential candidacy, even among supporters of the old regime. After being physically attacked at a gathering in Mexico City, Reyes and his followers called for a postponement of the elections. Congress refused to grant the request, leading Reyes to withdraw his candidacy amid charges that Madero was employing dictatorial methods which precluded an honest election.[34] Reyes then decided to retire to San Antonio to become the latest and the most prominent in a long line of exiled opponents of the Mexican government.

Reyes left Mexico City for Veracruz where he boarded a ship for New Orleans. On the trip from New Orleans to San Antonio, Reyes had as his traveling companion Francisco Chapa, the leader of San Antonio's Mexican American community who had been a major force in swinging his constituency's vote to Colquitt in the gubernatorial election of 1910. One of the Governor's most trusted political advisors, Chapa at the time served as a lieutenant colonel on Colquitt's personal staff. General Reyes received a warm welcome in San Antonio and established himself at 817 San Pedro Avenue, the home of Manuel Quiroga, a business partner and close personal friend of Francisco Chapa.[35]

The general set up his revolutionary headquarters at 701 San Pedro and received a steady stream of anti-Madero exiles and Mexican Americans. Influenced by the earlier lack of action on the part of American authorities against the Madero conspiracy, Reyes openly began to organize a revolutionary movement in San Antonio. He publicly announced his intention to overthrow the Madero regime and recruited personnel and purchased arms which he then shipped to the border. These blatant activities attracted the attention of federal authorities in both the United States and Mexico. The United States Bureau of Investigation kept Reyes under constant surveillance and had succeeded in planting informers within his group. With its own intelligence agents operating in the city, the Mexican government was well aware of the revolutionary proceedings in San Antonio. The interim president of Mexico, Francisco León de la Barra, even went to the extent of sending his brother, Luis, to San Antonio to try to persuade Reyes to put an end to his plotting. Reyes, not surprisingly, refused.[36]

Reyes' refusal to maintain a low profile extended to his nonpolitical activities as well. The mayor of San Antonio, Bryan Callaghan, officially welcomed the general to the city on October 14. Several local clubs bestowed memberships on him; appropriately enough, the memberships were all temporary. Reyes responded to the attention, taking time off from his revolutionary plotting to follow a busy social calendar. He was guest of honor at a reception at the San Antonio Club, attended a fair, and even reviewed cavalry maneuvers at Fort Sam Houston.[37]

As the political-legal storm clouds gathered, Reyes embarked on one of his most important public ventures: a visit to Austin on October 16 to confer with Governor Colquitt. Accompanying Reyes to the interview was the ubiquitous Francisco Chapa who had arranged the meeting. The fact that Texas' most prominent resident revolutionary was visiting the state's chief executive aroused considerable public interest. Official accounts of the gathering conveyed the impression that Reyes merely was paying a courtesy call on the governor. The available evidence indicates, however, that Reyes and Chapa hoped to influence the governor's choice of personnel for the expanded Ranger force to insure the appointment of men sympathetic to Reyes; failing that, Reyes hoped to persuade the governor to employ the Rangers in a manner that would not interfere with his revolutionary activities. If Reyes had hoped to influence the composition of the expanded Ranger force, he had arrived too late; the expansion process had already been completed by October 1, almost a week before Reyes' arrival in San Antonio. There was still, however, the possibility of using the Chapa connection to determine how the Rangers would be employed.[38]

The Reyes conspiracy expanded steadily throughout the month of October. The general and his supporters established additional revolutionary juntas at the border towns of Brownsville, Laredo, and El Paso. The plan called for actual invasions of Mexico at these points, with the main effort to be centered on Laredo. Reyes had powerful allies in Laredo, most notably the local long-time political boss, Amador Sánchez. Sánchez had served as mayor of Laredo from 1900 to 1910, at which time he was elected sheriff of Webb County in which Laredo was located. Sánchez was not only a close political ally of General Reyes; he too was a prominent political supporter of Governor Colquitt. Sánchez had actively campaigned for Colquitt in 1910 among the Spanish-speaking population and had worked to deliver the Mexican

Francisco A. Chapa. *Photograph courtesy of the Barker Texas History Center.*

American vote in the Rio Grande Valley. Sánchez was sufficiently confident of his political connections to use the Webb County jail as the headquarters of the *reyista* junta in Laredo.[39]

As the Reyes conspiracy grew, there was increasing pressure from the Madero administration upon the U.S. government to enforce the neutrality laws and break up Reyes' budding revolutionary organization. Even the United States ambassador in Mexico City, Henry Lane Wilson, who was no supporter of Madero, urged the State Department to take "energetic measures." The initial response was similar to its earlier response when the Díaz administration had demanded that action be taken against the Madero conspiracy: without strong evidence that the neutrality laws had been violated, there was no action that the U.S. government could take.[40]

Federal authorities worked to gather such evidence against Reyes and his fellow revolutionaries while state officials demonstrated little concern over the burgeoning conspiracy. Governor Colquitt reminded Texans that his neutrality proclamation was still in force and that the Rangers would continue to aid federal officials in the enforcement of neutrality legislation. The governor sent additional Rangers to Laredo, but they took no action against the revolutionaries in the city that had become the focus of reyista activity. Frequent reports cited the growing number of "refugees" that were appearing in various towns in South Texas. The *San Antonio Express* observed that "at no time in the history of Mexican revolutions has San Antonio had so many refugees within her bounds."[41] Only after federal authorities moved against the conspirators would Colquitt send the Rangers into action.

The reyistas were so open in their revolutionary activities that federal officials soon collected the evidence needed to indict the rebels for violation of U.S. neutrality statutes. Since Madero earlier had been able to operate for several months before American authorities took action, Reyes incorrectly assumed that he too would be given a similar period of grace within which to develop his revolutionary organization. Doubtless Reyes also believed that his close ties with the Colquitt administration precluded action by state authorities even though they were theoretically committed to enforcing the federal neutrality laws. Further, he apparently thought the Chapa-Sánchez connection guaranteed friendly inaction on the part of the Rangers.

The Collapse of the Conspiracy

These optimistic but inaccurate assumptions disappeared with a series of federal indictments beginning in November. Three days earlier a federal grand jury had convened in Laredo to investigate the alleged Reyes conspiracy. The jury issued its first indictments on November 16, but Reyes was not among the accused. This federal action, however, forced Reyes' hand. On November 16 and 17 he withdrew a total of $60,000 from the First National Bank of San Antonio, but the conspiracy was unraveling too rapidly for the general to save it. On November 18 the grand jury at Laredo indicted Reyes for violation of federal neutrality laws.[42]

Other federal agencies were also closing in on the conspirators. The War Department dispatched additional cavalry forces to the Rio Grande with orders to block any armed groups from crossing the river and to confiscate any arms or ammunition which they believed would be used against the Madero government.[43] With federal forces on the move, Governor Colquitt hurried state forces into action with an eye toward sharing in the credit for breaking up the conspiracy. Colquitt failed to realize at the time that the pursuit of the revolutionaries would ultimately lead to the office of the governor.

Colquitt had been reluctant to take action against Reyes and his supporters; once the decision had been made to intervene, however, the governor pressed the matter vigorously. When authorities moved against the conspiracy, the focus of attention fell on Laredo rather than San Antonio. On November 17 Colquitt ordered most of the Ranger force to convene at Laredo, and the following day dispatched the state adjutant general, Henry Hutchings, there to supervise the operation. Hutchings took a room at the Ross Hotel which was also the headquarters for the local Reyes junta. The instructions given to Hutchings were to seize all arms and ammunition in the possession of the conspirators, to arrest all persons violating federal neutrality laws, and to "notify any citizens of Mexico who may be members of a revolutionary junta that they have forty-eight hours to leave Texas."[44] The governor also instructed Hutchings to try to enlist the support of the local army commander, General J. W. Duncan, in clearing Laredo of revolutionary elements.[45]

Local, state, and federal officials subsequently engaged in a series of raids that effectively destroyed the reyista conspiracy in South Texas. There were major confiscations of arms, ammunition, and horses, especially in the Laredo area. Suspicious of the large number of funerals taking place in Laredo on November 20, authorities stopped four funeral processions and found that three of the four coffins contained rifles.[46] To escalate the campaign against the revolutionaries, Governor Colquitt asked President Taft for permission to use the Rangers to enforce federal immigration laws as well as neutrality legislation: "If we can deport the alien Mexican population coming here for revolutionary purposes, we will save both the State and the Nation much expense."[47] While the governor's request brought an incredulous and negative reply from the federal government, Colquitt later was able to report that his request had led to greater activity on the part of federal immigration agents and that the Rangers had "been cooperating with them thoroughly."[48]

The destruction of the Reyes movement highlighted the growing problem of federal-state cooperation in maintaining border security. Federal officials were particularly disenchanted with Governor Colquitt's eagerness to take the credit for breaking up the conspiracy, especially when there was talk that the federal government had taken action only after it had decided to "pursue the Colquitt program" of getting tough with border revolutionaries.[49] In reality state officials had reluctantly followed the lead of federal authorities in dealing with the conspirators. Colquitt had ordered the state forces into action only when it had become clear that federal officials were prepared to move on their own. While the governor tried to convey the impression that the Rangers played the leading role in the crackdown on the reyistas, they had actually played only a supporting role to the various federal agencies involved: the U.S. Army, federal marshals, and the Bureau of Investigation.[50]

Jockeying for the limelight was only one aspect of the growing problems associated with coordinating a federal-state response to the situation on the border. It was clear that the joint federal-state operation against the Reyes movement had been a technical success; equally evident was the general confusion surrounding the limits and nature of this cooperative effort. Adjutant General Hutchings summarized the problem when he openly acknowledged his uncertainty about the legality of state officials aiding in the enforcement of federal laws.[51] The contradictory position of the federal government further confused the issue. President Taft actively recruited Colquitt's assistance in enforcing federal neutrality laws, but his administration reacted with disbelief when the governor suggested state aid in implementing the immigration laws, an action which might have been even more beneficial from the viewpoint of the State of Texas.

All parties involved were unsure as to their exact spheres of jurisdiction and of how far they should go in assisting one another. Since state officials were helping to enforce federal laws, Governor Colquitt assumed that federal officials would help enforce state directives. When the governor requested U.S. military assistance in clearing Laredo of revolutionary elements, the local military commander, General Duncan, asked his superiors for instructions concerning the extent of cooperation envisioned. The response from the War Department was that neutrality matters were the responsibility of federal officials, not state authorities. The army adjutant general informed Duncan that there would probably be "substantial indirect cooperation" between army officers and state officials but that "you are not authorized to support Texas authorities in the execution of state laws. I am responding to you so that you may fully understand the nature of the cooperation contemplated."[52]

Governor Colquitt was obviously among those who did not fully understand the nature of the cooperation contemplated. Colquitt contended that a breakdown in communication between the White House and the War Department had resulted in the federal government following contradictory policies. The governor told President Taft that the secretary of war did not "seem to be familiar with the actions taken by me at your request" to assist in enforcement of the federal neutrality laws.[53] Colquitt complained in a similar vein to Adjutant General Hutchings, instructing him to avoid "any jealousies or friction that might arise" between federal and state authorities over enforcement matters. The governor also cautioned Hutchings to continue the past policy of assisting with implementation of the neutrality laws but to make no effort to enforce federal immigration laws.[54] Thus the first major effort at federal-state cooperation ended with all parties thoroughly confused as to what their working relationship was to be.

State and federal officials came to divergent conclusions about the joint operations launched against the reyistas. Governor Colquitt adopted an optimistic stance, noting that most of the revolutionaries had departed and that the "energetic measures" of state and federal authorities had ended the "embryo revolution" of Reyes. The governor did worry, however, that "another revolution in Mexico is imminent" and promised President Taft that he would continue to enforce federal neutrality laws vigorously.[55] Adjutant General Hutchings displayed even greater caution during a newspaper interview in San Antonio. When questioned about state enforcement of federal laws, he replied: "I don't know anything, and I am not positive about that."[56]

Federal authorities looked to the future with even greater uncertainty. Secretary of War Henry Stimson acknowledged the successful repression of the Reyes movement but indicated that he was not particularly impressed with the performance of either Governor Colquitt or the Texas Rangers.[57] The growing confusion extended beyond the War Department to include the Department of State. One bemused State Department official wrote: "The Governor of Texas, upon receiving the President's assurance of cooperation, seems to have proceeded to do most of the cooperating himself. He appears to be a little mixed [up] as to the respective functions of the Federal and State authorities."[58] Governor Colquitt's problems with the Reyes conspiracy, rather than being over, were only just beginning.

The Legal Aftermath

When Reyes was first arrested on November 18, Francisco A. Chapa appeared to post his bond of $5,000. Federal authorities dropped the original charge against Reyes on November 20 but immediately arrested him on another neutrality violation. Friends of the general posted a $10,000 bond to guarantee his appearance at his trial scheduled for April 1912 in Laredo.[59] The overwhelming evidence assembled against Reyes seemed almost certain to lead to his conviction. Even if he were found not guilty, the legal process would require several months which Reyes could ill afford to lose with the Madero administration attempting to establish itself in Mexico. Realizing this, both state and federal officials feared that Reyes might jump bond and flee to northern Mexico. Adjutant General Hutchings provided a good summary of Reyes' position: "Reyes has gone too far to retrace and will forfeit bond and come down around here [the border] and get his loose ends together."[60]

Agents of both the Mexican and U.S. secret services kept Reyes under constant surveillance in San Antonio in order to prevent any effort by the general to leave the city. Despite these precautions, a disguised Reyes was able to leave San Antonio by train on December 4. Reyes cautiously made his way toward the border, reaching the Rio Grande opposite the Mexican town of Camargo on the night of December 10. Delayed by patrols along the river, Reyes made what he expected to be his triumphal return to Mexico on December 13. It was to be his last appearance in Texas.[61]

Although Reyes was no longer a factor in the border revolution, the political and legal fallout from the reyista conspiracy continued. While Reyes was making his way from San Antonio to the border, federal officials arrested Francisco Chapa on December 11 for violation of the neutrality laws. Chapa and almost two dozen other accused conspirators went on trial in federal court in Brownsville in January 1912. The defendants were represented by some of the best and most politically influential legal talent in Texas. Marshall Hicks, former mayor of San Antonio, served as counsel for all of the accused except Chapa, who was represented by Jake Wolters, another "lieutenant colonel" on Governor Colquitt's personal staff and successful manager of the governor's anti-prohibition campaign in 1911.[62]

Thirteen of the accused, including Sheriff Amador Sánchez, changed their pleas from innocent to guilty; the presiding judge, Waller T. Burns of Houston, dismissed the charges against nine other defendants. This left only Chapa, whose case was to go through the entire legal process. The evidence produced in the Chapa trial was both legally incriminating and politically embarrassing. Federal attorneys demonstrated the close ties between Chapa and Reyes, disclosing that Chapa endorsed Reyes' bank drafts. Adding to Governor Colquitt's discomfiture was the fact that his private secretary, John T. Bowman, was called upon to testify about the October meeting between Reyes and Colquitt. The governor's embarrassment was complete when Bowman's account of the meeting contradicted the testimony which Chapa had given under oath. Wolters countered by arguing that Chapa was the victim of a political frame-up, and Sheriff Sánchez testified that Chapa had not been involved in the plot. After extensive deliberation the jury found Chapa gulity, but only after Judge Burns assured the jurors that he would not sentence Chapa to the penitentiary.[63]

The legal proceedings against the convicted conspirators ended on an appropriately bizarre note. Observing that "the penitentiary is not the place for men of your kind," Judge Burns assessed a token fine of $1,500 against Chapa, which was immediately paid. His Honor also noted that it "distressed the court" to have to impose any penalty upon those who had entered guilty pleas. Before fining Amador Sánchez $1,200, Burns praised Sánchez' distinguished service as mayor of Laredo and sheriff of Webb County. The remaining defendants were sentenced to pay a $600 fine or serve six months in jail. When eight of the group could not produce the necessary funds, Burns ordered them to serve their sentences in the Webb County jail under Sheriff Sánchez' supervision despite the fact that they had been found guilty only of violating federal law. In order to deal with this increased inmate population, Sheriff Sánchez had to hire his brother José—a fellow convicted conspirator—to serve as jailer. Judge Burns brought this South Texas legal drama to a humanitarian conclusion. He paid the fine of one of those jailed so he could return to Mexico to be with his children after the death of their mother and invited all the convicted to visit with him at home if they were ever in Houston.[64]

State and federal officials could find little that was encouraging in the trial of the Reyes conspirators. For Governor Colquitt the trial had been a dual embarrassment. Not only was a member of his personal staff now a convicted felon; his personal secretary inadvertently had helped produce the conviction. Chapa immediately resigned his position on Colquitt's staff, but more than three months passed before the governor publicly acknowledged the resignation. Colquitt and his political allies lobbied strongly with President Taft to grant presidential pardons to both Chapa and Sánchez. Taft reluctantly granted the pardons even though one Bureau of Investigation report indicated that Chapa was still involved in revolutionary plotting. Both Chapa and Sánchez campaigned actively for Colquitt's reelection in 1912. Their gratitude, however, did not extend to Republican President Taft; both supported the Democratic nominee for the presidency in 1912, Woodrow Wilson. After receiving the pardons, Chapa resumed his position on the governor's staff while Sánchez continued in his position of sheriff of Webb County.[65] For federal authorities on the border, the aftermath of the Reyes conspiracy was a discouraging experience. Not only did the governor have someone on his personal staff who had been convicted of violating the neutrality laws; the federal government had also undercut its own position by granting presidential pardons to Chapa and Sánchez. The biggest political loser in the proceedings was Governor Colquitt; it was difficult to reconcile his law-and-order policy for the border with the fact that there was a convicted revolutionary holding an important position in his adminstration.

A Reevaluation of Border Policy

The collapse of the reyista movement led to a reevaluation of border policy by both state and federal governments. With Reyes in jail and his revolutionary organization in Texas destroyed, fiscal matters increasingly influenced policy-making in both Austin and Washington. The first indication of the changing situation came on January 12 when Governor Colquitt cancelled the neutrality proclamation which he had issued the previous February. The status of the expanded Ranger force also came under review. The Taft administration informed Colquitt that it was the conclusion of federal authorities that "normal conditions" prevailed along the border and that it was therefore ending its subsidy for the enlarged force as of January 31, 1912. Colquitt responded by ordering the Ranger force reduced to its size prior to the agreement of September 1911. While ordering the reduction, the governor expressed a theme that would increasingly influence federal-state relations on border policy: "I doubt, however, that the secretary of war has fully investigated conditions just across the border in Mexico."[66] This suspicion that federal authorities in Washington were not well informed on border conditions would soon develop into a conviction that would produce a bitter feud between Colquitt and federal officials.

The governor's fears seemed justified when revolutionary action again threatened in the Juárez-El Paso area. On January 31, the day the federal subsidy ended for the expanded Ranger force, the garrison at Juárez mutinied when the Madero government attempted to discharge some of the troops. The rebellious troops originally claimed to be supporters of Emiliano Zapata, the first major revolutionary figure to come out in opposition to the Madero administration. Later they announced that they were aligned with Emilio Vásquez Gómez who had been plotting in Texas for some time and who was the most important exile figure since the failure of the Reyes conspiracy. State and local officials were primarily concerned that this latest revolt might lead to the kind of heavy fighting in Juárez that had produced casualties in El Paso in May 1911. The El Paso city council briefly considered a resolution calling upon President Taft to send U.S. troops into Juárez. Cooler heads prevailed, and the council settled for a milder resolution asking the president to take whatever measures were necessary to prevent firing into El Paso.[67]

While the El Paso city council sought action from the federal government, state authorities were moving forward on their own. With the Ranger force contracting, Governor Colquitt was in a weakened position in dealing with this latest revolutionary threat. Nevertheless, the governor took a firm stand with both Mexican and U.S. federal authorities. Colquitt immediately ordered Ranger Captain John Hughes at El Paso to "notify contending forces at Juárez that they must not shoot into El Paso."[68] The governor made an equally strong representation to President Taft: "I ask that you give notice that they must not shoot into El Paso as they did at the last battle of Juárez. If necessary I will take drastic steps to prevent this recurrence."[69]

Colquitt's threat to take "drastic measures" brought a quick response from Washington. President Taft's initial reply to Colquitt was both mild and vague; the President informed the governor that he had issued orders "with a view to meeting the difficulties at Juárez and have invited the attention of the Secretary of War to the necessity for action."[70] The actual orders sent out by the War Department to army commanders on the border did not represent any major departure from earlier federal policy. Under a directive from his superiors, Steever, commander of U.S. forces at El Paso, notified military authorities in Juárez that they were to prevent any firing into U.S. territory. The commander of the Department of Texas received permission to dispatch additional troops to the border in case of "sudden emergency." There was considerable discussion about "enforcing the neutrality laws," which did not apply to the current problem in any case. There was no change in the most important policy restriction of all: American forces were still not permitted to cross the border.[71] This federal action won the "cordial approval" of Governor Colquitt, who thought it indicated a more aggressive policy on the part of the federal government. The governor's favorable evaluation was influenced by the misconception that Taft was seriously considering military intervention as a result of the Juárez crisis.[72]

While Colquitt's belligerent policy did not ultimately determine the outcome of the latest Juárez crisis, it certainly caught the attention of the other parties involved. U.S. federal authorities were clearly concerned about the possibility of state military action at El Paso. Colonel Steever reported that he would need a full battalion at El Paso "if the Governor of Texas initiates the drastic measures he boasts of."[73] While the War Department and the Department of State appreciated the difficult position in which Colquitt found himself, they wanted the governor of Texas "to understand that this is a matter which must be attended to by the Federal authorities, and not those of any State."[74] Officials on the other side of the border had also taken heed of the governor's warnings. The rebel mayor of Juárez, Santiago Mestas, informed Ranger Captain John Hughes that, in the event of a fight for the city, the contending forces would meet outside Juárez to "avoid any complications relative to the adversity which might take place in your town."[75]

The much-feared struggle for Juárez never took place. Pascual Orozco, the leading general in the Madero revolt and commander of the rural forces in Chihuahua, enjoyed considerable popularity among the federal troops in Chihuahua and was able to talk the rebellious garrison into surrendering without a shot being fired. Orozco, well known on both sides of the border, also met with local officials and federal authorities in El Paso. The general cheerily observed on his arrival: "I am glad to be in El Paso. I always had a good time here."[76] Orozco ordered the rebellious troops removed to the south, and what passed for calm briefly returned to the area. Orozco had solved one problem but would soon create another. In less than a month he would initiate his own revolt against Madero which would disturb the border region even more. At the same time, Governor Colquitt's independent attitude and more belligerent policy did not augur well for future federal-state relations. At least there was one bright spot; the horse races were on again in Juárez.

Governor Colquitt soon found himself again at odds with federal authorities in both Washington and Mexico City. The Madero administration had requested permission from the U.S. Department of State for Mexican troops to cross over Texas territory from Eagle Pass to El Paso. The purpose for this movement was to replace the soldiers at the Juárez garrison ordered south by Orozco and to suppress additional revolts which had broken out in Chihuahua on behalf of Emilio Vásquez Gómez. The troops would not be armed, and the U.S. army was to provide an "honorary escort" for the Mexican forces. The U.S. government had granted permission for similar passages on two earlier occasions, and the latest request was considered a "matter of routine." Both state and federal authorities had given their blessing to the project as a good method of restoring calm to the border.[77]

Governor Colquitt, however, began to have second thoughts about the movement after a strident protest by the *El Paso Morning Times*. Under the headline "El Paso Is in Grave Danger," the *Morning Times* dismissed the Mexican troops as "little brown soldiers who fought for the dictator Díaz" and warned that the reinforcements would be attacked "in the very streets of El Paso before they cross to Mexican soil."[78] With the *Morning Times* doing its best to raise the level of hysteria on the border, Governor Colquitt informed the secretary of state that the State of Texas was withdrawing its approval for the troop movement.[79] Colquitt was uncertain whether the U.S. federal government had the authority or the will to go ahead with the movement even in the face of state opposition. Confronted with this uncertainty, Colquitt instructed the Texas Rangers not to interfere with the proposed passage of troops as long as they were unarmed and escorted. The Rangers did have orders to block any movement of armed Mexican forces since "no armed force will be permitted to enter Texas without permission of the governor unless such force is part of the U.S. Army."[80]

This latest disagreement between state and federal authorities was to a great extent manufactured by the governor. The U.S. government had never intended to permit the passage of armed or unescorted Mexican troops across Texas soil nor was it prepared to allow the movement of Mexican forces under any conditions if there was opposition on the part of state or local authorities. Colquitt's position proved embarrassing for both the U.S. and the Mexican governments. As the Taft administration began to back away from its original approval of the project, the Madero administration attempted to save face by withdrawing its request before it could be officially refused. The Mexican government's public explanation for its action was that the troop movement envisioned would require the approval of the Mexican senate, which was not in session at the time, and that the situation in northern Mexico had improved, making the transfer of troops unnecessary.[81]

The *El Paso Morning Times* did little to improve the strained relations with its public gloating over the cancellation of the troop movement. The newspaper's headlines on February 10 told the story: "Governor Colquitt Gets Busy with Washington Authorities" and "El Paso Protests Cancel Contemplated Violation of Neutrality Laws Which Would Have Endangered This City and American Lives and Property in State of Chihuahua." In an editorial that same day entitled "President Taft Put Wise," the *Morning Times* rejoiced that President Taft had had his "eyes opened" on the question of the troop movement and congratulated Governor Colquitt for the "energetic steps" he had taken in the dispute. More accurately than it realized, the paper referred to the "diplomatic complications" that had arisen involving the State of Texas, the U.S. government, and the Mexican government.[82] Federal-state disagreement over border policy had evolved to the point that the State of Texas under Governor Colquitt was in effect pursuing its own policy. The governor summarized his position in a letter to Adjutant General Hutchings in El Paso immediately after the troop-movement incident: "I want it understood that the State of Texas or any of its officials will not take part or parcel in the politics of Mexico but that we are determined to protect the people from the results of fighting between various revolutionary bands and troops of the Mexican government."[83]

The Streetcar "Invasion"

Although the *vasquista* revolt had come to a peaceful conclusion, the volatility of the El Paso-Juárez area continued to complicate relations on the border. The nervousness which prevailed on both sides was clearly shown in an incident which took place on February 15, 1912. U.S. Army Lieutenant Ben W. Fields, who arrived in El Paso only three days earlier, was to lead a detail of soldiers for guard duty at one of the international bridges linking El Paso and Juárez. The detail was to make the first part of the journey by special streetcar from Fort Bliss and cover the last part on foot. After examining a map, Fields correctly determined that the entire trip could be made by streetcar, but he failed to realize that the car would loop through Juárez before returning to the American side near the position the men were to occupy. Fields realized his error only after leading a patrol of nineteen armed men approximately 100 yards into Mexican territory. Even though armed Mexican customs officials stopped the streetcar, a near panic ensued as word spread through Juárez that the Americans were invading. Mayor Mestas soon appeared on the scene, "brandishing a large pistol." Following close behind the irate mayor came an armed mob, ready to repel the gringo invaders.[84]

Fields, who could not speak Spanish, engaged in a lengthy and heated discussion with his captors. Convinced that the *yanquis* were not invading by streetcar, Mexican authorities released Fields and his men. The embarrassed lieutenant lamely explained that he "had heard that the Rio Grande was a large river and not the small one that it was."[85] Although the initial incident was resolved, it had set in motion a series of other incidents. Adjutant General Hutchings, who was already in El Paso investigating the local situation, ordered the local unit of the Texas National Guard to active duty. American visitors in Juárez hastily returned across the border as the saloons and gambling houses closed due to the intervention scare. Even the horse races, which had shown an amazing durability in earlier revolutionary upheavals, were suspended in the face of the "gringo invasion." Ironically, the quick release of the Americans sparked disturbances in El Paso. Mexican mobs in El Paso—angered by the fact that armed Mexicans caught earlier on the U.S. side had been held for a week—engaged in street demonstrations, provoking a response by National Guard forces.[86]

While the Mexican government expressed no alarm over the incident, the U.S. government did issue a formal apology, attributing the episode to the fact that Lieutenant Fields was "ignorant of the topography of El Paso."[87] As for Fields himself, army authorities had arrested him on February 17. A group of prominent El Paso businessmen intervened with the secretary of war on behalf of Fields, urging leniency for the inexperienced lieutenant. The army court-martialed and reprimanded Fields but quickly returned him to duty.[88] It was indicative of the unsettled conditions along the border that an inexperienced junior officer in the U.S. Army could provoke an invasion scare that would close the border and lead to the call-up of the Texas National Guard simply by taking the wrong streetcar.

Local and state authorities were not amused by the streetcar confrontation or its aftermath. Mayor Kelly of El Paso asked the federal government to send U.S. troops into Juárez to restore order. Secretary of War Stimson declined to intervene militarily although he did dispatch additional troops to the border.[89] Governor Colquitt also wrote to President Taft urging U.S. military intervention in Juárez. Characterizing the situation at El Paso-Juárez as "critical," Colquitt called for the "friendly occupation" of Juárez by American troops until order was restored. In his concluding remarks, the Governor indicated how far he had moved in the direction of military intervention: "I do not see how we are going to avoid taking a hand in this unfortunate Mexican situation."[90]

Colquitt vs. the U.S. Army

During his first year in office, Colquitt's disagreements with federal authorities had been restricted almost exclusively to civil officials. In particular the governor was at cross-purposes with the U.S. attorney general and the secretary of war over the issue of state involvement in the enforcement of neutrality legislation. Colquitt generally had maintained good relations with the army, especially with field commanders assigned to the Department of Texas with headquarters at Fort Sam Houston in San Antonio. The latest round of difficulties at Juárez-El Paso, however, taxed the amicable working relationship that had developed between state officials and army officers during the first year of the border revolution.

In the course of the latest crisis at Juárez, Colquitt had dispatched Adjutant General Hutchings to El Paso to provide direct information on the situation and to supervise personally the actions of the Texas Rangers and the National Guard. While at El Paso, Hutchings visited nearby Fort Bliss and held discussions with the post adjutant who informed him that Governor Colquitt's intervention in the border dispute might be construed as a violation of the federal neutrality laws and that the governor consequently was running the risk of arrest. Colquitt immediately wrote President Taft of the incident and took the occasion to criticize the past performance of certain federal officials along the border, accusing some not only of failing to enforce the neutrality laws but also of actively aiding certain revolutionary elements. The governor also dashed off a letter to Hutchings instructing him to inform the post adjutant at Fort Bliss that the state administration had the right and responsibility under the state constitution to "protect the frontier from hostile incursions" and that Colquitt was not afraid of arrest for doing so.[91]

Colquitt's latest literary effort soon brought a written response from Brigadier General Duncan. While Duncan "deplored" and was "astonished at" the remarks made by the post adjutant at Fort Bliss, the general also provided a defense of the army's record during the border revolution. Duncan expressed his regret that Colquitt had "felt it necessary to take the matter up over my head with the President of the United States" and said that he interpreted Colquitt's letter to the President as "a criticism of my actions during the recent Reyes rebellion." Promising to investigate the "alleged discourtesy" of the post adjutant at Fort Bliss, General Duncan asked Colquitt to inform him of what past failures the army was guilty so that he would be able to avoid any "future errors."[92]

Duncan's blend of conciliation and contrition produced an immediate softening of the governor's position. On February 19 Colquitt called and also wrote the general. The governor apologized for going directly to President Taft with the problem rather than through channels to General Duncan, offering the rather improbable explanation that he did not realize that the troops at El Paso were under Duncan's command. Colquitt also explained that his criticism of the conduct of federal officials during earlier revolutionary activities did not refer to the army nor to the Reyes rebellion; it was rather a reference to the conduct of certain civil officials of the federal government during the Madero revolution. After reviewing the history of state involvement in the enforcement of federal neutrality legislation, the governor concluded his communication with the observation that "I went further in my letter to the President than I should have done out of courtesy to you."[93] General Duncan seemed equally eager to end the controversy. In a conciliatory letter to Colquitt, Duncan praised the governor's earlier neutrality proclamation and assured him that the "average army officer is generally conversant with the rights of states."[94]

More Crises at Juárez

Colquitt made his peace with the U.S. Army just in time for the next crisis at Juárez. By late February rebel forces supporting Emilio Vásquez Gómez again were threatening Juárez. Like many other Mexican rebels, Vásquez Gómez originally had supported Madero but turned against him in 1911 over Madero's choice for a vice-presidential running mate in that year. Emilio's brother, Francisco, had run on the Madero ticket in the unsuccessful presidential effort of 1910; in 1911 Madero bypassed Francisco Vásquez Gómez in favor of José María Pino Suárez as the vice-presidential nominee. After the break with Madero, Emilio Vásquez Gómez followed the well-worn exile trail to San Antonio where he established his residence and a revolutionary junta. Later, another revolutionary junta was organized in El Paso. Vásquez Gómez immediately attracted the attention of federal agents of both the Mexican and the U.S. governments, especially after issuing a "manifesto" to the Mexican people. The manifesto was not a call to arms but rather an expression by Vásquez Gómez of his willingness to accept the provisional presidency if the people of Mexico wanted him. Vásquez Gómez denied any connection with the revolutionaries in Chihuahua and maintained that he would not take part in a violent revolution. U.S. federal authorities were at least partially convinced of the truth of his pronouncements; they maintained that there was no concrete evidence that the neutrality acts had been violated.[95] With the collapse of the Reyes conspiracy, Vásquez Gómez had become the dominant exile figure in South Texas.

The vasquista threat soon had local, state, and federal officials at odds with one another. The wrangling on the American side began when Mayor Kelly of El Paso asked Secretary of War Stimson to send additional troops to protect the border. Stimson declined, as he had done on earlier occasions, on the grounds that there were sufficient troops available to deal with the situation. Although Stimson quickly relented and sent additional troops, local authorities began to organize for their own defense. Sheriff Edwards issued a public appeal for "responsible citizens" to sign up at his office for a "posse" which was being formed to protect El Paso in the event of fighting in Juárez; the sheriff quickly enlisted 500 persons to serve in the posse.[96]

Edwards' organizational activities immediately attracted the attention of Mexican and U.S. federal authorities. Mexican officials did not protest the formation of the posse itself but were upset by reports that blacks and foreigners were being allowed to join it. When the Mexican consul at El Paso presented an official protest to the local U.S. Army commander, Colonel Steever then forwarded the complaint to his superior, General Duncan, in San Antonio. Duncan in turn passed the message on to Governor Colquitt for action. Colquitt wired Sheriff Edwards, urging him to pursue a cautious policy and to purge the posse of any "undesirable elements."[97] Colquitt, however, did not recommend the disbanding of the posse.

Mayor Kelly's complaints and Sheriff Edwards' posse produced a show of force by the U.S. government. El Paso took on the appearance of an armed camp after Colonel Steever ordered all troops at Fort Bliss into the city. General Duncan dispatched additional army units from San Antonio, bringing the total number of troops in El Paso to more than 2,500. The local company of the Texas National Guard was also on duty, and the sheriff's posse was waiting for the call to action. As a final measure, eleven Texas Rangers were also in El Paso.[98] When a reporter asked Colonel Steever what would be done if shots were fired into El Paso, he replied, "You ask President Taft."[99]

The mobilization at El Paso led many, including Governor Colquitt, to the mistaken conclusion that President Taft was seriously considering intervention in Juárez, a course of action advocated by both the governor and Mayor Kelly.[100] When Kelly had asked Secretary of War Stimson to send troops into Juárez, however, Stimson had refused the request and said that he did not foresee any circumstances under which it would be necessary to do so.[101] The army chief of staff, General Leonard Wood, publicly stated that there had been no orders issued authorizing any crossing of the international boundary by U.S. troops and that their commanders were still operating under the same instructions that had been in effect in May 1911 during the first major incident at Juárez.[102] Under those instructions, U.S. forces could fire across the border but could not cross it.

While El Paso bristled with military activity and rumors of intervention, a considerably different scene was unfolding across the river in Juárez. Again fearful that a struggle over Juárez might provoke an international incident and possible American intervention, President Madero directed that the city be surrendered to the vasquista rebels without a fight. In ordering the evacuation, Madero specifically cited the need to avoid any shots being fired across the border. Rebel forces under General Emilio Campa took possession of Juárez on February 27 without loss of life on either side of the river.[103]

The peaceful transfer of Juárez did not restore calm to the border region nor did it produce an end to the bickering among officials at different levels of government. Mayor Kelly, who was an enthusiastic supporter of the harder line advocated by Governor Colquitt, was not satisfied with the response of the federal government in the latest Juárez crisis. In an angry letter to President Taft, Kelly attributed the "deplorable state of affairs in El Paso to the continued anarchy in the city of Juárez" and maintained that the increased U.S. forces in the area had been used primarily "to prevent American citizens from defending themselves." After consulting with his attorney, · the mayor reached the conclusion that he had the power to protect lives and property in El Paso even if the threat originated on foreign soil. It therefore followed that any federal officer who interfered with the mayor while exercising this power would be in violation of the law. According to Kelly, federal officials spent too much time trying to "avoid irritating the Mexicans" rather than protecting American lives and property. The mayor closed on a note that echoed on a local level sentiments expressed earlier by Governor Colquitt: "I do not propose to maintain order in the City of Juárez, Mexico, but I do intend to protect life and property in the corporate limits of El Paso, Texas."[104]

The Taft administration could scarcely let such an exposition go unchallenged, and Kelly's outburst brought a quick reply from the State Department. Acting Secretary of State Huntington Wilson responded to what he referred to as "certain intimations" in the mayor's letter which had been referred to him by President Taft. Wilson indicated to Kelly that Article I, Section 10, of the United States Constitution prohibited states from waging foreign wars.[105] Rather than ending the discussion, Wilson's comments provoked a rejoinder from Kelly, who informed the acting secretary that he had that very section of the Constitution in mind in his earlier remarks. "Whatever may be its interpretation by the [State] Department (and our cemeteries contain evidence as to what that interpretation is)," the mayor's interpretation was that the firing of shots into American territory constituted an "actual invasion" under the provisions of the Constitution and that he intended to take action if El Paso was the "point invaded."[106]

While the State Department and Mayor Kelly debated the Constitution, a major new threat appeared along the Texas-Chihuahua border; the revolution on behalf of Emilio Vásquez Gómez had phased into a much more serious revolution under Pascual Orozco. There had been major disagreements between Madero and Orozco as early as the first Battle of Juárez in May 1911. After the revolution succeeded, Madero and Orozco continued their alliance and their disagreements. One of the principal causes for the ultimate break between the two was competition over future control of the state of Chihuahua. Orozco, the state's leading military figure, had openly sought the governorship, but Madero supported Abraham González who was elected governor after Orozco withdrew his candidacy under extreme political pressure. Orozco's growing estrangement from the Madero administration fueled rumors that he was connected with the unsuccessful Reyes conspiracy. In early March 1912, Orozco pronounced against the Madero government; the poorly organized vasquista revolt had become the much more dangerous *orozquista* movement.[107]

For authorities of the State of Texas, the most immediate problem posed by the Orozco rebellion was the rebel control of Juárez. There were fears that forces of the central government might attempt to retake the city, bringing a repetition of the events of May 1911. The concern of state officials increased when rumors began to circulate that the rebels might deliberately provoke an international incident to avoid defeat at the hands of the Madero forces. Colquitt again dispatched Adjutant General Hutchings to El Paso to assume command of state forces and directed him to warn the Mexicans that they must not fire across the river into El Paso.[108] Colquitt also telegraphed the secretary of war, asking what instructions had been given to army officials in the El Paso area in the event that the Mexicans fired into the city. As in the past, the secretary replied that Mexican forces had been warned not to do so, but he declined to give any specifics about instructions to army commanders on the grounds that it was against "public policy."[109] The instructions actually given field commanders had not changed from the earliest days of the border revolution: If Mexican forces fired into American territory, U.S. Army troops could return fire across the border but were not allowed to cross the international boundary under any circumstances.

Uncertain as to what the federal response might be, Colquitt and Hutchings were prepared to take drastic action. Hutchings had already conferred with the local army commander Steever. Steever had informed Hutchings that he had received orders to warn Mexican forces about firing into El Paso but had refused to tell Hutchings what his instructions were should the warning be ignored. The adjutant general indicated that there were at least some military preparations underway; he wired the governor that "I believe U.S. troops will return fire if there is shooting into Texas, and I know that Rangers and citizens will."[110] Hutchings also took the occasion to complain to the governor about the lack of cooperation by other federal officials: "If the War Department had any courtesy, it would send the Adjutant General of the Department from San Antonio to make personal representations to you. However, you have forced their hand, and I am gratified."[111]

The crisis over Juárez lingered into the summer of 1912. Instead of using military force, the Taft administration decided to use economic pressure to try to keep the rebel forces in check. Federal authorities first blocked the shipment of arms from El Paso to Juárez; in May all trade between the two cities was terminated. With the embargo in force, Juárez lost much of its economic significance for the rebels and became a strategic liability.

While Taft was applying economic pressure on the rebels, Governor Colquitt had embarked on a more belligerent approach. During June and July periodic rumors suggested that Madero forces would attempt to retake Juárez. Colquitt was particularly disturbed by a Ranger report that indicated it was "a sure thing that El Paso will be fired into" in the event of an attack on Juárez.[112] The rebels, angered by the trade embargo, refused to give assurances that they would not fire into El Paso, claiming that they could not be held responsible for what might happen as long as the U.S. government continued to aid the Madero regime.[113]

Colquitt again approached the secretary of war for information concerning instructions given to army commanders in the event of firing into El Paso. In asking about federal plans, the governor offered the secretary some insight into what the state projected: "I have ordered the Adjutant General of Texas to take the necessary steps to defend the citizens of this state." These "necessary steps" included preparations to order the Texas National Guard's only artillery units from Dallas to El Paso with instructions to "defend the people of El Paso" if army troops did not prevent firing from the Mexican side into El Paso.[114] Colquitt sent an even more strongly worded message to Adjutant General Hutchings instructing him that the National Guard artillery unit must be ready to go "at a moment's notice"; the extent of Colquitt's agitation was evident from the fact that the financially pressed governor even authorized the renting of a special train to carry the unit to El Paso. If U.S. troops failed to prevent firing into El Paso, then Hutchings was to station his artillery "at convenient places to protect lives and property of Texas people." The only restraining note in the governor's instructions to Hutchings was to "wire me before you take any final action or do any shooting."[115]

Without informing Governor Colquitt, President Taft continued his efforts to find a peaceful solution to the Juárez situation. With the economic pressure on the rebels at Juárez continuing, Taft exerted diplomatic pressure on the Madero administration to avoid a conflict that might endanger American lives and property. The president summarized his views on any effort by the Madero forces to recapture Juárez in a letter to the secretary of state: "Indeed the situation is such that unless they can insure American safety they ought to refrain from attacking Juárez altogether.[116] The Mexican ambassador assured Acting Secretary of State Huntington Wilson that there would be no firing by Mexican federal forces that would result in bullets falling on the American side.[117]

Unaware of Taft's diplomatic efforts, Governor Colquitt continued to worry about what instructions had been given to U.S. Army officers along the Rio Grande. In his search for information, Colquitt still found Secretary of War Stimson unresponsive. Answering an inquiry by the governor, Stimson said that it was "not consistent with the public interest" to tell Colquitt what specific instructions had been issued but that he was confident that they would be "effective in preventing an invasion of American rights." Secretary Stimson recommended that Colquitt take up the matter with President Taft since "the situation is under the personal direction of the

President."[118] Colquitt acted on Stimson's recommendation, writing the president concerning the instructions given to Colonel Steever at El Paso. While asking for information, the governor again indicated that the State of Texas was prepared to take action: "If I cannot be assured of adequate protection in case of attack on Juárez, I shall mobilize enough state troops at El Paso to properly resist any movement on either side to endanger the lives of our people."[119]

President Taft's vague reply to the governor's inquiry was a good indication that federal-state relations had advanced very little after more than a year of trying to cope with the effects of revolution on the border. Taft dismissed the whole problem of the ongoing crisis at Juárez-El Paso with the uncertain but optimistic assurance that "the matter with the Mexican government had been arranged so there is substantially no danger to the people of Texas along the Mexican border with reference to an attack on Juárez."[120]

From the governor's viewpoint, Taft's response to Colquitt's latest query was unsatisfactory on several counts. First, the governor needed specific information concerning the federal government's intentions so that he could formulate the state response to the problem. Taft and Secretary of War Stimson consistently refused to give any insight into what the federal government's contingency plans might be in regard to using military force along the Rio Grande. Second, while the president might have assurances from the "Mexican government"—that is, the Madero administration in Mexico City—it was the rebels who held Juárez that primarily concerned the governor. State officials also had received assurances from Madero's representatives in El Paso that the Mexican federals would avoid shooting into El Paso. The threat came from the rebels who demonstrated increasing anger with what they considered the "unneutral" acts of the U.S. government and who had made a point of refusing to give any assurances concerning this issue. Finally, one of Colquitt's biggest concerns was the financial implications of a confrontation. With federal aid to the Rangers ended and with the state treasury in strained circumstances, Colquitt was eager to avoid incurring additional expenses for the Rangers or the Texas National Guard. If the federal government was prepared to take a firm stand for the protection of lives and property on the Texas side of the river, the governor would evade the financial burden of concentrating the Rangers in El Paso or calling out units of the Texas National Guard. Without adequate information about federal plans, however, Colquitt felt that he was in a political and financial dilemma. If the federal government failed to adopt a firm stand and state forces were not on the scene, then lives and property in El Paso would be in danger; if federal contingency plans called for a strong response and state forces had also been mobilized, then unnecessary expenses would be incurred.

A State Border Policy

Colquitt's subsequent actions in the summer of 1912 indicated his intention to press forward with his own border policy in the absence of what he considered satisfactory guarantees of federal action. Units of the Texas National Guard were scheduled to engage in joint maneuvers in July with National Guard units from Louisiana and Arkansas in Louisiana. On June 29 the governor postponed the maneuvers on the grounds that it was "unwise for the Texas National Guard to leave the state at this time due to unsettled conditions on the border that may require early mobilization of a large portion of state forces."[121] The National Guard company at El Paso began to drill three times a week rather than the customary once a week. Ambulances and additional military equipment were sent to El Paso.[122]

The governor also demonstrated that he was not bluffing about ordering National Guard artillery to El Paso. Colquitt ordered Captain F. A. Logan, commander of the artillery unit at Dallas, to go to El Paso to determine weapon positions and potential targets in the area. Later statements by Logan indicated that state authorities were thinking in offensive as well as defensive terms. Captain Logan reported to Adjutant General Hutchings that he had been looking for "gun positions which would command the bridges in order to cover the advance of infantry" and that he knew "to within a yard" the ranges to potential targets in Juárez.[123] With such actions going on, there was little doubt that the governor's independent, hard-line policy was complicating federal-state relations. In a letter that was both cautionary and congratulatory, Adjutant General Hutchings informed Colquitt that the people of El Paso were "looking to the Governor for protection," not to federal authorities, and that it might be a good idea for the governor and the adjutant general to meet to discuss "possible federal complications" resulting from this situation.[124]

Once again the long-feared struggle for Juárez never materialized. The decline of the Orozco movement had started as early as April 1912 when federal forces launched a major offensive in northern Mexico under the leadership of the tough Porfirian general, Victoriano Huerta. Orozco was severely restricted in his military activities by a shortage of arms and ammunition, a partial product of the U.S. embargo. Huerta steadily drove Orozco's forces north, capturing Juárez on August 16, 1912, without loss of life or major property damage in El Paso. Orozco briefly engaged in guerrilla warfare in northern Chihuahua but went into exile in the United States in September.[125]

The decline and ultimate defeat of the Orozco movement permitted Governor Colquitt to soften his position on border policy. Ranger Captain Hughes at El Paso reported as early as mid-July that "most all danger of trouble in Juárez in the near future is over."[126] The governor rescheduled the postponed National Guard maneuvers for August.[127] But even with more peaceful conditions returning to the Rio Grande region, Colquitt could not resist one final tweaking of federal authorities. He ordered the Texas Rangers to arrest Orozco, who had violated no state laws, in the event that he entered Texas, and he wrote a personal letter to Francisco Madero asking the Mexican president whether he wished to extradite Orozco.[128]

Governor Oscar B. Colquitt at the christening of the battleship *Texas. Photograph courtesy of the Barker Texas History Library Collection.*

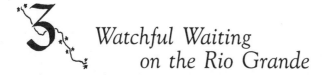

Watchful Waiting
on the Rio Grande

Just as elections in 1910 had done a great deal to influence border developments, the Texas gubernatorial and the U.S. presidential campaigns of 1912 were central factors in determining federal-state relations on border policy for the next few years. Traditionally Texas governors had encountered little opposition in running for a second term. Colquitt, however, generated substantial opposition to his reelection because of the same issue that had bedeviled him in 1910: prohibition. Originally Colquitt had hoped that the 1911 referendum, which had resulted in the defeat of a prohibition amendment to the state constitution, would eliminate prohibition as an issue in the 1912 governor's race. The prohibitionists were not prepared to let the issue die, however; led by Colquitt's predecessor in the governorship, Thomas M. Campbell, they attempted to block Colquitt's renomination by the Democratic Party.

While the "progressive" elements of the Democratic Party continued to denounce Colquitt for his conservative approach, the incumbent governor actually defied easy political classification. Colquitt opposed the introduction of the initiative, referendum, and recall—all items strongly favored by progressive elements. At the same time, the governor favored the highly progressive policies of educational and prison reform, workmen's compensation, compulsory arbitration of labor disputes, and financial aid for farmers. Colquitt's vigorous border policy won the support of residents in the Rio Grande region but attracted minimal attention in the campaign as a whole. Most of his critics focused on the governor's continuing opposition to statewide prohibition. Despite this unusual opposition, Colquitt handily won renomination, which was tantamount to winning the governorship, and crushed his opponents at the State Democratic Convention that went on record as endorsing the governor's "Mexican policy."[1] As indicated earlier, in the political struggle Colquitt had the solid backing of the Mexican American vote mobilized by such leaders as Francisco Chapa and Amador Sánchez.

An even more unusual race was developing for the U.S. presidency in 1912. For the first time since 1860, there would be a serious campaign waged by a third party. A major split had developed in the Republican Party between the progressive wing, which supported the nomination of former president Theodore Roosevelt, and the conservative wing, which backed the renomination of the incumbent William Howard Taft. When President Taft used his control of party machinery to gain the nomination, Roosevelt launched his own Progressive Party, which promised the country one of the most extensive domestic reform programs in history under the banner of the "New Nationalism." Included in Roosevelt's progressive package were proposals for a minimum wage, child labor legislation, workmen's compensation, and federal health programs. The Democratic nomination went to Woodrow Wilson, who campaigned for his own brand of domestic reform under the slogan of the "New Freedom."

The race resolved itself into a contest between Wilson and Roosevelt, with Roosevelt's only hope for success to win over large numbers of Democratic progressives to his more advanced form of progressivism. When this hoped-for Democratic defection did not materialize, Wilson defeated Roosevelt easily, with Taft finishing a distant third.[2] The 1912 election had centered almost exclusively on domestic issues with little emphasis on foreign policy in general or Taft's Mexican policy in particular. Although the situation in Mexico continued to deteriorate throughout 1912, the situation on the border seemed relatively calm during the peak of the presidential campaign in the fall.

Before Wilson assumed the presidency in March 1913, he already had developed a relationship with Governor Colquitt which offered little hope for improved federal-state cooperation on border policy. In organizing and conducting his successful presidential campaign, Wilson—a native of the South—depended heavily upon southerners such as Walter H. Page, William F. McCombs, and William G. McAdoo.[3] Texas was one of the principal targets for the Wilson organization, and his supporters there "organized the most enthusiastic and successful Wilson state campaign in the country."[4] The leader of the Wilson movement in Texas was Thomas B. Love, prominent Dallas attorney and veteran state politician. Love bitterly opposed Colquitt for his antiprohibition and antiprogressive views and described the governor to Wilson as the "head of the reactionary and anti-progressive element of the Democratic party in Texas who lets pass few opportunities to proclaim his opposition to the essential things for which all progressives stand."[5] Colquitt was also a well-known political ally of Texas Senator Joseph Bailey who had waged a struggle to the bitter end to defeat the Wilson movement in Texas, claiming that a Wilson victory would bring the "triumph of socialism" in the Democratic Party within a decade.[6]

Governor Colquitt had an opportunity to join the Wilson campaign early when Wilson visited Dallas in October 1911 to deliver an address during the State Fair. Several politicians—such as Senator Charles A. Culberson—used the occasion to endorse his candidacy, but Colquitt restricted his public pronouncements to a "few meaningless platitudes" about Wilson's record and made no mention of supporting him for the presidency.[7] After Wilson carried both the state and national Democratic conventions, however, the governor belatedly assumed a prominent role in his campaign. Colquitt received an appointment to the Democratic Party's National Advisory Campaign Committee and was soon active in various fund-raising efforts. At one point Colquitt suggested raising $750,000 by obtaining pledges of $2,500 each from 300 people; the governor offered to start the campaign with his personal pledge of $2,500. Despite the demands of campaigning for himself and Wilson, however, the situation on the border was never far from the governor's thoughts. While discussing campaign financing with McAdoo, Colquitt suggested that fund-raising prospects would be enhanced if Wilson would make some critical comments about the "do-nothing" Mexican policy of the Taft administration.[8]

Privately the governor admitted that he did not agree with much of the program being advocated by Wilson. After Wilson spoke favorably of the initiative, referendum, and recall, Colquitt wrote to one of his political associates that "I had been assured by many friends that he had gone entirely away from this heresy."[9] His political support for Wilson was based on political expediency, not on philosophical agreement; Colquitt's main concern was to "get in touch with the [Wilson] organization and have some influence with the administration in the event of Wilson's election."[10]

The defeat of the incumbent Taft by Wilson made the formulation of border policy an even more complicated task; Taft indicated that he would make no major changes in border policy without the prior approval of President-elect Wilson. Colquitt attempted to take advantage of this ambiguous situation to press his own views on the border problem and emphasized a familiar theme: that the failure of federal authorities to deal sternly with the Madero revolt in 1910-1911 had been the source of much of the trouble along the border ever since that time. Colquitt described the border issue as a "most vexatious, perplexing, and dangerous question." The governor criticized federal authorities for failing to cooperate with each other and also with state officials. He flatly accused federal officials of "aiding and abetting" the Madero revolt for which they had been rewarded by Madero with gifts, "some of which are still held-up in the customs houses at Eagle Pass and perhaps at Laredo." Colquitt said that he would forego the usual patronage requests made of the president in favor of asking Wilson to assign federal officials to the border who are in "sympathy and harmony with the State Government of Texas in its efforts to preserve law, order, and neutrality on the border."[11]

Wilson's response was encouraging if somewhat vague. Saying that he would always welcome the governor's suggestions, Wilson informed Colquitt that he was "very much interested in what you say of the situation on the Mexican border and should like to know anything further that is in your thought in that matter."[12] Having dealt with federal authorities for two years who did not seem to be particularly interested in his views on border policy, Colquitt quickly responded to Wilson's overtures. In a partisan letter to the president-elect, Colquitt complained of the lack of cooperation between state and federal officials because of the "jealousy of some of the Army officers for the Texas Rangers." He claimed that additional troubles along the Rio Grande were due to "Republican office-holders who are out of harmony and out of sympathy with the State administration." With the national and state governments under the control of the Democratic Party, the governor expressed confidence that there would no longer be federal officials along the border who were "antagonistic to and will not cooperate with the State Democratic administration in preserving law and order."[13]

The Fall of Madero

While Colquitt and Wilson were looking forward to a peaceful and scheduled transfer of presidential power in March 1913, Mexico was moving toward an earlier and unscheduled change in presidential administrations. From its inception, the Madero administration had aroused an impressive array of violent political opposition that ran the political spectrum from disappointed agrarian reformers under Zapata to former supporters of Porfirio Díaz who wanted to turn back the political clock. These incessant rebellions were often manifestations of the political opportunism that the Revolution of 1910 had encouraged or of the traditional regionalism that had influenced rebellions throughout Mexican history. Madero had always been more symbol than leader of the Revolution and never solved the equation of political, financial, and military factors needed for a stable government. In addition, the defense of his administration to a great extent depended upon an army that was basically a holdover from the Porfirian epoch.

By the time that Colquitt started his second term in January 1913, the political situation in Mexico was reaching a crisis. Disgruntled army officers in Mexico City were openly plotting the overthrow of Madero, and reports from U.S. Ambassador Henry Lane Wilson were increasingly pessimistic about the ability of the government to control the situation. Ambassador Wilson informed Secretary of State Knox that he regarded the "whole situation as gloomy, if not hopeless." The Madero regime was "suffering from universal unpopularity," could not arrange its finances, and received only "contempt and dislike" from the federal army. The economic situation was "hourly assuming more threatening proportions," with the government resorting to "all sorts of quack economic remedies" to deal with the deterioration of the economy.[14]

As opposition to the Madero government grew, conditions on the border — especially at Laredo and El Paso — steadily worsened. Governor Colquitt became more belligerent in both his public and private pronouncements, urging President Taft to take measures to protect the border and pressing for U.S. military intervention in Mexico.[15] As in past troubles, Colquitt concentrated the Rangers along the Rio Grande in order "to have as many as possible on the firing line" and directed the commander of the Ranger force at El Paso, Captain Hughes, to "keep me advised of situation and shoot straight if necessary."[16] The governor assumed that, as in past rebellions, Juárez would be a prime point of confrontation with a corresponding threat to El Paso. Unlike earlier and unsuccessful revolts on the periphery, this latest one would strike directly at the heart of the government in Mexico City.

The long-expected coup against the Madero government finally materialized on February 9 when forces in Mexico City rebelled under the leadership of two long-time opponents of the Madero regime, General Bernardo Reyes and General Felix Díaz. Reyes was rallying after his earlier unsuccessful revolt plotted in Texas while Díaz—nephew of the former dictator—was also a veteran of a previous rebellion against Madero. Reyes was killed on the first day of the revolt in an attack on the National Palace, but the coup produced a ten-day battle in the heart of the capital that saw many civilian casualties. Ambassador Wilson called for American intervention, and, showing some appreciation for the local situation, not only demanded protection for American personnel from the Madero administration but also requested that "all saloons and pulque shops be closed."[17] The coup successfully ended on February 18 when General Victoriano Huerta—who had earlier defeated Pascual Orozco and was currently commanding Madero's forces in Mexico City—went over to the rebels and ordered the arrest of Madero and Vice-president José María Pino Suárez.[18]

The unfolding crisis in Mexico City provoked new activity from Governor Colquitt, who wrote President Taft urging that the United States had the duty to intervene in Mexico under the Monroe Doctrine. The secretary of state politely rejected the governor's novel interpretation of the Monroe Doctrine but indicated that "precautionary naval dispositions" had been made to deal with the situation.[19] With less than a month remaining in office, Taft was not about to abandon the cautious policy that had marked his administration. So, with no military response from Washington, the governor began his own preparations. Colquitt was disturbed about the shortage of federal troops along the border, especially the lower Rio Grande, and informed President Taft that if additional federal troops were not provided, he would "send the Texas troops to take charge of the situation on the Rio Grande."[20] The War Department initially declined to send additional forces, which prompted more communications from the governor. Colquitt telegraphed the Democratic senator from Texas, Charles Culberson, that the Taft administration "did not seem to understand the seriousness of the local situation" and that the current federal policy on protection of the border was an "outrage" to the State of Texas.[21] Senator Culberson paid a personal visit to the president, and the Taft administration finally relented and announced that more troops would be dispatched to the border.[22]

Invasion Scare at Brownsville

Disagreement between Taft and Colquitt over protection of the border led to a near-confrontation at Brownsville in late February. On February 24, state authorities at Brownsville received a report that the Mexican military commander across the river in Matamoros was holding Americans for ransom and that there had been a threat to blow up the American consulate in that city. Captain F. A. Head, commander of the local Texas National Guard company, asked Colquitt whether he was authorized to protect Americans across the river. The governor ordered Head's unit to active duty but specifically directed him not to cross the Rio Grande. He also instructed Head to convey a warning to Mexican officials: "Notify Mexican commander at Matamoros who is demanding money that if he harms a single Texan his life will be demanded as forfeit."[23]

Colquitt ordered additional units of the Texas National Guard at Houston, Corpus Christi, and Austin to be prepared to entrain for Brownsville. Before dispatching additional state troops, Colquitt called General Steever, former commander at El Paso and now commander of the Southern Department at Fort Sam Houston, to determine whether federal troops might be dispatched to the scene. The governor also informed Steever that he had no intention of ordering state troops across the river. Steever agreed with the need for federal troops at Brownsville but had to request authorization for the movement from the War Department. When officials in Washington did not move rapidly enough for the governor, he took it on himself to order the alerted Texas National Guard units to proceed to Brownsville. The additional state forces had scarcely been dispatched when Steever received authorization to send federal troops to the area. Apparently fearing that the state troops might intervene in Matamoros regardless of the governor's assurances, the secretary of war ordered the troop movement to Brownsville to prevent any violations of the neutrality laws, not for the purpose of protecting Americans in Matamoros. Since the enforcement of neutrality laws would mean the blocking of any movement of armed men across the border, the War Department seemed to be more concerned about the intentions of the governor of Texas than about the actions of the Mexican military commander at Matamoros.[24]

The sending of federal troops required new negotiations between state and federal authorities. Expecting a jurisdictional rather than a military clash, Colquitt telegraphed General Steever: "I hope your instructions from Washington will not require you to interfere with the orderly discharge of their duty by state troops which have been forwarded to Brownsville."[25] After being informed by Steever that federal forces were being sent to prevent violations of the neutrality laws, Colquitt complained to the general that such instructions were "entirely unnecessary" since state troops had been directed from the beginning not to cross the river. In concluding his latest telegram to Steever, Colquitt indicated that the matter was far from closed: "We will not hesitate to use state troops to protect Texas people."[26] Steever immediately notified the governor that the army would not interfere with state troops "in the orderly performance of state duties within the state."[27]

All the negotiations and troop movements ultimately proved unnecessary. Subsequent reports indicated that there was never a "ransom demand" made for Americans nor had any threat been made to blow up the American consulate. The Mexican commander at Matamoros had placed a levy upon Mexican residents for the support of his troops and had specifically exempted Americans from the impost. Instead of a threat to destroy the American consulate, the commander only had warned that he would withdraw his troops if the levy was not paid, leaving Matamoros undefended.[28] The rapid evaporation of the "crisis at Matamoros" permitted Colquitt to return to another perennial preoccupation: state finances. One of the main reasons Colquitt had attempted to get federal troops sent to Brownsville was to avoid the expense of sending state troops. With no threat to lives or property, the governor wanted to release the National Guard units as quickly as possible. On February 27 he wired Adjutant General Hutchings: "If state troops are no longer needed, pay them off and send them home."[29] The next day Hutchings demobilized all of the National Guard companies at Brownsville.[30]

This demobilization, however, did not bring an end to federal-state squabbling over the Matamoros incident. Colquitt complained to the secretary of state that reports given by federal authorities to "northern newspapers" made it appear that state troops were sent to Brownsville for the purpose of invading Mexico which was "without foundation and wholly untrue." The governor also repeated his claim that he had acted only after an appeal for assistance by the American consul at Matamoros, J. H. Johnson, and after requesting without success that federal troops be dispatched.[31] The Department of State investigation into the affair presented a much different picture of the incident. Consul Johnson denied that he had ever appealed for assistance to state or local authorities. He attributed the confusion to an "exaggerated report" sent to Governor Colquitt, although he admitted that the dispatch of state and federal troops had provided a "good moral effect" on the Brownsville-Matamoros area.[32]

Colquitt as usual wanted the last word in the argument. In a speech at Dallas on March 2, he fired a parting shot at the border policy of the outgoing Taft administration. Colquitt began by observing that the "vigorous policy" followed by state officials had met with a "fair amount of success." Control of Mexico's army was now in the hands of "anarchists," and the northern Mexican states were "infested by bandits who look on Texas property as a reserve from which they can draw at will." Texans along the Rio Grande had "the utmost contempt" for federal border policy because "the powers at Washington have not at any time opened their eyes to the dangers." The governor dismissed as "absurd and ridiculous" reports that the Texas National Guard would invade Mexico but vowed that he would "protect Texas people in Texas. If any person at any time thinks my people will be left to the mercy of cutthroats and robbers, they are badly mistaken."[33] Having failed in repeated efforts to spur the Taft administration to stronger action along the border, Colquitt could only look forward to the arrival of the presumably friendlier and more cooperative administration of his fellow Democrat, Woodrow Wilson.

New Administration, Old Problems

The confusion and disunity that marked the final days of the Taft administration carried over into the Wilson presidency. Madero's overthrow put General Victoriano Huerta in the Mexican presidency, but the United States government had not extended diplomatic recognition to the new regime. Two reasons for withholding recognition had to do with the short time remaining in Taft's term as well as a desire to use it as a bargaining tool in obtaining concessions from any new Mexican government. The killing of Madero and his vice-president while being transferred to prison further complicated the problem of recognition. General Huerta maintained that Madero and Pino Suárez were accidentally killed when a group of Madero's supporters attempted to free them. Ambassador Henry Lane Wilson supported this official version in the face of widespread reports that Huerta had ordered the executions.[34]

In the midst of this confusion, President Wilson had to establish his own administration, develop a general foreign policy, and formulate a particular program for coping with the revolution in Mexico and border problems. Wilson and his Secretary of State, William Jennings Bryan, were both politicians who had risen to power and prominence essentially on domestic issues. Wilson had remarked shortly before his inauguration that it "would be the irony of fate if my administration had to deal chiefly with foreign affairs."[35] When that irony was realized, Wilson often showed himself philosophically and temperamentally ill-suited to cope with international problems, whether it was border policy with Mexico or submarine warfare with Germany.

Wilson had demonstrated little knowledge of, or even interest in, foreign affairs prior to assuming the presidency. Instead of compensating for this deficiency by selecting a secretary of state experienced in diplomatic affairs,

Wilson compounded the problem by appointing Bryan, who was even less equipped to deal with foreign affairs and whose appointment was strictly a product of party politics. Both Wilson and Bryan were idealists when it came to international relations and attempted to conduct foreign policy based on eternal verities rather than practical political concerns. Such idealism was sadly out of place in the rough and tumble politics in revolutionary Mexico or even in South Texas where Wilson had garnered many votes. The evangelical nature of Wilsonian diplomacy, in which the president tried to spread the true gospel of American democracy to the political heathens, brought out the pedantic side of Wilson's character. The former history professor and college president often seemed to be lecturing his international colleagues, rather than negotiating with them.

In addition to these philosophical limitations, Wilson's foreign policy also suffered from his personalistic approach to the conduct of international relations. Such an approach caused confusion within his own administration and complicated efforts to promote cooperation between state and federal authorities in the formulation and implementation of border policy. The president distrusted the State Department, which he considered vaguely aristocratic if not downright Republican, and feared that Bryan was not capable of handling delicate diplomatic negotiations. The result was that the president often bypassed regular diplomatic channels in favor of operating through his advisors and special agents. This approach took what had been a frequent difficulty with border policy—namely, communications—and converted it into a pervasive problem that virtually guaranteed a maximum of jurisdictional disputes and federal-state friction. There had been complaints from the earliest days of the Madero revolution that federal and state authorities had difficulty communicating and coordinating their actions; the incident at Matamoros had clearly demonstrated the problem. Even among federal agencies there were problems of coordination and cooperation in carrying out border policy because of the number of agencies involved; with Wilsonian diplomacy yet another set of operatives would have to be taken into account. But in March 1913 these difficulties were not as obvious as they would later become; for the time being Governor Colquitt was optimistic that a Democratic administration in Washington would mean a tougher and better coordinated border policy.

The governor's initial optimism soon gave way. In the face of growing friction late in the Taft administration, Colquitt had ordered state officials to stop aiding federal officers in the enforcement of neutrality legislation. New revolts in the northern border states, occasioned by Huerta's seizure of power, once again caused major problems with the neutrality laws. The rise of the so-called "men of the North"—Venustiano Carranza in Coahuila, Pancho Villa in Chihuahua, and Alvaro Obregón in Sonora—would keep the border region in an almost continuous uproar until long after the end of Colquitt's administration. When the Mexican consul general at San Antonio, J. A. Fernandez, complained to the governor about enforcement of the neutrality laws, Colquitt could only reply that state officials were no longer involved in the implementation of federal neutrality laws and that there was a "disinclination on the part of U.S. civil authorities to cooperate with those of the State of Texas in the enforcement of law along the Rio Grande." The governor did indicate that he was prepared "at any and all times to use the National Guard to protect the citizens of the State."[36]

Colquitt's disenchantment with federal border policy increased as the result of another dispute over the passage of Mexican troops through Texas. A group of Mexican soldiers loyal to President Huerta had been driven out of Sonora into Arizona by rebel forces. The U.S. government proposed to get rid of these unwanted intruders by transporting them to El Paso where they would be permitted to return to Juárez, which was still under the control of forces friendly to Huerta. When the government transported the Mexican soldiers to El Paso without consulting authorities in any of the states involved, Governor Colquitt immediately took exception. A highly agitated Colquitt wired Ranger Captain John R. Hughes that "these Mexican soldiers have no right to pass through Texas without permission from me" and directed Hughes to arrest any of the Mexican soldiers that attempted to cross at El Paso.[37]

The governor then turned his attention to the authorities in Washington, directing strongly worded communications to President Wilson, Secretary of State Bryan, and Secretary of War Lindley Garrison. Colquitt wired the president insisting upon the "rights of the State of Texas to protest against the harboring or introduction of troops of a foreign country" and demanding that the Mexican soldiers be returned to Arizona.[38] With the secretary of state, Colquitt resurrected an objection made in connection with earlier troop movements: that the introduction of Mexican troops into Texas, especially at El Paso, would invite an attack by a rival faction. The governor protested to Bryan that "we have been laboring diligently to preserve order on the border, observe neutrality laws, and afford contending parties equal treatment."[39] Colquitt complained to Secretary of War Garrison that border troubles had already caused Texas "much trouble and expense" and that he was surprised by the introduction of Mexican troops into Texas "where we already have more trouble with this element than we desire."[40]

The dispute dragged on for months with the Mexican soldiers interned at Fort Bliss outside of El Paso. The governor had the last word on the subject literally and figuratively. He sent a blistering telegram to Secretary of State Bryan on August 4, declaring: "I do not wish to assent to any course which will aid, increase, or encourage the barbarous and inhuman warfare which the policy of the United States government is permitting across its border and in the Republic of Mexico generally toward our own citizens."[41] The federal government later moved the confined soldiers to California, and the War Department issued an order that all Mexican soldiers crossing the border during battle be returned immediately to Mexico.[42]

Wilson and "Watchful Waiting"

Colquitt soon concluded that although there might be a new Democratic administration in Washington, there was no indication that President Wilson intended to pursue a more aggressive policy along the border. Wilson's policy became known as "watchful waiting," a composite of two phrases used by the president in a message to Congress in late August 1913. Wilson had told the Congress that he would "wait" and "vigilantly watch" political developments in Mexico.[43] Such an attitude was unlikely to please Governor Colquitt, whose principal criticism of the Taft administration had been that it did too much waiting and watching.

The refusal of the Wilson administration to recognize any of the contending factions in Mexico further complicated border policy. With various parts of the Texas-Mexican border in the control of both the rebels and the Huerta forces, Colquitt was unsure of the extent to which he could engage in normal relations with Mexican officials; indeed, the governor was uncertain as to who were "officials" in the northern Mexican states. With small-scale raids taking place almost constantly across the Rio Grande, Colquitt was particularly interested in initiating extradition proceedings with the governors of the Mexican states along the border; extradition, however, was virtually impossible as long as diplomatic recognition was withheld.

The uncertain situation along the Rio Grande was the product of larger policy goals being pursued by the Wilson administration. While the president was reluctant to intervene militarily in Mexico, he was not the least bit reluctant to interfere in Mexican affairs. President Wilson repeatedly rejected Ambassador Wilson's suggestions to recognize the Huerta regime and recalled the ambassador, who then resigned in August 1913.[44] Through a series of personal representatives sent to Mexico, President Wilson worked to obtain a promise from Huerta that he would not be a candidate for the presidency in the elections which were scheduled for the fall of 1913; unsuccessful in obtaining such a commitment, Wilson then initiated a policy of seeking the elimination of Huerta from the presidency.[45]

While President Wilson focused his attention on Mexico City, the governor was more concerned with deteriorating developments on the border. Colquitt believed that the only way to relieve the situation was for the federal government to issue an ultimatum to the Mexican government that it restore order on the international boundary or face American intervention.[46] In a letter to President Wilson on the question of intervention, the governor observed: "I know your desire for peace, but this country owes to itself and to Christianity a duty which it ought not hesitate longer to perform." Drawing upon "a fair knowledge of the situation," Colquitt assured the president that American intervention would be welcomed by the "better class in Mexico" and even by the lower classes "whose lives are daily being sacrificed by most inhumane warfare." Colquitt discounted any ideological content to the revolution, maintaining that "the troubles in Mexico are largely fomented by desperados and selfish leaders desiring a license to loot, rob and murder."[47]

Colquitt's requests that the federal government adopt what he euphemistically referred to as a "firm policy" met with only polite acknowledgments from Washington and assurances that everything possible was being done to protect American lives and property along the border.[48] Within the Wilson administration, there was considerable doubt about the advisability or even feasibility of American intervention in Mexico. Secretary of State Bryan strongly opposed intervention, saying that it would put "property rights above human rights" and that the United States would no longer be looked to as "the leader of the peace movement and as the exponent of human rights."[49] Edward House, Wilson's closest advisor, expressed doubts about the readiness of the army and navy to intervene in Mexico.[50]

Military officials were also worried about the practicality of intervention, especially defense of the border if the United States moved into Mexico. General Tasker Bliss, recently appointed commander of the Southern Department headquartered at Fort Sam Houston, pointed out the dangers that intervention posed for the border region in a lengthy letter to the president of the War College. Bliss warned that intervention would almost certainly unite the warring factions in Mexico; should they unite, their combined forces would greatly outnumber U.S. troops along the international boundary. The general believed that the success of a local invasion of U.S. territory by Mexican forces was a "foregone conclusion" and flatly stated that the "present regular force cannot guarantee the integrity of the border."[51]

Secretary of War Garrison wrote in a similar vein to Secretary of State Bryan. Garrison warned that it was possible and even probable that American intervention would result in a Mexican invasion. Garrison's fears were particularly relevant to those living along the Texas-Mexican border. The U.S. Army had no more than 4,000 troops along the entire border from California to Texas while there were 5,000 *huertista* soldiers in the vicinity of Juárez alone. The combined national guards of Texas, New Mexico, and Arizona would number only about 3,700 men. The secretary of war singled out El Paso, Laredo, Eagle Pass, and Brownsville—all Texas border towns—as likely targets for Mexican attack, and noted that Mexican forces had also been concentrating recently at points where railways crossed the border.[52]

Had Colquitt known of the military problems confronting the federal government, he might have adopted a less belligerent and less independent stance. As it was, the governor was content to pursue his own policy despite the limited military resources available to the state government. Although the Rangers had an authorized strength of eighty-eight men, there were only sixteen actually serving. As for the National Guard, Texas ranked seventh among the states in terms of total financial assistance from the federal government but ranked forty-sixth in terms of money appropriated by the state legislature on a per capita basis.[53] Financial considerations further restricted the governor's military response as he was reluctant to incur the additional expense involved in calling out units of the Texas National Guard. Although Colquitt frequently voiced his concern about border security, border disturbances resulted in the National Guard being mobilized on only four occasions during 1913; on three of those four occasions, local officials—not the governor—called it out.[54] Despite his military shortcomings, however, Colquitt continued his tough talk. After another change of control at Juárez in November, he commented: "In the event Mexicans start any trouble, we will protect our citizens and not wait for Washington to act."[55]

The Vergara Incident

As resistance to the Huerta regime in Mexico increased in late 1913 and early 1914, both the situation on the border and relations between state and federal authorities worsened. The growing antagonism between Colquitt and the Wilson administration came to a head in the so-called "Vergara incident" of February 1914. Clemente Vergara, a Texas citizen, owned a ranch at Palafox, Texas, across the Rio Grande from the Mexican village of Hidalgo which was in a region under the control of the forces of President Victoriano Huerta. Vergara customarily pastured his horses on an island in the Rio Grande that he had attempted to buy; the state land commissioner, however, had refused the purchase request on the grounds that it was uncertain whether the island belonged to Texas or to Mexico. On the morning of February 12, 1914, Mexican federal troops removed eleven of Vergara's horses from the disputed island.[56]

Vergara's political and legal problems brought him into contact with a prominent figure on the border: Sheriff Amador Sánchez of Laredo. Sánchez had remained as sheriff of Webb County and had continued to dabble in Mexican politics despite his own legal problems arising out of the Reyes conspiracy. A supporter of the Huerta regime, Sánchez had made a strenuous effort to block arms shipments to the Constitutionalists, the name applied to those who opposed Huerta and who followed at least nominally the leadership of Venustiano Carranza. Vergara approached Sánchez about using his influence with the huertistas to obtain the return of the stolen horses. Sánchez agreed and, after a meeting with the local Huerta commander, arranged for Vergara to cross the Rio Grande and recover his horses. As soon as Vergara arrived on the Mexican side, huertista soldiers arrested him and took him to Hidalgo. On February 14 Vergara's wife and daughter saw him alive for the last time in the Hidalgo jail. According to reports, Vergara was tortured and hanged the following day by Mexican federal troops.[57]

Colquitt seized upon the Vergara incident as an illustration of the failure of Wilson's Mexican policy and of the inability—or unwillingness—of federal authorities to protect American lives and property on the border. The governor sent a sharply worded telegram on February 26 to President Wilson in which he brought up two controversial issues. First, after complaining about border conditions in general and the Vergara hanging in particular, Colquitt asked for permission to send the Texas Rangers into Mexico in pursuit of persons who committed crimes in Texas and then returned to Mexico. The governor's request was clearly in relation to the Vergara incident; it, however, ignored the doubtful jurisdictional status of the island where the removal of the horses took place and the fact that the killing of Vergara had occurred in Mexico. Colquitt also challenged Wilson's policy of nonrecognition by asking whether he should deal with rebel officials or Huerta's officers in trying to obtain action on the Vergara case. The federal government's response to Colquitt was both negative and evasive. Secretary of State Bryan emphatically refused permisson for state officers to cross into Mexico, stressing that only the federal government could send troops across the border. Bryan also declined to give a definitive answer as to which faction the governor ought to deal with in Mexico. President Wilson answered that no forces would be sent into Mexico without the consent of Mexican authorities and that the U.S. government had not sought, and would not seek, such consent.[58]

The federal reply provoked the bitterest rejoinder to date from Colquitt. The governor issued a lengthy statement in which he charged that "there seems to be a deliberate effort at Washington, in dealing with the Mexican border question, to make me appear ridiculous before the people of the country." He denied any intention to sensationalize the situation, saying he was only interested in apprehending "the murderers of Texas citizens." Colquitt said that it was impossible to "proceed intelligently" with such matters if he did not know who the recognized authorities in Mexico were and asserted that there were certain questions, such as the refugee problem, that "cannot be determined by the Federal Government but must be handled by the State Government of Texas."[59]

Bryan and Colquitt continued their mutually unsatisfactory correspondence over the Vergara incident. In another telegram to the secretary of state on February 27, the governor again broached the two issues he had raised in his previous communication. On the question of sending the Rangers across the border, Colquitt observed: "I do not want to invade Mexico with military force. I asked your consent to allow me to send Texas Rangers, who are peace officers, in pursuit of those who are constantly transgressing our law." The governor again raised the sensitive issue of who was the recognized authority in Mexico so that he could begin extradition proceedings.[60]

In his reply Secretary of State Bryan did little to clarify the position of the federal government or to appease Governor Colquitt. Bryan repeated his refusal to sanction a Ranger crossing of the international boundary on the grounds that "no distinction should be drawn between them and any other armed force." He also stated that the United States did not recognize any government in Mexico but that Colquitt should direct his request for extradition to the governor of Nuevo León, the Mexican border state where Vergara had been killed.[61] Bryan's suggestion conveniently ignored the fact that there were two governors of Nuevo León—a rebel governor and one loyal to the Huerta regime.

Colquitt responded to the secretary of state with a 3,000-word letter, much of which was devoted to a denunciation of Wilson's border policy. The governor wrote that he did not contemplate a "military expedition against the territory or people of Mexico" but only wanted to use the Rangers to "compel respect and inflict punishment on lawless elements." Colquitt also offered another one of his novel legal interpretations guaranteed to upset officials in Washington. One of the provisions of the state constitution gave the governor the power to repel foreign invasions; Colquitt interpreted the provision to include the implied right of pursuit across the border by state forces. The governor again questioned the Wilsonian policy of nonrecognition and charged that it "encouraged the anarchy that prevailed" in the Mexican border states. Colquitt concluded that such a policy was in effect intervention in the internal affairs of Mexico and that, once involved, the United States would not be able to withdraw "except in blood."[62] When Colquitt asked the secretary of state which of the two governors of Nuevo León he should deal with, he received no reply.[63]

With little assistance or guidance from the federal government, Governor Colquitt increasingly formulated and implemented his own policy. He requested the extradition of six Mexican federal soldiers reportedly involved in the Vergara incident from the huertista governor of Nuevo León, General Joaquín Maas, who immediately ordered their arrest. Although Governor Maas appeared willing to cooperate, the huertista commander at Nuevo Laredo whose troops were involved maintained that Vergara was still alive and serving with the Constitutionalist rebels. In requesting extradition, the

State of Texas charged the men with horse theft rather than murder, since the theft had taken place on U.S. soil while the murder had occurred in Mexico. Colquitt later commented: "I have just begun my fight to uphold the rights of the citizens of Texas. To say I am going the limit to protect the Americans in Texas from any harm but mildly expresses it."[64] When Mexican federal officials asked to survey the island in the Rio Grande where the Vergara incident began in order to determine whether it belonged to the United States or Mexico, they made their request to Governor Colquitt rather than to federal authorities. The governor readily granted permission for the survey.[65]

The actual extradition request furnished two valuable insights into the Vergara incident. First, the fact that Colquitt made the request of the huertista governor indicated that his dispute with Secretary of State Bryan involved philosophical disagreements rather than practical legal problems. Since the Vergara incident occurred in an area under huertista control and involved huertista soldiers, there was no real question as to whether application for extradition should be made to the huertista governor or the rebel governor. Colquitt instead was trying to use the extradition question to force the Wilson administration's hand on the issue of nonrecognition. Second, the attitude of the huertista commander at Nuevo León is more revealing than the cooperation extended by the huertista governor, General Maas. The explanation offered that Vergara was alive and serving with the Constitutionalists signified why Vergara had been seized and executed. Huertista authorities suspected that Vergara had been aiding the Constitutionalists, primarily by running guns across the border. The involvement of Sheriff Sánchez, whose pro-Huerta views were well known, further indicated that Vergara was set up to be captured by the huertistas rather than being victim of random violence on the border.

The Vergara incident suddenly escalated on March 8 when a group of armed Texans crossed into Mexico, exhumed Vergara's body, and returned it to the Texas side of the Rio Grande. Even more sensational was the original report that Texas Rangers had been involved in the operation. Texas Ranger Captain J. J. Sanders had originally telegraphed the governor: "Have just returned from Hidalgo, Mexico. Have the body of Clemente Vergara on Texas soil."[66] When President Wilson picked up his *Washington Post* on March 9, he was greeted by the following headlines on the front page: "Armed Texas Rangers Boldly Invade Mexico and Bring Back Mutilated Body of Vergara. Charred Hand of American Rancher Evidence of Brutal Torture by Federal Troops. Shot Three Times, Skull Crushed and Then Hanged." The *Post* went on to report that the Rangers, "determined that for once American manhood should not truckle to Mexican trickery and deceit," had led a group of ninety men into Mexico like a "Cossack horde." The Rangers had only "their

carbines as their warrants and their six-shooters as their passports." The president must have been particularly struck by the report that the Rangers were
ready for a "repeat performance" if necessary.[67]

If President Wilson had read the *San Antonio Express* the same day, he
would have gotten a more subdued account of what supposedly had taken
place. Under the headline "Armed Texans Cross Border," the *Express* reported
that "nine heavily armed men" had crossed into Mexico early in the morning
of March 8, recovered Vergara's body, and returned it to Texas. The recovery
operation had been made by "friends and relatives of the dead man." As to
actions by the Rangers, the newspaper account said that there had been
Rangers in the vicinity but that their exact role was not known.[68]

If Governor Colquitt was upset by reports that Texas Rangers had been
wandering around northern Mexico digging up bodies, his subsequent
actions failed to indicate it. The governor released Sanders' telegram to the
newspapers with the observation that he had "no complaint to make" about
Sanders' actions. When questioned further about any official involvement in
the recovery of Vergara's body, Colquitt merely replied: "We wanted
Vergara's body to determine the manner of his death, and we have it. Some

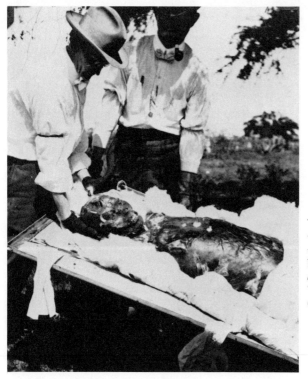

Two Texans with
what was purported
to be Vergara's
body. *Photograph
courtesy of the Barker
Texas History Library
Collection.*

people may call this an 'invasion,' but it was not."[69]

The recovery of Vergara's body converted a border incident into a national political issue that called into question Wilson's entire Mexican policy. Morris Sheppard—Democratic antagonist of Colquitt elected in 1913 to serve out the unexpired term of Colquitt ally Texas' U.S. Senator Joseph Bailey—bitterly denounced the governor's border policy in a Senate speech. Sheppard said that President Wilson and Secretary of State Bryan had handled the Mexican situation "in the best possible manner" and that the critics of the administration "would have plunged the country into war with Mexico." Sheppard contended that the people of Texas "almost unanimously" supported the Mexican policy of Wilson and Bryan and "deplored the attitude" assumed by the governor of Texas. The freshman senator even accused Vergara of "voluntarily inviting trouble" by crossing the Rio Grande and hinted that Vergara had been involved in the internal politics of Mexico. Sheppard concluded by saying that there was "no excitement over the Vergara incident except in the imagination of the governor of Texas and a few adventurous spirits along the river."[70]

The controversy over the recovery of Vergara's body had hardly started before a considerably less sensational version began to emerge. Governor Colquitt issued an official statement denying that Texas Rangers had ever crossed the border and claiming that Captain Sanders had found the body of Vergara on the Texas side of the river after being notified by those actually involved in the recovery operation. Colquitt denied that he had ever ordered Sanders to go into Mexico to recover the body. The official state account of the incident at this point was that a small group of Vergara's friends had actually recovered the body, left it on the Texas side of the Rio Grande, and notified Sanders where it could be found. As to Sanders' telegram that he had just returned from Hidalgo, Nuevo León, the explanation was that Sanders had asked the American consul at Nuevo Laredo to send the telegram for him and the consul had incorrectly wired that Sanders had just returned "from Hidalgo" rather than "to Laredo" as Sanders had wanted.[71] Even the story about Vergara's mutilation came in for some revision. Sanders had originally reported to Adjutant General Hutchings that "there were two bullet holes in the head, one hand was burned to a crisp and the head looked like it had been mashed in."[72] Dr. O. J. Cook, health officer at Laredo, examined the body and reported to Governor Colquitt that there were no signs of torture.[73] The Huerta administration even tried to save face by issuing a statement that Mexican federal authorities had delivered the body to Americans on the international bridge between Laredo and Nuevo Laredo.[74]

Regardless of what the true story might have been, the incident accelerated the deterioration in federal-state relations over border policy. Newspapers throughout the country seized on the incident, making an instant celebrity out of Colquitt and contrasting his aggressive policy with the "watchful waiting" of the Wilson administration. Several newspapers wrote the governor asking for his picture in Ranger attire, but he modestly declined. One journalist photographed Colquitt leaving the capitol followed by other reporters and said that he would caption the photograph "Governor Leaving Capitol with Texas Rangers."[75]

Even after the more subdued version of the recovery became public, Colquitt continued to use the Vergara incident to attack Wilson's Mexican policy. At the same time that he denied any Ranger involvement in the recovery action, Colquitt on March 9 said that he preferred not to express any opinion "as to what might be done by the Rangers in case of emergency in the future." The governor maintained that "Texas has not committed an act of aggression against Mexico, but Mexico is consistently committing acts of aggression against the citizens of Texas." Colquitt concluded by charging that Wilson's Mexican policy was "largely responsible" for murders and outrages such as the Vergara case and that he would make no official report of the incident to Washington unless specifically requested to do so. Colquitt's mild denials that the Rangers were involved in the Vergara recovery were met with some skepticism in Washington, particularly when Colquitt displayed such enthusiasm for keeping the controversy alive. Colquitt held out the possibility of further violations of the international boundary when he offered a $1,000 reward for any of Vergara's killers who might be delivered on Texas soil.[76]

At a meeting of the Texas Cattle Raisers' Association in Fort Worth on March 10, the governor asserted that he had already "opened negotiations" with Mexican authorities and would deal directly with them in matters relating to the rights of Texans. On this occasion, it seemed as if Colquitt were not only going to follow his own foreign policy but also was considering taking Texas out of the Union once again. As the governor entered the auditorium to address the cattlemen, the band struck up a spirited rendition of "Dixie" which soon had the crowd roaring. In response to cries from the audience to "tell us about Mexico," Colquitt discarded his prepared speech on the Livestock Sanitary Commission and quarantine regulations in favor of an extemporaneous and belligerent discourse on states' rights and Wilson's Mexican policy.

Colquitt began his speech with some complimentary remarks about the efforts of General Bliss, commander of the Southern Department, to protect Texas citizens and his cooperative attitude toward state officials. Those were to be the only favorable comments directed at federal authorities that day. The governor hurled a direct challenge at the Wilson administration: "I defy any authority or any power on the face of the earth to take from the governor of Texas the right to protect its citizens from wrong. The defense of the rights of the people along the border belongs to Texas, and they shall have its full protection while I am governor." Colquitt also responded to Morris Sheppard's attack on him in the U.S. Senate: "If little Morris Sheppard will resign his seat in the U.S. Senate tomorrow, I will resign as governor and see whether the people of Texas endorse him or me—or Woodrow Wilson."[77]

The governor then returned to his extraordinary exposition on states' rights: "The Governor of the State of Texas is superior to the President of the United States on matters entrusted to his care and keeping. The Democratic Party has forgotten that State lines exist." Colquitt also offered a hypothetical situation in which President Wilson or Secretary of State "Billy" Bryan was kidnapped, taken across the Rio Grande, and "butchered as other Texas citizens have been butchered: How many of you would have gone across the border with the Rangers to bring his body back?" Colquitt denounced his fellow politicians who did not "have the nerve to stand and defend Texas" and who had criticized the governor because he would not "bow down and kiss the golden idol at Washington. I may retire from office, but I'll never kiss anybody's toe at Washington." Colquitt's speech was well received by the cattlemen who spent the rest of the day "debating the foreign policies of the President of the United States and the Governor of Texas" instead of selecting the site for their next convention.[78]

Tacked to a wall is a cartoon of Colquitt standing along the border. *Photograph courtesy of the Barker Texas History Library Collection.*

Federal authorities, meanwhile, helped to reduce the growing tension by exonerating state officials of any involvement in the recovery of Vergara's body. Reports from both the civil and military sides indicated that the recovery operation was strictly a private action and that no state officials were involved in the actual crossing of the river. Piecing together the different reports, federal officials concluded that the recovery operation had been carried out by private citizens who were either relatives or employees of Vergara and that the Rangers had not been part of the recovery team. The Wilson administration, in effect, was prepared to accept the revised version of the incident as the true account.[79] In a further effort to placate the governor, the War Department announced that it was sending two additional regiments of infantry to aid in patrolling the border; the latest troop movement brought the total number of U.S. Army troops in Texas to almost 18,000 — a number larger than the force that had invaded Cuba in 1898. That the War Department was more influenced by political considerations than military requirements was evident from the fact that the commander of the Southern Department had indicated that he did not need additional troops to patrol the border.[80]

Rather than being pleased by the additional federal troops which he had often requested, Colquitt said that two more regiments would not aid in the protection of life and property in Texas. The governor contended that "100 Texas Rangers were worth more than 10,000 U.S. troops" when it came to maintaining law and order on the border. Colquitt indicated that he wished only one thing from the federal government: "I want Washington to send me only three words — 'Go after them.' "[81] The governor also announced that he was sending the entire Ranger force to the border and that he was going to expand the force by recruiting men "who can shoot and will shoot when necessary." If the governor was going to pursue a more vigorous policy on the border, the Rangers certainly needed additional recruits; the entire force numbered only fifteen men.[82]

Despite a considerable amount of talk and even some action by state and federal authorities, there was never a satisfactory resolution of the Vergara incident. No one ever took up the governor on his offer of a $1,000 reward for the delivery in Texas of those sought in connection with the Vergara kidnapping. In fact, the reward offer only served to worsen relations between Washington and Austin. When federal officials worried that it might lead to illegal acts and international complications, Colquitt bitterly riposted: "It is strange to me why the authorities at Washington should be so solicitous about the kidnapping of Mexicans and fear international complications as a result when they so indifferently regard the kidnapping and murdering of Texans and the taking of their property by Mexican marauders and kidnappers."[83] The Huerta administration refused to surrender the soldiers involved in the incident and even denied that Vergara was dead. The official Mexican version was that Vergara was a "bandit by profession" who had been captured but later escaped to fight with another bandit gang.[84] The only positive action taken by the Huerta regime was the return of some of the stolen horses which had been the occasion for the incident in the first place.[85] There was never an investigation at the state or federal level to determine whether Clemente Vergara was an innocent rancher caught on the wrong side of the river or a bandit and revolutionary aiding the Constitutionalist forces. The federal government also declined any further investigation into the recovery of Vergara's body and said that it would not prosecute anyone connected with the operation.[86] For Governor Colquitt it was sufficient that the Vergara incident seemed to epitomize the problems that the border region had suffered since the beginning of the Mexican Revolution in 1910.

The Veracruz Occupation and the Border

Problems in federal-state relations presented only one aspect of growing difficulties with Wilson's Mexican policy in general. The president's plan of trying to eliminate Huerta but avoid intervention was both generating friction within the Wilson administration and complicating efforts to restore calm to the border. U.S. Army chief of staff, General Leonard Wood, complained to British Ambassador Sir Cecil Spring Rice that the White House was not keeping the army and the navy informed of changes in the Mexican situation and said that he "did not believe for a moment that the Administration had now, or ever had had, a deliberate plan in Mexico."[87] As President Wilson moved toward a more belligerent position in regard to Huerta, it became increasingly difficult to synchronize foreign policy with military policy and to harmonize the demands of U.S.-Mexican relations with the problems of border policy.

Wilson began his escalation of the campaign against Huerta as early as August 1913 when the State Department "earnestly urged" that all Americans leave Mexico at once.[88] In October 1913, Huerta dissolved the Mexican congress and arrested 110 congressmen, an action which completed the transition of the Huerta regime to a military dictatorship and prompted new thoughts about intervention on the part of the Wilson administration. Wilson considered the possibility of extending belligerent status to the Constitutionalist forces under Carranza and of blockading Mexican ports to deprive Huerta of his principal sources of revenue. The president even contemplated sending U.S. troops into northern Mexico in the unlikely event that the Mexican border states would agree to the action.[89] Wilson took more direct action in February 1914 when he partially lifted the embargo on arms shipments from the United States to Mexico, which had been in effect since March 1912. Under the revised edict, the Constitutionalists would be permitted to import arms legally but not the Huerta administration.[90]

Wilson hoped that his selective arms embargo would serve as a substitute for American intervention by providing the Constitutionalists with the means to overthrow the Huerta regime and thus restoring peace to Mexico and to the border region. Certainly many of the Constitutionalists felt that this would be the result; Wilson's action brought an effusive response from Pancho Villa, one of the leading Constitutionalist generals: "I think President Wilson is the most just man in the world. All Mexicans will love him now, and we will look upon the United States as our greatest friend because it has done us justice."[91] The action did lead to increased military activity by the Constitutionalists; ironically, this new military activity would help precipitate rather than preclude American intervention. When intervention finally did occur, it would be over an incident far removed from earlier border incidents which had threatened to bring American intervention, and it would take place at a location far distant from the Texas border which had been the scene of so many earlier confrontations.

The occasion for American intervention involved a minor incident at Tampico on April 9, 1914. Constitutionalist advances in the north had led to a siege of the vital oil center at Tampico which was still under Huerta's control. The threat to the oil supplies and the presence of large numbers of foreigners in the area prompted substantial activity in the region by the U.S. Navy. On April 9, huertista soldiers detained a small party of American sailors who had come ashore to purchase gasoline but had disembarked in a restricted area. When higher-ranking Mexican officers learned of the incident, they immediately ordered the release of the Americans and made a formal apology. Rear Admiral Henry T. Mayo, commander of the American squadron at Tampico, informed the Mexican authorities that the apology was not adequate and that he wanted a twenty-one gun salute to the American flag as well. President Wilson and Secretary of State Bryan supported Mayo's demand.[92]

Wilson's support for Mayo's demand was both inconsistent and revealing. Although Wilson refused to recognize the Huerta government, he nevertheless expected it to discharge an international obligation. The president's response provided an important insight into his growing frustration with his own Mexican policy. The Wilson administration had anticipated that the partial lifting of the arms embargo would lead to a rapid Constitutionalist victory; instead, while Wilson's action led to greater military activity by the Constitutionalists, there was no indication by April that the military demise of the Huerta regime was at hand. John Lind, Wilson's personal representative in Mexico, had written Secretary of State Bryan that, "if the revolutionists fail to take active and efficient action by the middle of March, it will be incumbent on the United States to put an end to Huerta's saturnalia of crime and oppression."[93] Wilson's dissatisfaction with the lack of success in bringing about Huerta's downfall indirectly was leading to greater consideration of direct American action to bring about the desired change in government. International pressure was also building for Wilson to resolve the impasse with the Huerta regime one way or another. The British in particular were disenchanted with Wilson's Mexican policy, which they often viewed as no policy at all, and they desired some sort of normalization of relations between the United States and Mexico to protect their own oil interests.[94] All of these factors induced President Wilson to consider an option he had long tried to avoid: the use of large-scale American military force to produce political change in Mexico.

Huerta's response to the American demand was to agree to render the twenty-one gun salute if American forces pledged in advance to return the gesture. This led to additional frenzied negotiations between the Wilson administration and the Huerta regime. Huerta subsequently proposed that the salute be rendered simultaneously and that the matter be submitted to the Hague Tribunal if the United States did not agree. The United States refused a simultaneous salute or a prior promise but indicated that it would return the salute "in accordance with accepted international practices." Huerta then asked the United States to sign a protocol promising to return the salute. Declining on the grounds that it could be construed as recognition of the Huerta government, the United States repeated its oral pledge to return the salute.[95]

Although the U.S.-Mexican wrangling over the diplomatic niceties of exchanging salutes might have struck some as humorous, it was in fact the prelude to American intervention. The Tampico affair became Wilson's diplomatic last straw, and the president submitted the matter to Congress, asking for authority to use military force to obtain redress if necessary. While the Congress debated the president's request, the crisis took a new turn. The State Department received word that the German steamer *Ypiranga* was about to arrive at Veracruz with a large shipment of arms for the Huerta government. Without waiting for congressional authorization, Wilson ordered the army to move into Veracruz and block the unloading of the *Ypiranga*. On April 21 American troops seized the customs house and the dock facilities; the following day, in the light of unexpectedly heavy opposition, U.S. forces moved to occupy the remainder of the city. Expecting only token opposition from the huertista defenders, the occupation had instead produced American losses of nineteen dead and seventy-one wounded. Mexican casualties included 126 killed and 195 wounded, according to the official American count; some Mexican reports put the casualty figure as high as 500. After the initial fighting, Americans settled in for an occupation that was to last for more than six months.[96]

The intervention at Veracruz—although at some distance from the Rio Grande—did have a major impact on the border region. The secretary of war authorized the dispatch of additional troops to the border and alerted all military commanders to the possibility of reprisal attacks along the international boundary. Since Mexican forces still outnumbered American forces in the region, the government feared that the potential invasions spoken of earlier by General Bliss might come to pass.[97] The military situation on the border basically depended upon whether the various Mexican factions would unite behind Huerta in the face of U.S. intervention. With the exception of Pancho Villa, the major Constitutionalist leaders denounced the occupation of Veracruz but offered no military response. Villa publicly said that he would not make war on the Americans and privately told President Wilson that he approved of the occupation. The leadership finally agreed that they would oppose U.S. forces only if they invaded Constitutionalist territory.[98] Since the Wilson administration had no intention of broadening the occupation, the Constitutionalists—especially strong in the north—were effectively neutralized.

In the meantime, Governor Colquitt was making some military plans of his own. He sent President Wilson a list of Mexican cities that he felt should be seized at once should the decision be made to invade Mexico; the list included Matamoros, Nuevo Laredo, Ciudad Porfirio Díaz [Piedras Negras], and Juárez. The governor argued the necessity of the occupation of these towns because of the presence of some 20,000 to 30,000 refugees living along the border who posed an immediate threat to lives and property in Texas. Colquitt also publicly expressed the hope that federal authorities would warn him in advance of any future intervention since "there may be numerous assassinations unless proper protection has been arranged for before the declaration of war."[99] He also called for the formation of "home guards" along the Rio Grande to supplement the Texas National Guard and the Rangers. His plan would divide the border into three districts with a home guard unit of twenty to forty men for each district. A Ranger captain would command each home guard unit, and the adjutant general of Texas would furnish arms and ammunition.[100] The governor received a number of offers from Texans volunteering their military services in the current crisis. E. L. Blackshear, the head of the all-black Prairie View College, offered to organize and lead "at least one negro regiment in the movement to Mexico." George F. Howard, an inmate at the state prison in Huntsville, sent a list of convicts with military experience who were willing to volunteer for the "war with Mexico." Howard acknowledged to Colquitt that a convict regiment would be a "radical move, but you have never faltered in the face of adverse criticism."[101]

The additional state and federal troops provided improved security for the border, but there was no improvement in federal-state relations. While Colquitt continued to praise military authorities in Texas for their cooperation, he complained that "Washington does not appear to realize the true situation on the border and is not giving Texas the protection it should have."[102] New strains appeared in the federal-state relationship as the result of an incident at Brownsville in late April and early May.

Continuing Federal-State Conflict

The incident began on April 23 when Governor Colquitt requested additional federal troops for Brownsville where there were fears that the American intervention at Veracruz might lead to isolated attacks by Mexican troops or to disturbances by Mexicans residing on the Texas side of the river.[103] Further complicating the maintenance of order was a longstanding political feud between the city police force and the sheriff's department; this split between local law enforcement agencies was so bad that Texas Rangers in the vicinity had been ordered to "stay away from the city of Brownsville."[104] When Colquitt did not receive an immediate response to his request for federal troops, he dispatched several units of the Texas National Guard to Brownsville, including the Guard's only artillery battery. Meanwhile General Bliss at Fort Sam Houston had ordered additional federal troops to Brownsville without notifying Governor Colquitt of his actions.[105]

When Secretary of War Garrison became aware of the situation, he became alarmed that there might be some sort of federal-state incident resulting from what he called "conflicting military jurisdiction." Garrison promised Colquitt that he would send more troops if the Guard units were withdrawn; the governor, always looking for a way to reduce expenses, readily agreed. Colquitt gave the order only to have to countermand it when the federal units did not arrive on time. The Guard finally withdrew from Brownsville after serving from April 24 to May 17. Ironically, during the interval the greatest fear of conflict had been the possibility of an altercation between state and federal forces. No major problems resulted from actions on the Mexican side during the same period.[106]

Colquitt's Mexican policy kept Texas politics stirred up as well. The governor's additional efforts to protect the border raised the old problem of financing. Colquitt asked influential Congressman John Nance Garner from South Texas to intervene with the Wilson administration for federal aid to finance state border protection, but Secretary of War Garrison refused to help with state expenses. When a reporter asked Governor Colquitt whether he would call a special session of the state legislature to ask for more funds for border protection, he bluntly replied: "I would rather have war with Mexico than a [special] session of the Texas legislature." The governor's response reflected not only his ongoing political problems with the legislature but also practical financial considerations; it would cost more to call a special session of the legislature than to increase state defenses along the border.[107]

While Colquitt continued to lash out against Wilson's Mexican policy, both Texas senators maintained their support of the president's policy. Colquitt's nemesis, Morris Sheppard, offered his "military services" to Wilson in the event that intervention turned into a war between the United States and Mexico as many believed would happen; there was even a rumor in Washington that Sheppard would be given a commission as a brigadier general and authorized to raise a volunteer cavalry regiment for service in Mexico along the lines of the "Rough Riders" of Spanish-American War fame.[108] Even the more restrained Senator Charles Culberson said that he agreed with the president's refusal to recognize the Huerta regime and that it was the duty of every citizen, "and especially every Democrat," to support Wilson's Mexican policy.[109]

Colquitt refused to do his duty as outlined by Senator Culberson and continued sniping at Wilson's Mexican policy. When informed that Argentina, Brazil, and Chile had agreed to mediate the Huerta-Wilson dispute, Colquitt responded, "I am not advised what questions are to be submitted for mediation. I do not believe that Argentina, Brazil, or Chile will consent to humiliate us more than has already been done."[110] Even when a relative degree of calm returned to the Rio Grande region, the governor attributed it to his forceful policy and said that there had been "too much watchful waiting." Colquitt ended his latest tirade on a menacing note: "If there should be any attempt to renew depredations on Texas soil or bullets are fired into Texas territory by the Mexicans, I will promptly send the State Rangers to give protection to our citizens, and these Rangers will shoot to kill."[111]

While federal and state authorities might dispute the credit for improved conditions along the border, there was no disputing that Wilson had finally achieved his goal of ousting Huerta. Huerta's resignation in July 1914 was due to a great extent to the cumulative effect of actions taken by Wilson since he entered office in March 1913—actions which often provoked criticism from foreigners and the governor of the State of Texas. Wilson's refusal to recognize the Huerta government complicated its foreign relations with many European and Latin American countries which preferred to follow the American lead in dealing with revolutionary regimes in Mexico. Denial of recognition effectively shut off American financial institutions as sources of financing for the Huerta administration and made European financiers more hesitant to make loans to Huerta. When the Americans occupied Veracruz, Huerta lost his most important source of revenue—the customs duties from Mexico's busiest port. Wilson's selective arms embargo ultimately helped produce the Constitutionalist military victories that led to Huerta's downfall. Wilson's "victory" over Huerta, however, did little to pacify critics of his Mexican policy, one of the more prominent of whom, of course, was Colquitt.

Colquitt kept up his verbal attacks on Wilson's Mexican policy until he stepped down from the governorship in January 1915. The governor sent New Year's greetings to the Wilson administration by publicly describing it as "the greatest failure in the history of the presidency" and by labeling Wilson's foreign policy as "imbecilic." Colquitt summed up the Wilson-Bryan management of Mexican affairs as an "egregious failure."[112] The governor's latest broadside brought a response from the Wilson administration. Cone Johnson, who had been defeated by Colquitt for the Democratic nomination for the governorship in 1910 and who was currently serving as State Department solicitor, launched a biting counterattack on the governor's Mexican policy. Claiming that the state government under Colquitt "had collapsed into great confusion," Johnson said that the governor's comments on Wilson's Mexican policy "displayed vast ignorance and an amazing recklessness of statement." Colquitt's "troublemaking in the Mexican situation" had started under the Taft administration and had carried over into the Wilson presidency. As for the governor's continuous criticism of border policy, "Colquitt has long been gnawing that file and his teeth are about worn out."[113]

When Governor Colquitt delivered his last message to the state legislature in January 1915, it was the longest ever delivered by a governor up to that time. Colquitt devoted most of the message to state matters, including such diverse items as the establishment of state parks and the extension of the governor's term to four years. His only reference to his Mexican policy was a defense of the increase in the Ranger force to protect the border; even after the increase, the Ranger force was still far under its authorized strength.[114]

A company of Texas Rangers along the border.
Photograph courtesy of the Barker Texas History Center.

An Evaluation of Border Policies

Colquitt's two terms as governor had seen a stormy period in federal-state relations deriving from basic disagreements over border policy. Much of the friction resulted from poor communications, a not surprising development in view of the fact that border policy involved three levels of government and a number of different agencies. While the lack of communications might be partially attributed to "demands of public policy" as federal authorities maintained, much of it was motivated by a preoccupation with jurisdictional concerns and an ill-concealed disdain that many federal officials had for state authorities.

Coordination among the different federal agencies created a particular problem. The Republican President Taft decided to form the Maneuver Division in Texas without consulting with or informing his own secretary of state in advance. Communication problems became greater after the advent of the Wilson administration. Wilson's penchant for personal diplomacy often left federal officials as confused as state officials about foreign policy direction. The White House frequently kept the War Department uninformed, and even the State Department was often unaware of the course Wilson was pursuing in Mexico, since the president operated through a series of personal representatives. Wilson did not trust the State Department and lacked confidence in Secretary of State Bryan, who was often absent in any case. In Bryan's absence much of the responsibility for running the Department devolved upon Assistant Secretary of State Osborne, "a former governor of Nebraska and an apothecary."[115] The number of federal agencies involved in border policy also complicated communications; the Departments of State, Justice, War, Treasury, and Commerce and Labor all had jurisdictional concerns relating to various aspects of border policy. State authorities, on the other hand, had the advantage of being closer to the scene and of having fewer agencies whose actions had to be coordinated. Colquitt maintained virtually unilateral control over formulation of border policy and operated through only one person, Adjutant General Henry Hutchings, who commanded the two state groups directly involved in border policy—the Rangers and the Texas National Guard.

Poor communications only accentuated the basic problem in federal-state relations over border policy: the fact that Governor Colquitt favored a much tougher stance than federal officials. Colquitt could afford to think in terms of a border policy; Presidents Taft and Wilson had to formulate a broader-based Mexican policy which in turn was only a part of their general foreign policy. The governor could advocate occupation of Juárez without worrying about its impact on American investments in southern Mexico or British oil interests in the Tampico region.[116] At the same time, Texans along the border understandably demonstrated an interest in Mexican affairs that was difficult for the European-oriented State Department and the domestically oriented Wilson administration to comprehend. In June 1914, while the assassination of Archduke Franz Ferdinand was making headlines around the world, the lead item in the *El Paso Morning Times* was "Aguascalientes Evacuated by Federals without a Fight."[117] Federal officials also underestimated the support in Texas for Colquitt's tough position on border policy. Encouraged by Colquitt's prohibitionist critics, they often consoled themselves with the idea that Colquitt's views were atypical of his fellow Texans when in reality there was substantial agreement with them. The reaction to the Vergara incident in 1914 clearly indicated that the governor was not so far out of step with his constituents as his critics liked to imagine.

Colquitt, Taft, and Wilson did have one thing in common when it came to formulating border policy: policy was to a great extent conditioned by domestic political considerations. Ignoring the border controversy, Colquitt's tenure as governor was a colorful and controversial one. Beset by financial problems and confronted by a largely hostile state legislature, Colquitt aroused strong opposition on issues ranging from prohibition to prison reform to public warehouses for cotton. The Texas Democratic Party was badly split along conservative-progressive lines, with the governor being identified with the conservative faction primarily because of his views on prohibition. Much of the criticism of Colquitt's Mexican policy came from persons such as Morris Sheppard and Cone Johnson who viewed the governor's actions in the broader context of the conservative-progressive split. Future as well as current political considerations also influenced the governor's position on border issues. After stepping down from the governorship in 1915, Colquitt intended to run in 1916 for the U.S. Senate seat held by Charles Culberson. As early as 1914, during his bitter attack on Wilson's Mexican policy at the Texas Cattle Raisers' Association meeting, Colquitt had said that "I have a good mind to say this morning that I'm going to be a candidate for the U.S. Senate."[118] Certainly an independent stand on border policy had a certain amount of political mileage in it for the governor; a federal-state confrontation on the scale that ensued, however, could only have hurt his future political career.

Personalities also came to play an important role in the growing split over border policy. Ironically, Colquitt found it easier to get along with the Republican Taft than with his fellow Democrat Wilson. Congressman Rufus Hardy of Texas identified the problem when he observed that the "governor has for some time had the Wilson-phobia."[119] Wilson's attitude toward Colquitt may have been prejudiced from the beginning by leaders of the Wilson movement in Texas who were anti-Colquitt primarily because of the governor's stand on prohibition. Colquitt also generally found it easier to cooperate with U.S. Army commanders along the border than with federal civil authorities, especially those in Washington. With a few notable exceptions— such as the Brownsville incident in the spring of 1914—Colquitt worked in harmony with the various commanders of the Southern Department. The governor believed that there was a simple explanation for his good relations with the local military and his poor relations with officials in Washington: the military was more familiar with the border situation and therefore understood the need for a firmer policy.

From the standpoint of the citizens of Texas, the most important consideration about Colquitt's Mexican policy was whether it provided increased defense of life and property in the Rio Grande region. On repeated occasions the governor demonstrated his willingness to furnish additional protection by either sending the Rangers or calling out the National Guard—both actions involving important budgetary considerations. Whether the governor was bluffing with his tough talk and military maneuvers is impossible to determine because neither the various Mexican factions nor the U.S. government ever called Colquitt's hand. There is ample evidence that on several occasions the federal government sent additional troops to the border strictly to pacify the governor rather than out of any military necessity.[120] Whether these troops could have been used more effectively elsewhere is debatable, but Texas was by far the scene of the greatest number of border incidents.

Colquitt could also be accused of overreacting to several crises on the border, thereby contributing to the general anxiety and sometimes outright hysteria that affected the region. The loss of life in El Paso in May 1911 during the maderista capture of Juárez was the single biggest factor influencing the governor's response to future border incidents. Colquitt had been in office fewer than four months when this violence took place, and he was determined that there would be no repetition of it during his administration. In his correspondence with federal officials, Colquitt made frequent references to the El Paso affair and his intention to avoid further such occurrences. When similar episodes erupted along the border outside of Texas without any strong military response by the United States, the governor appeared only further convinced of the correctness of his policy.

Colquitt's decision to pursue his own Mexican policy was also partially a product of a vacuum in federal border policy. Taft's cautiousness and Wilson's "watchful waiting" often had the effect of being no policy at all. Given Colquitt's energetic nature and the fact that Texas was "on the firing line," as he phrased it, the governor was not reluctant to move into that vacuum. This in turn led to some rather bizarre interactions between state and federal authorities, including federal fears that the State of Texas was prepared to invade Mexico. As one of Woodrow Wilson's harshest critics said in reference to his attitude toward the Huerta regime: "An animosity is not a policy."[121] Although Colquitt's departure from the governorship ended the Wilson-Colquitt feud over Mexican policy, it did not mean that peace had returned to the border region. The situation along the Rio Grande was about to take a dramatic turn for the worse as a result of raids arising out of the so-called Plan of San Diego.

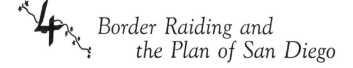

Border Raiding and the Plan of San Diego

The Mexican American and Mexican populations residing in the Rio Grande Valley had been a source of concern to authorities at all levels since the outbreak of revolution in 1910. These two groups far outnumbered the Anglo Americans in the region, were unassimilated culturally, and lived a marginal lower-class economic existence. They were suspicious of Anglo authorities, most especially the Texas Rangers who were often accused of using unnecessary force when dealing with non-Anglo groups in South Texas. The advent of revolution in Mexico led to growing political involvement by Mexican Americans and Mexicans, many of whom had relatives living in areas affected by revolutionary activity or who lived close enough to the border to be directly affected by events in northern Mexico. Beginning with the Madero revolution in 1910, such persons often supported one of the various military factions by smuggling weapons or by furnishing intelligence information. The influx of political refugees and illegal immigrants into the border area further disturbed the traditional politics of the region and encouraged some to seek more radical solutions for their political and economic problems.[1]

The growing unrest in the Rio Grande Valley assumed its most spectacular form in the so-called "Plan of San Diego" discovered in late January 1915. On January 24, 1915, local officials at McAllen, Texas, arrested Basilio Ramos, Jr., a supporter of the ousted Mexican president, General Victoriano Huerta. At the time of his arrest, Ramos had in his possession a number of documents, including a copy of the Plan of San Diego, a revolutionary manifesto supposedly composed and signed at the South Texas town of San Diego. The Plan—which had actually been drafted in a jail in Monterrey, Mexico, rather than in Texas—called for a combination revolution, race war, and separatist movement. According to the document, the revolution was to begin at precisely 2:00 A.M. on February 20, 1915. The ultimate goal of the revolution was to liberate the states of Texas, New Mexico, Arizona, California, and Colorado, which had been taken from Mexico in a "most perfidious manner by North American imperialism." The "Supreme Revolutionary Congress" at San Diego was to appoint a military commander and organize an armed force known as the "Liberating Army of Races and People." The Liberating Army would welcome into its ranks Mexican Americans, blacks, and Japanese and would restore to the Indians their lost lands. Blacks would be rewarded for their participation by receiving aid in conquering six other adjacent states where they could establish their own black republic. The liberated states bordering on Mexico would be organized into an independent republic which could later seek annexation by Mexico if such an action was considered "expedient." The Plan also called for a no-quarter race war with summary execution for all Anglo males over the age of sixteen as well as for all prisoners and "traitors to the race." The revolutionaries specifically rejected any form of aid from the Mexican government.[2]

After interrogation by federal officials, Ramos admitted that he had been one of the signatories of the Plan and that he had the authority to organize revolutionary juntas under its auspices. Federal authorities charged Ramos with conspiracy to levy war against the United States and had him bound over for action by a federal grand jury. Ramos was unable to post bond, which had been set at $5,000, so he remained in the Brownsville jail. Authorities originally tried to keep the arrest of Ramos a secret in the hope of increasing the chances of apprehending his fellow conspirators. The Associated Press, however, broke the story on February 2, and Texas newspapers immediately publicized it.[3]

Despite the fantastic nature of the Plan, authorities did not treat the threat lightly, and the U.S. Army increased its patrol activities along the Rio Grande. As the February 20 date for revolution approached, tension grew along the border, especially in the lower Rio Grande Valley. The arrival of the day, however, produced only another manifesto rather than the feared insurrection. The revolutionary congress was the supposed source of this "Manifesto to the Oppressed Peoples of America" which was datelined February 20 at San Diego.[4]

The revised Plan retained the basic features of the original one but introduced new focus, rhetoric, and personnel. It called for the liberation of the non-Anglo proletariat and for equal distribution and communal ownership of property. The movement would focus its activities on Texas where a "social republic" would be established which would serve as a base for spreading the revolution to the states of Arizona, New Mexico, Colorado, California, Utah, and Nevada. The triumph of the revolution would bring an end to racial hatred and the introduction of the "principles of Universal Love." Only one of the signatories of the original plan signed the revised plan; Agustín Garza, also known under the alias "León Caballo," signed both documents and received the title of "General in Chief" under the provisions of the new Plan.[5]

For the next few months attention focused on the federal courts rather than on the revolutionary struggle. In May a federal grand jury in Brownsville indicted Basilio Ramos and several other plotters on charges of conspiring to "levy war against the United States of America and to seize certain property of the United States, to wit, the states of Texas, Oklahoma, New Mexico, Arizona, Colorado, and California." The indictment modestly concluded that such actions were "against the peace and dignity of the United

States of America."⁶ Although the indictment mentioned Oklahoma as a target, neither the original nor the revised Plan had referred to that state. After Ramos was indicted, his bond was reduced from $5,000 to $100, an indication that authorities had concluded that the Plan of San Diego was mostly revolutionary rhetoric and not a threat to border security. Ramos was able to meet the reduced bail, posted bond, and promptly fled across the river to Matamoros. Although Ramos had been publicly identified as a supporter of Huerta, he was well received by local carrancista officials in Matamoros.⁷

The Beginning of the Raids

Beginning in July 1915, a series of raids in the lower Rio Grande Valley connected with the Plan of San Diego shattered the border complacency about the revolutionary movement. One of the most disturbing features was that the raiders—supposedly huertista in their sympathies—could operate freely in areas of northern Mexico controlled by the carrancistas who were concerned about a possible political comeback by Huerta. This revolutionary offensive in the Rio Grande Valley brought with it another modification of the Plan. The newest version cited the "criminal acts and insults of the miserable Rangers who guard the banks of the Rio Bravo" and called for the creation of a "Republic of Texas" composed of Texas, New Mexico, California, Arizona, and parts of Mississippi and Oklahoma. The movement would continue to focus its attention on Texas with revolutionary headquarters now moved to San Antonio from San Diego. New leadership emerged with the position of "First Chief of Operations" going to Luis de la Rosa, a former deputy sheriff in Cameron County (Brownsville); his second-in-command was Aniceto Pizana, a member of a well-known ranching family near Brownsville.⁸

As the bandit raids multiplied and assumed a pattern of guerrilla warfare, state and federal authorities attempted to mount a response. Governor James E. Ferguson, who had taken office in January, found himself in a position similar to his predecessor, O. B. Colquitt. Since the Ranger force numbered only sixteen, Ferguson wanted federal aid in order to rapidly expand the force. Ferguson requested that President Wilson provide financial assistance for the doubling of the Rangers but expressed fears that the president had not received the information that he needed to make sound decisions on the border situation.⁹

The governor also asked that additional federal troops be sent to the border. General Frederick Funston, commander of the Southern Department, initially declined this request on the grounds that the raids were the result of local political feuds and cattle rustling. Practically speaking, Funston's ability to respond was limited by a severe manpower shortage. Even though the U.S. Army was concentrated on the border, much of the international boundary was still poorly defended. The Brownsville military district, the primary area of the San Diego raids, included almost 300 miles of border with only 1,100 troops to patrol it.[10] Many of the troops were infantry, which were virtually worthless in pursuing the highly mobile raiders. In addition, as earlier, U.S. troops were not permitted to pursue raiders across the international boundary without prior permission from authorities in Washington, a policy which in effect gave the raiders a privileged sanctuary in northern Mexico since the carrancista forces did not interfere with their activities.[11]

Federal interpretation of the nature of the raids also complicated the response. Army officers on the border, reluctant to acknowledge the international character of the raids, initially classified them as criminal activity by

Governor James E. Ferguson.
*Photograph courtesy of the Barker
Texas History Center.*

Texas citizens. Since rustling and banditry were well established pastimes along the Rio Grande, the U.S. military simply viewed the San Diego raids as extreme examples of those traditional activities. General Funston wrote to the army adjutant general, H. P. McCain, that "most of the bandits operating in Texas counties along the border are Americans" but that he would continue to use army forces to pursue the raiders since some of them might be "armed marauding bands which have crossed the border into U.S. territory."[12] Secretary of War Lindley Garrison indicated that federal forces would be used if the bandit raids involved "repelling invasions of American territory or border uprisings." Garrison had informed state authorities that "internal disturbances" were a state responsibility and that federal authorities would not intervene unless Governor Ferguson "certified" to President Wilson that such disturbances were beyond state control.[13]

While Ferguson had requested federal assistance in the form of both troops and financing, he agreed that the raids by Mexican bandits were a localized problem and should be dealt with by state authorities. Even without promises of federal financing, Ferguson increased the Ranger force by twenty, more than doubling its size. On August 8, a band of approximately fifty raiders attacked Norias Ranch, part of the King Ranch, with five bandits killed in the assault. This attack prompted Ferguson to order another twenty-man increase in the Ranger force and to dispatch the entire force to the Rio Grande.[14]

The growing frequency and intensity of the raids soon forced both state and federal authorities to modify their views on the border situation. U.S. Army troops, Texas Rangers, local law enforcement officials, and armed citizens' groups fought regular engagements with the raiders. There was even talk of a "war zone" and a "battle front" along the Rio Grande. Federal officials in particular feared that the situation was getting out of control. Frequent exchanges of fire across the Rio Grande sometimes involved U.S. troops and carrancista forces. General Tasker Bliss, now acting army chief of staff, warned Secretary of War Garrison that some "reckless and desperate Mexican military commander" on the border might order his troops to cross into American territory, causing "great damage and loss of life." Bliss singled out Brownsville and Laredo as likely places for such an incident.[15] General Funston drastically altered his interpretations of the origin and motivation of the raids. Funston, who had previously attributed most of the raids to residents on the Texas side, now believed that carrancista officials in northern Mexico were connected with the raiders. The general had earlier opposed the dispatch of additional army troops because of the expense involved; on August 30, however, he wrote Adjutant General McCain that the "time for economy has passed; more troops should be supplied regardless of expense."[16]

The international character of the raids especially alarmed both state and federal officials. Governor Ferguson wired President Wilson, claiming that most of the raiders were from the Mexican side of the river, and he expressed doubt that even the expanded Ranger force could control the situation. Ferguson warned that "a reign of terror exists on the Mexican border and that any unusual occurence now would cause a disastrous invasion of Texas from Mexico."[17] Army reports themselves indicated that many of the raids originated in Mexico, and there was growing suspicion of some sort of official Mexican support for them. Since portions of the Mexican side of the river were controlled by rival factions under Venustiano Carranza and Pancho Villa, it was difficult to determine which faction might be the source of "official" support even if such support were being provided. Further complicating the situation was the fact that the United States had not extended diplomatic recognition to any of the contending groups so there was no "government of Mexico" to which to appeal. Whether the raids were officially supported or not, there was no doubt that northern Mexico would continue to be used as a sanctuary by the raiders as long as the United States maintained its policy of not permitting its forces to cross the international boundary, even in hot pursuit.

The Carrancista Connection

The carrancista commander at Matamoros, General Emiliano P. Nafarrate, had been at the center of charges of Mexican complicity in the raids since the first discovery of the Plan of San Diego. Testimony in the Ramos case indicated that Nafarrate had been connected with the Plan since its original formulation. As noted earlier, after Ramos jumped bail, he immediately fled to Matamoros where he was given sanctuary by Nafarrate.[18] A steady stream of official and unofficial reports reaching the American side indicated that Luis de la Rosa and Aniceto Pizana were openly recruiting in Nafarrate's district and that some of the San Diego raiders had been seen in carrancista uniforms. There were even accusations that Nafarrate's troops provided protective fire for raiders returning from Texas to Mexico.[19]

Although originally dismissing charges that Nafarrate was connected with the raids, General Funston increasingly viewed him as the carrancista connection. Funston later acknowledged that carrancista officers and soldiers made up a "considerable portion" of the raiders but felt that such persons were operating "without the authority of their chiefs." By late September General Funston was reporting to Adjutant General McCain that the raiders had a "military organization" and that Nafarrate was "in sympathy with or afraid of the bandits."[20]

For his part Nafarrate offered a variety of explanations for the raids, none of which involved him. Nafarrate had originally blamed them on the ousted

Huerta's supporters, who were supposedly trying to block U.S. recognition of the Constitutionalist faction under Carranza. This explanation had a certain plausibility given the origins of the Plan of San Diego and the continuing negotiations between Carranza and the U.S. government. Nafarrate later attributed the raids to "outlaws on the Texas side" who had been shooting at persons on both sides of the river in an effort to provoke an incident. He attributed much of the unrest in the area to the Texas Rangers whom he charged with mistreating both Mexicans and Mexican Americans and characterized as "causing trouble all the time." In the midst of the controversy, Nafarrate received a promotion to general of brigade in September 1915, which increased suspicion that there was official support for the raiders. The dispute over Nafarrate's role in the Plan came to an end in early October when he and his entire command were transferred from the border. Nafarrate's replacement, General Eugenio López, promised to cooperate in maintaining order, but within a matter of days after the change of command General Funston was complaining to the army adjutant general that "we can expect no help from the new commander in preventing these raids."[21]

The carrancista connection under the Plan of San Diego hinted at the link between the raids and diplomatic recognition of the Carranza regime. After the United States government extended de facto recognition to Carranza on October 19, 1915, the raids came to an abrupt halt. Federal officials and Governor Ferguson consented to the movement of carrancista forces through Texas to Sonora to aid in the defense of the town of Agua Prieta which was under attack by forces of Pancho Villa. Carranza responded by replacing the recently arrived commander at Matamoros, General López, with General Alfredo Ricaut who was Carranza's nephew and who had a more favorable attitude toward the United States. Luis de la Rosa and Aniceto Pizana received large cash payments from Carranza to cease their revolutionary activities under the Plan of San Diego; de la Rosa also obtained a commission in the regular Mexican army.[22]

Ferguson and the Raids

Governor Ferguson's handling of border policy soon involved him in a public dispute with Senator Morris Sheppard, one of the more vocal critics of Colquitt's border policy. Sheppard—who had consistently dismissed Colquitt's earlier warnings about the border situation—dramatically reversed his position in the wake of the raids under the Plan of San Diego. He wrote to Secretary of State Lansing on October 23 that the border situation was "desperate," that "vigorous representations" should be made to the Carranza government about it, and that there should be "redoubled vigor and attention on our part" to the situation on the Rio Grande.[23] Sheppard's problems with Ferguson began when the senator decided to make a personal inspection of the Rio Grande Valley to gain first-hand knowledge of the problems of the region without advising the governor of his intentions. When Sheppard telegraphed the governor that a "state of panic" prevailed along the border, Ferguson wired in reply: "Am glad that you have at last become interested in the troubles of Texas." Ferguson went on to complain that he had received "plenty of general recommendations but few specific suggestions" about how to deal with border problems. The governor acidly concluded his telegram with the observation that "you can readily understand that general expressions and useless platitudes will not suffice as a basis for official action."[24]

Sheppard attempted to avoid a major confrontation with Ferguson by immediately telegraphing the governor that he had "misconstrued the spirit" of the first telegram and that the senator did indeed have some "specific suggestions" about border policy. Ferguson rejected the opportunity to let the misunderstanding die, informing Sheppard that he "resented the second telegram more than the first" and accusing the senator of insinuating that state authorities had not acted in the matter, "a piece of crude politics." The governor closed with an accusation of his own: Sheppard had helped to get federal officials appointed on the border "who persecute our worthy citizens with Mexican perjury and who have not helped to relieve us from Mexican treachery."[25]

In a speech at Brownsville on October 29, Sheppard said that the border problem should not become a partisan political issue and urged Governor Ferguson to come to the border and personally investigate the situation, "for it is impossible for any man to understand the true significance of this situation unless he comes on the ground." Sheppard telegraphed the governor the same day offering the "specific suggestions" that he had spoken of in his earlier telegram. Observing that conditions on the border were "full of tragic possibilities," Sheppard called for additional army posts, a roadway linking the posts, and a centralized command. The senator, however, was vague as to what role state authorities were to play: "the State of Texas should hold itself in readiness to supplement and support Federal action in such manner as its authorities think advisable."[26]

Sheppard's latest pronouncements offered little that would placate Ferguson. When former Governor Colquitt had earlier suggested that Sheppard needed to be "on the ground" to appreciate the border situation, Sheppard had rejected the idea and had even implied that such direct involvement led to a distorted view of border conditions.[27] Sheppard's specific suggestions offered nothing new and concerned actions that only could be taken by the federal government. Both Governors Colquitt and Ferguson had lobbied for additional army troops and stations along the Rio Grande; while this pressure often produced results, the final decision on such matters lay with federal authorities. As to the idea of a military road in the Rio Grande Valley, such a road had been under discussion for more than a decade. The central-ized command suggested by Sheppard already existed at Fort Sam Houston. Sheppard's specific recommendations, in fact, were all beyond the pale of state authorities, and his only suggestion for state action was vague and rec-ommended a policy which had been followed by every governor since the outbreak of the Mexican Revolution in 1910.

While Sheppard and Ferguson continued their unproductive public debate, the governor was also negotiating with the other two principal fig-ures involved: the recently recognized president of Mexico, Venustiano Car-ranza, and President Woodrow Wilson. On October 30 Ferguson met with Roberto Pesqueira, Carranza's personal representative, to discuss the situa-tion along the Rio Grande. When Ferguson stressed the need for carrancista authorities to cooperate with Texas and federal officials in stopping the cross-border raids, Pesqueira promised the full cooperation of the carrancistas in ending bandit activities. The interview left the governor sufficiently optimis-tic to predict that "conditions on the border will rapidly improve."[28]

Communications between Ferguson and Wilson presented a much differ-ent picture. Shortly before the meeting with Pesqueira, Ferguson wrote the president that the border situation was "growing more serious" and that the raiders were operating out of northern Mexico without interference from the carrancista authorities. As Colquitt had done before him, Ferguson pointed out the handicap that U.S. Army forces and Texas Rangers encountered in not being able to pursue the raiders across the international boundary; unlike Colquitt, Ferguson stopped short of asking permission for the Rangers to cross the border. President Wilson referred Ferguson's message to Secre-tary of State Lansing who wrote to the governor in reassuring terms on November 3. Lansing informed Ferguson that Carranza had promised a per-sonal investigation of the border situation and had pledged to remove any troops "that may be inclined to instigate trouble." He also claimed that the Mexican Secret Service would cooperate with U.S. military authorities in locating and punishing bandits and that Carranza had ordered the arrest of Luis de la Rosa and several others involved in the recent raids.[29]

Carranza and Governor Ferguson met at Nuevo Laredo in late November specifically to discuss border problems. U.S. officials expressed concern over a state governor conducting negotiations with the head of a foreign govern-ment, especially since Governor Ferguson had issued a proclamation on October 27 in which he offered a $1,000 reward—dead or alive—for Aniceto Pizana or Luis de la Rosa. Ferguson, however, conveniently chose to ignore the carrancista connection with the recent raids, and the meeting between the governor and Carranza ended in an "absolute and complete understand-ing" on border problems. They agreed to cooperate in suppressing banditry along the Rio Grande "without going into details to fix the cause of the trouble or to assign responsibility." Thoroughly impressed with Carranza's deter-mination to restore order, Governor Ferguson optimistically wrote Secretary of War Garrison that "border conditions have at last become normal."[30]

The federal and state negotiations with Carranza led to a temporary "demilitarization" of the border problem. The federal government reverted to its original position that the raids were essentially a state, not a federal, problem and should be dealt with by civil officials, not military authorities. Although the army had been used to pursue the raiders, even that action had gone beyond a strict interpretation of orders; henceforth, army forces would continue to operate under directives which prohibited crossing the international boundary without prior authorization from Washington.[31]

At the same time that the federal government assigned primary responsi-bility for dealing with the raiders to the State of Texas, it took action which in effect reduced the capability of state officials to cope with the situation. The War Department advised Adjutant General Henry Hutchings of the Texas National Guard that the annual federal allowance for the Texas Guard was being reduced from $100,000 to $9,000. The basis for this reduction was the allegation that certain guard officers had designated uniforms and other military equipment as unfit for service, claimed to have destroyed the mate-riel involved, and then sold it to Mexican revolutionaries. Subsequently, a federal grand jury indicted three officers of the Guard—including Captain F. A. Head who commanded the Brownsville unit—for defrauding the federal government.[32]

In early December Governor Ferguson traveled to Washington to discuss border policy with federal authorities. During his visit Ferguson met with the three persons most responsible for formulating federal border policy: Presi-dent Wilson, Secretary of State Lansing, and Secretary of War Garrison. Ferguson emerged from this round of interviews in an optimistic mood. Gar-rison promised to try to restore the funding for the Texas National Guard, returning federal assistance to its original figure of $100,000 per year; Garri-son later promised additional federal funding to finance the establishment of two new artillery units in the Texas National Guard. In his talks with Wilson and Lansing, the governor expressed his confidence in Carranza's ability to deal with the border situation, characterizing Carranza as a "man of the safe and sane type." After his trip to Washington, Ferguson was convinced that federal authorities now had a better understanding of the conditions existing in the border region.[33]

By the time of Ferguson's trip to Washington, the situation on the border seemed to be substantially improved. A Bureau of Investigation survey of sheriffs and postmasters in South Texas indicated that activity in connection with the Plan of San Diego had virtually ceased. Typical of the responses was that of Sheriff J. C. Guerra of Starr County who stated that "I have not found, heard, or know of any man in my county connected with or in favor of the Plan of San Diego or any socialistic order." Sheriff A. W. Tobin of Duval County reported no revolutionary activity in his region, saying that the Plan of San Diego must refer to San Diego, California, "if there ever was any plan at all."[34] In a three-day period carrancista forces captured fourteen bandits who had been raiding Texas, executing two and sending the remainder to Matamoros and Reynosa for trial. Carranza also issued an order that de la Rosa and Pizana were to be shot immediately if captured.[35]

The Return of Villa

This relatively peaceful interlude in late 1915 and early 1916 soon dissipated. The latest problems were not connected with the plan of San Diego but rather with the declining military fortunes of Pancho Villa who had long been in violent opposition to Venustiano Carranza. Although Villa had been forced to surrender the key border town of Juárez on December 20, 1915, he was still a major military figure and leader of regional importance. The Mexican state of Chihuahua was the scene of continued revolutionary activities by the villistas, which in turn posed a serious threat to the border region. Villa, who had spoken so highly of Wilson's Mexican policy in 1914, was becoming increasingly anti-American in his pronouncements and actions as a result of U.S. recognition of the Carranza regime. This growing antagonism showed itself in early 1916 in the massacre at Santa Ysabel, Chihuahua.[36]

A group of American and Mexican employees of the Cusi Mining Company who had left Mexico in the fall of 1915 at the urging of the United States government were returning to their mining operations in Chihuahua. They had the assurance of carrancista officials that the area had been evacuated by the villistas and was now under the control of forces loyal to Carranza. On the afternoon of January 10, 1916, a band of villista raiders stopped the train carrying the group at a spot west of Chihuahua City, near Santa Ysabel. The bandits forced the Americans off the train and then executed all but one who escaped after pretending to be dead. The Mexicans on board were robbed but not physically harmed.[37]

The initial response of the U.S. government was firm and even threatening. Secretary of State Lansing informed Carranza that the massacre had caused "intense excitement" in the United States and called into question the ability of the Carranza administration to fulfill its international obligations. Lansing called for "prompt and vigorous" measures to capture the bandits, warning that failure to do so might lead to a "grave crisis with far-reaching consequences."[38]

The excitement on the border was especially pronounced. When the bodies of the massacre victims were returned to El Paso, a series of disorders erupted. Clashes between Mexicans and Americans in the city forced local officials to call out the police reserves; even U.S. soldiers joined in the attacks on Mexicans and Mexican Americans. With a full-scale riot impending, General John J. Pershing, commander at Fort Bliss outside of El Paso, ordered regular army forces into El Paso to restore order. The troops sealed off the Mexican area of the city and searched it for weapons. El Paso police captain, W. D. Green, announced that "every Villa leader in El Paso will be run out of town." Law enforcement officials arrested several prominent villista sympathizers, charging them with vagrancy. Some hotels even sent away their Mexican musicians to avoid further disturbances. At nearby Fort Hancock, local citizens were reported to be "cleaning out" the local Mexican population."[39]

As the situation worsened, Governor Ferguson found himself in the midst of another dispute with the federal government over National Guard finances. Ferguson accused Secretary of War Garrison of "attempting to unload on my administration debts that have been accumulating since 1900 amounting to $102,025.24."[40] The figure involved represented an amount equal to the entire budget for the Texas Adjutant General's office for the fiscal year ending in August 1916. The governor described these accumulated shortages and defalcations as the "sins of former administrations, State and National." In an angry letter to the secretary of war, Ferguson described Garrison as an "autocrat lacking in appreciation and not willing to do as much for my administration as I am doing for yours."[41] Ferguson wrote to influential South Texas congressman John Nance Garner that Garrison was an "autocrat of the first degree," observing that it was "difficult to explain to friends why they should be loyal to the [Wilson] administration."[42] Ferguson, however, would soon have more pressing problems with which to deal; a villista raid in New Mexico in March 1916 was to lead to a revival of activity under the Plan of San Diego.

Pancho Villa's pre-dawn attack on Columbus, New Mexico, on March 9 had caught off-guard both civilian and military authorities. As had been the case in the past, officials were predicting normality in the area. Only a few weeks earlier the secretary of state had reported to President Wilson that "conditions along the border are practically normal."[43] President Wilson's special agent to Villa, George Carothers, had reported that Villa and his forces were close to the border but apparently heading west into Sonora.[44] The last weekly report from the army unit stationed at Columbus before the attack consisted of only one sentence: "Border conditions in this patrol district for the week ending March 4, 1916 have remained normal."[45] Obviously, the residents were unprepared when Villa's force struck. Almost 500 villistas burned and looted the town and then withdrew under a heavy counterattack by U.S. Army troops. Seventeen Americans died during the raid while Villa's casualties were estimated to have been as high as 100.[46]

The response of the American government to the Columbus raid was to launch a major military operation in northern Mexico under the command of General Pershing. Officials optimistically hoped that Carranza would cooperate with the so-called "punitive expedition" in eliminating one of Carranza's longtime antagonists. Instead of cooperating, Carranza prepared an armed resistance in the event of a broader intervention and classified any U.S. troop movement into Mexico as an "invasion of national territory."[47] As the Pershing expedition grew in size and penetrated more deeply into northern Mexico, Carranza began to think in terms of military operations against United States territory; part of this new strategy involved a revival of the raids into South Texas under the Plan of San Diego.[48]

The Resumption of the Raids

When raids under the Plan of San Diego ended in October 1915, Carranza had pensioned off Luis de la Rosa and Aniceto Pizana while simultaneously assuring American officials that he was pursuing the two and would have them executed when captured. Despite Carranza's assurances, frequent reports indicated that both de la Rosa and Pizana were operating without interference in northern Mexico and were organizing forces for possible future raids into South Texas. In November 1915 a Bureau of Investigation report claimed that both de la Rosa and Pizana were "openly recruiting around Monterrey" and that the Plan of San Diego had the support of a

A detachment of the 7th Cavalry scouting for Pancho Villa on the Mexican border in 1916. *Photograph courtesy of the Arizona Historical Society.*

"large number of Carranza forces."[49] Army intelligence also indicated that the San Diego raiders were reorganizing, with even reports of German assistance for the raiders. Carranza's sincerity came more into question when forces under General Ricaut, Carranza's nephew, captured Pizana but did not execute him.[50]

The Pershing expedition into Mexico led to demands by Rio Grande Valley residents for increased federal troops out of fear of retaliation. General Funston received numerous requests from South Texas towns for their own army military units, but with the additional demands on army resources caused by the Pershing expedition he was forced to admit that he did not have sufficient troops to meet the requests. Funston instead recommended that the towns form local defense forces, and many followed his advice. There were additional reports that de la Rosa was continuing to organize forces near Monterrey and Ciudad Victoria, causing further uneasiness among Valley residents.[51]

During April and May the connection between the Pershing expedition and events on the Rio Grande became more pronounced. American military leaders were increasingly uncertain about the prospects for success for the expedition. General Pershing warned War Department officials not to be "optimistic over the capture of Villa" as it was going to be "a very difficult matter to run him down."[52] General Funston, Pershing's immediate superior, warned Army Chief of Staff Hugh Scott that the expedition was in danger of

United States soldiers in front of the adobe cookhouse at Glenn Springs. *Photograph courtesy of the Harry Ransom Humanities Research Center, The University of Texas at Austin, Smithers Collection.*

becoming "stalled" because of supply problems and that the whole situation was "fraught with the gravest dangers."[53] The longer the expedition remained in Mexico, the greater the likelihood grew that there might be some incident involving expedition forces and carrancista troops. This warning proved true when an American cavalry unit exchanged fire with carrancista officials and local citizens at Parral, Chihuahua, on April 12. Two Americans were killed and several wounded; Mexican casualties totaled approximately forty.[54]

Efforts to negotiate an early end to the American intervention also proved unsuccessful. Generals Scott and Funston began meeting with General Alvaro Obregón, Mexican secretary of war, in El Paso in late April. The conference, however, broke up in early May over the Mexican demand for immediate withdrawal of the Pershing expedition. Large-scale raiding had resumed on May 5, when a group of approximately eighty bandits crossed the Rio Grande and raided the small towns of Glenn Springs and Boquillas, Texas, in the Big Bend region. Both settlements had general stores whose supplies would attract the raiders and a cavalry detachment of only nine men serving as a border patrol at Glenn Springs. When the raiders struck at Glenn Springs, there was a brief but fierce exchange of fire with the troopers stationed there; the attack resulted in the deaths of three soldiers and one civilian. At Boquillas, the Mexicans raided the general store, capturing the owner, Jesse Deemer, and his clerk, Monroe Payne. When the raiders returned across the Rio Grande, they took Deemer and Payne with them. The group also attacked the company store of the American-owned mine at Boquillas, Mexico, directly across the river from the Texas town of the same name. The bandits took several more prisoners, including the mine physician and superintendent.[55]

State and federal officials were preparing for the worst even before the raiding was renewed. On May 1, Secretary of War Newton Baker notified Governor Ferguson to "take such steps as could be taken without publicity to expedite action if a call-up [of the Texas National Guard] should become necessary." Only a few hours before the raid on Glenn Springs, Baker informed Ferguson that "the need for increased troops on the border seems to be passed." This particular raid—in which three American soldiers died and American troops crossed the Rio Grande in pursuit of the raiders—drastically changed the situation on the border. The simultaneous collapse of the Scott-Obregón talks led to a decision by the Wilson administration to federalize the National Guards of Texas, New Mexico, and Arizona. Secretary Baker ordered the federalization on May 9, citing the need to prevent "further aggression upon the territory of the United States from Mexico and to properly protect the frontier." Ferguson directed the entire Texas National Guard to mobilize at San Antonio; more than 3,500 guardsmen reported to San Antonio for federal service. Ferguson also increased the Ranger force to forty and promptly dispatched them to the border.[56]

These new raids were taking place in a much more volatile context than earlier raids under the plan. After the attack on Glenn Springs, federal authorities made a major change in border policy and authorized U.S. Army troops to follow raiders across the international boundary when in "hot pursuit." Major George T. Langhorne, leading one of the units pursuing the Glenn Springs raiders in his own Cadillac, indicated his enthusiasm for the new policy: "I am clear of red tape, and I know no Rio Grande." The major promised to press the chase with "no pause for orders or State Department negotiations." Langhorne's troops crossed the Rio Grande on May 11; two days later another force under Colonel Frederick W. Sibley also crossed into Mexico on the trail of the Glenn Springs raiders. The only operational restriction was that all forces had to be back on American soil no later than May 26.[57]

The newest punitive expedition quickly produced results despite a three-day headstart by the raiders. The Americans captured on the Mexican side of the river had escaped even before the troops crossed the Rio Grande. Closely pursued by Langhorne's forces, the bandits left Deemer and Payne behind at the village of El Pino, Coahuila, where they were found on May 15 by U.S. troopers. With all captives liberated and the raiders dispersed, Langhorne faced the difficult decision of whether to continue the chase or return to American soil; the major elected to continue the pursuit. Some minor skirmishes ensued with several bandits killed or wounded and the recovery of some of the loot from Boquillas, Texas. Since the expedition had accomplished its mission, Colonel Sibley—the nominal commander of the operation—issued orders for the withdrawal of the expedition beginning on May 17; all members of Langhorne's and Sibley's commands had returned to American soil by May 21. This second punitive expedition had penetrated more than 100 miles into Mexico, traveled more than 550 miles, recovered the captives, and dispersed the raiders—all without suffering any casualties.[58]

Turning their attention elsewhere, high-ranking military officials were also concerned that the continued presence of the Pershing expedition in northern Mexico might promote additional raids along the Rio Grande. Generals Scott and Funston warned the secretary of war that they expected many attacks along the border similar to the one at Glenn Springs. Funston wired Pershing that there were "suspiciously large" troop movements on the part of carrancista forces in the North and ordered him to destroy any carrancista forces that attacked the expedition.[59] Funston believed that it was impossible to prevent raids into Texas with the troops at his disposal operating only from U.S. territory. He recommended that his troops move across the international boundary and occupy "strategic points" forty or fifty miles below the border; only by placing the "bandits and the Mexican troops" on the defensive could the border be protected.[60]

The growing tension between the United States and Mexico returned to prominence two persons associated with the original series of raids under the Plan of San Diego: Luis de la Rosa and General Emiliano Nafarrate. Agents of the Bureau of Investigation reported that Nafarrate and de la Rosa were organizing troops for an invasion of Texas sometime between May 10 and May 15. The Bureau also indicated that certain Germans and German Americans along the border were involved in the plot and were organizing in large numbers at Houston and San Antonio. Federal investigations also indicated that two other figures were involved in a plot similar to that of the Plan of San Diego. Two former villistas, General José Morín and Victoriano Ponce, were attempting to promote a revolution by the Mexicans of South Texas. Morín and Ponce proposed to destroy railroad lines and engage in bombings in several South Texas cities, with San Antonio being the principal target. The date for the Morín-Ponce uprising was supposedly May 10.[61]

State and federal authorities moved quickly to deal with the new threats. Governor Ferguson increased the Ranger force to fifty and directed that the new personnel be used along the border. The Texas Rangers became involved again in the enforcement of neutrality legislation as they had been during the Colquitt administration. Federal agents infiltrated the Morín-Ponce conspiracy and arrested the two leaders, who then were turned over to state authorities at Kingsville. On May 23 Texas Rangers removed Morín and Ponce from the Kingsville jail; no trace was ever found of the two conspirators although there was widespread speculation that the Rangers had executed them. The May 15 deadline for the Nafarrate-de la Rosa invasion of Texas also passed without incident. There were continuing reports, however, that de la Rosa and Pizana were still recruiting along the border in anticipation of new raids into Texas.[62]

Carrancista Invasion Plans

U.S. Consul Garrett at Nuevo Laredo had further disturbing news for state and federal officials; the carrancistas were busily repairing a railroad line running into Nuevo Laredo, apparently to facilitate the movement of troops to the border for an invasion. Garrett believed that Carranza was planning a surprise attack on certain U.S. border towns that would be coordinated with a major assault on Pershing's forces. According to Garrett, the invasion was to take place no later than June 10.[63]

The general direction of U.S.-Mexican relations added credibility to Garrett's views. In a note composed on May 22 but delivered on June 2, Mexican Minister of Foreign Relations Aguilar bitterly denounced the Pershing expedition and the pursuit of the Glenn Springs raiders as an "invasion of our territory." Aguilar called for the immediate withdrawal of U.S. forces from

Mexico, saying that failure to do so would leave Mexico with "no further recourse than to defend its territory by appeal to arms." The minister was especially critical of the artillery and infantry units accompanying the Pershing expedition, pointing out that such units were not suitable for chasing bandits but rather "exclusively destined for use against regular Mexican forces." Aguilar even blamed the prolonged civil war in Mexico on the "decided aid" given to Pancho Villa by American officials. The Mexican government characterized the raiding of bandit groups into American territory from Mexico as a "lamentable affair" but said that it could not be held responsible for such activities. Aguilar also criticized the U.S. government for failing to take effective action against anti-Carranza exiles who were "cared for and armed on the American side under the tolerance of the authorities of the State of Texas."[64]

While the possibility of a large-scale Mexican invasion of United States territory seemed improbable, carrancista officials were in fact planning such an operation in conjunction with the Plan of San Diego. General Pablo González, one of Carranza's most prominent generals, had developed a plan calling for an attack on Laredo by regular carrancista troops with simultaneous raids under the Plan and an uprising in South Texas. In immediate command of the operation was Colonel Esteban Fierros, an officer in González' Army Corps of the East and a Mexican American from Laredo. Fierros received a regular-army promotion to brevet general and also a commission as a brigadier general in the Plan of San Diego's Liberating Army. He assembled at Monterrey a brigade of approximately 450 men, composed of about 300 cavalry and 150 infantry. Luis de la Rosa also served as a brigadier general with the brigade, which was typically top-heavy with two other brigadier generals in addition to Fierros and de la Rosa. The brigade itself was a motley collection of veterans of the San Diego raids, new recruits, and carrancista regulars. By early June the brigade was ready for action; indeed Fierros had already set the operation in motion by infiltrating part of his forces across the Rio Grande in small parties.[65]

The final design called for an uprising in South Texas under the banner of the Plan of San Diego. Fierros' brigade was to cross the Rio Grande above and below Laredo, isolate the city, and then attack in conjunction with regular carrancista forces at Nuevo Laredo. At the same time raids would be launched from Matamoros in the lower Valley region. The members of the Fierros brigade who had infiltrated earlier would engage in guerrilla warfare in the Valley. This grand design for invasion and revolution, however, fortunately never went beyond the planning stage. Federal authorities through informants were found to have detailed information of the entire operation. Learning of this, carrancista officials cancelled the invasion portion of the plan in early June. Not content to drop all elements, they decided to renew raids under the Plan of San Diego so that at least one phase of the operation would be put into effect.[66]

The renewal of the San Diego raids represented a return to a policy that had proved successful for the carrancista regime in 1915 when it had exploited the raids to help obtain diplomatic recognition. At this point, raids, in combination with other forms of diplomatic and military pressure, were designed to encourage the withdrawal of the Pershing expedition. The results produced something quite different; a series of raids in the lower Rio Grande Valley in June led instead to additional "punitive expeditions" across the international boundary. The initial confrontation was on June 14 when a group of approximately twenty-five raiders encountered an army patrol near Brownsville; a brief firefight ensued in which one of the Mexicans was killed. When the remaining Mexicans fled across the river, General James Parker, commander of the Brownsville military district, ordered a troop of cavalry to pursue. Parker later sent additional cavalry units and machine gun troops to reinforce the first group. Although the expedition killed only two bandits on the Mexican side of the river, the presence of such a large force—approximately 400 troops—caused a near panic in Matamoros. The most serious event of the incursion occurred four days later. As American troops were withdrawing, carrancista troops fired upon their rear guard. The remaining troops then counterattacked, killing two of the carrancistas.[67] On June 15, another bandit group numbering about 100 attacked two troops of cavalry at San Ignacio, Texas, forty miles from Laredo. In this incident, the raiders had eight killed while the Americans suffered three killed and six wounded. A detachment of cavalry crossed into Mexico in pursuit but returned after only two hours without further encounters with the bandits or carrancistas.[68] The army response at Brownsville and San Ignacio represented the new general policy that U.S. forces had the authority to cross into Mexico when in "hot pursuit" of raiders. This was not only a pronounced departure from the earlier policy; it carried with it the possibility of major military confrontation since most of the crossings were taking place in areas along the Rio Grande where there were large numbers of carrancista forces.

By mid-June the new raids and the continuing U.S. military activity in northern Mexico had produced a situation which might lead to a full-scale war between the United States and Mexico. Certainly the United States was preparing for such an eventuality. On June 16 General Hugh Scott directed the War College to draw up a new plan for the invasion of Mexico "on the lines of the various railways from the north," which would support the existing invasion plan, known as the "Alternative Plan." The original plan, which had called for a landing at Veracruz followed by an overland march to Mexico City as had taken place during the Mexican War, was now outdated since most of the Mexican army was concentrated in northern Mexico. Scott wanted a new strategy that would have provisions for both an invasion and for protection of the border zone. The new plan "should be ready to be put into force at once."[69]

The clearest indication of the seriousness of the situation and the importance of the border region in any future conflict was the federalization of the National Guard units of the remaining forty-five states on June 18. The Wilson administration ordered all of the units to the border to join the earlier federalized guards of Texas, New Mexico, and Arizona. The order involved more than 100,000 men who would free the approximately 30,000 regular Army troops on the border for any further military operations in Mexico.[70]

During the same period, carrancista officials also took actions which threatened the Rio Grande Valley. The commander of the garrison at Juárez distributed weapons to more than 1,000 civilians in anticipation of new hostilities along the border. Furthermore, he suspended regular streetcar traffic in Juárez because all cars were needed to transport carrancistra troops to their positions. General Ricaut, whose command stretched from Nuevo Laredo to Matamoros, warned U.S. military officials that he would attack any American force encountered on the Mexican side of the river. General Jacinto Treviño, commander of carrancista forces in Chihuahua, issued a general call to arms and prohibited Mexicans from crossing the border into the United States.[71] Treviño also warned General Pershing that he had orders to resist any "new invasions" by American forces and to attack forces of the punitive expedition "if they move any direction except north."[72]

The whole environment portended a clash between U.S. troops and carrancista forces that could easily lead to full-scale hostilities. Such an incident occurred at Carrizal, Chihuahua, on June 21. Worried about the intentions of carrancista forces, Pershing dispatched two reconnaissance patrols to the vicinity of Villa Ahumada, Chihuahua. Pershing specifically ordered the patrols to avoid a fight if at all possible and not to enter any town garrisoned by Mexican forces. Since the reconnaissance involved troop movements which went against Treviño's warning, command of the operation was given to one of Pershing's most trusted field commanders, Captain Charles T. Boyd. Boyd later combined the two patrols before attempting to enter the town of Carrizal where there was a carrancista garrison under the command of General Félix Gómez. Boyd violated Pershing's orders by asking Gómez for permission to march through the town. When Gómez refused permission, Boyd angrily replied: "Tell the son-of-a-bitch that I am going through." Boyd promptly proceeded to do just that, provoking a major fight with heavy casualties on both sides. Twelve Americans were killed, including Boyd, and ten wounded; the carrancistas captured twenty-four others. Mexican casualties were estimated at a minimum of seventy-four.[73]

While both the United States and Mexico waited to see whether the Carrizal incident would lead to war, high-ranking Army officers were preparing for a wider conflict along the border. Adjutant General McCain wrote to General Funston to review the procedures for implementing martial law along the border should it become necessary. General Scott also wrote Funston in a somewhat excited tone that "things look as if they were going to pop now" and that he was rushing the mobilization of the national guard "in order to throw it on the border wherever you want it."[74] Troops at Fort Bliss were placed on alert in anticipation of a possible movement into Juárez.[75]

Neither Wilson nor Carranza could afford to let the fighting escalate. Wilson, seeking another term as president in 1916, was using as one of his chief issues that he had kept the United States out of war in Europe. Thus he could not afford to let the United States get involved in a war in Mexico. Another of his concerns was that U.S. forces might get tied down in a lengthy war in Mexico when they might be needed elsewhere. Certainly Wilson's two experiences with major interventions in Mexico—the Veracruz occupation and the Pershing expedition—demonstrated the danger of supposedly brief actions becoming prolonged military operations.[76] Carranza for his part was neither politically nor militarily prepared for a major conflict with the United States, a conflict which might very well lead to his ouster from the presidency. The "war crisis" evaporated very quickly when the Carranza administration announced on June 28 that it would release the Americans taken prisoner a week earlier at Carrizal. Mexico and the United States

The 10th Cavalrymen who were captured at the Battle of Carrizal, June 21, 1916. *Photograph courtesy of the Historical Museum, Fort Huachuca, Arizona.*

agreed in early July to submit their disagreements to a joint commission.[77]

During the June war crisis, carrancista officials were supporting raids into Texas under the Plan of San Diego and seeking additional funds to continue operations. Carranza, however, was moving in the opposite direction. Even before he announced that the Carrizal prisoners would be released, Carranza had taken measures to help defuse the border situation. On June 23 he ordered raids under the Plan halted and had Luis de la Rosa taken into custody. Carranza also ordered the Fierros Brigade disbanded, with some of its personnel being incorporated into regular carrancista forces. By July 1916, raiding under the Plan of San Diego had run its course.[78]

Racial Strife in South Texas

While raids across the border ebbed and flowed in response to other political and military considerations, one constant continued to disturb the Rio Grande Valley: growing racial antagonism between Anglos and Mexicans or Mexican Americans. As early as August 1915, General Funston was warning of a possible "race war" in the lower Rio Grande Valley.[79] Actually, the possibility of a large-scale racial conflict posed the threat of higher casualties for the border region than did the raiding. Fatalities from the raids had been surprisingly small; between July 1915 and July 1916, thirty raids into Texas had produced only twenty-one American deaths among both civilians and military.[80]

Although Mexican Americans constituted a majority of the population, the preponderance of political power and armed force was on the side of the Anglo minority. The Plan of San Diego led to a wave of summary executions by Texas Rangers, local law enforcement officials, and various armed citizens' groups. Typical of the approach was the attitude of Ranger Captain J. M. Fox who summarized the day's activities by telephoning: "We got another Mexican, but he's dead."[81] After three other Mexicans were found dead outside of Brownsville, a reporter for the *Washington Post* observed that any Mexican found armed was "under instant suspicion. If he is slow to explain, his life is in immediate danger; and if he makes any threatening move, his life is forfeited."[82] Numerous Mexicans or Mexican Americans were killed while "resisting arrest" or "escaping." In one six-week period, nine Mexicans were "killed while trying to escape" from the jail at San Benito, Texas.[83] After raiders attacked a train near Brownsville on October 18, 1915, a civilian posse summarily hanged or shot ten "suspicious Mexicans."[84]

Various vigilante groups burned the homes of suspected raiders, disarmed the non-Anglo population regardless of its political views, and forced Mexican Americans in rural areas to move to higher-populated areas where they could be more easily watched. Racial tensions became so acute that there was a mass migration of Mexicans and Mexican Americans out of the lower

Rio Grande Valley, many of them seeking refuge in northern Mexico. This exodus caused a severe labor shortage, threatening the rural-based economy of the region and posing even greater security problems. In response to the critical situation, mayors from towns in the region met at Mercedes in September 1915 and issued a statement calling for the protection of "good Mexicans" who were residing on the American side of the river.[85]

In reality there was little that state or federal officials could or would do to curb the excesses. Secretary of State Robert Lansing asked for Governor Ferguson's assistance in "allaying race prejudice and in restraining indiscreet conduct" when dealing with the border situation caused by the Plan of San Diego raids. Ferguson merely forwarded the communication to his personal staff, emphasizing that cooperation with federal officials was "essential."[86] Ferguson made no effort to rein in the Texas Rangers. While not condoning the summary killings carried out by law enforcement officials and citizens' groups, the governor attributed much of the problem to Mexican Americans themselves. In response to complaints by carrancista officials about the killing of Mexicans by the Rangers, Ferguson offered the observation: "The problem with the Texas-Mexican population is that their sympathies are with Mexico, and they never extend any cooperation to our authorities but are continually aiding and abetting the lawless element overrunning our country from Mexico."[87]

Although a final death toll from the racial strife in the Valley was difficult to calculate, General Funston estimated that approximately 300 "suspected Mexicans" had been summarily executed by hanging or shooting on the Texas side of the river as a result of the feelings caused by the Plan of San Diego.[88] The *San Antonio Express* reported that finding dead bodies of Mexi-

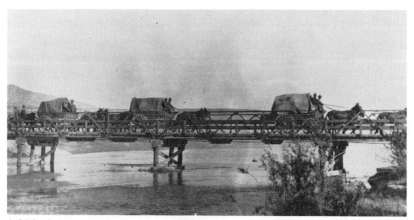

A U.S. Army wagon train crossing the Rio Grande at El Paso, ca. 1916. *Photograph courtesy of the Historical Museum, Fort Huachuca, Arizona.*

cans "had become so commonplace" that it "created little or no interest."[89]

By July 1916, raids under the Plan of San Diego had come to a halt, but the legacy of the Plan continued to influence economic activity and race relations long after that date. Several hundred people had died; economic damage running into the millions of dollars had been incurred; thousands of persons had seen their lives disrupted. Carranza had skillfully maneuvered the Plan to achieve diplomatic recognition in October 1915 but had dangerously overplayed his hand in reviving the raids in 1916. While anti-Anglo sentiment had helped to provide a foundation for the Plan from the beginning, it was the Mexican American population rather than the Anglo which ultimately suffered the most from the movement. The Carranza connection was the unifying factor in the raids, but the Plan of San Diego drew attention to two other disturbing elements on the border: revolutionary activities by supporters of General Huerta and espionage activities by the Germans.

5. Huertistas and "Huns" on the Border

After his resignation in July 1914, General Victoriano Huerta exiled himself comfortably in Spain, establishing residence in Barcelona. Huerta quickly tired of his new arrangements, however, and rumors emerged that he was planning a military comeback. Certainly the situation in Mexico encouraged aspiring revolutionaries, past and future. The ouster of Huerta had not led to an era of political stability and economic recovery but rather to the bloodiest phase of the Mexican Revolution. The Constitutionalist victory over Huerta eliminated the common enemy and at the same time the strongest link binding together the various factions. The revolutionary leaders soon fell out, with Carranza and a reluctant Obregón being matched against Villa and Zapata, allies who showed little allegiance. As revolution degenerated into civil war, exiles such as Huerta hoped to exploit Mexico's political and military chaos.

Since his departure had been partially due to outside intervention by the Wilson administration, Huerta felt that his political return would depend on substantial support from an outside source interested in undermining American influence in Mexico. Realizing that Britain and France would not challenge U.S. preeminence, his choice in such a situation was a limited one: Imperial Germany. When Huerta first came to power, Germany cautiously supported his regime while trying not to offend the Wilson administration. As the anti-American tone of his actions increased, however, German support grew correspondingly stronger. Eventually, though, Huerta's mounting financial and military problems forced Germany to withdraw its support. German diplomats even worked secretly to force his removal and put in his place Carranza, hoping to preclude more radical governments under either Villa or Zapata. Ironically, after Huerta decided to resign, he asked the German government to take him out of Mexico on one of its warships. German officials unenthusiastically granted Huerta's request but pointedly restricted the movement to his immediate family and General Aureliano Blanquet. A British ship would carry off the other members of Huerta's staff going into exile, a maneuver designed by Germany to involve Britain in Huerta's exit from the Mexican scene.[1]

Within a matter of weeks after Huerta's resignation from the presidency on July 15, 1914, World War I began in Europe, producing another vacillation in the German attitude toward Mexico and Huerta. German officials were greatly concerned by the role that the United States might play in the conflict. While the United States adopted a neutral position, American trade and loan activities worked strongly in favor of the Allies at the expense of the Germans. German plans to use submarine warfare to interrupt this trade ran into heavy criticism from American officials, forcing Germany to modify its use of submarines. Covert operations by German agents in the United States to disrupt the trade proved inept and politically embarrassing, with several agents being expelled or arrested.

German planners increasingly focused their attention on Mexico in an effort to interrupt trade between the United States and the Allies; the Germans hoped to exploit the revolutionary turmoil in Mexico first to reduce American arms shipments to the Allies and ultimately to provoke a war between the United States and Mexico. American military intervention on a large scale in Mexico would almost certainly preclude United States entrance into the European war and might produce the added benefit of interrupting the flow of Mexican oil to the British Royal Navy.[2] To help achieve these goals, the German government turned to a Mexican politician whose antagonism toward the Wilson administration in Washington was well known: General Huerta.

Early in 1915, while the supposedly huertista Plan of San Diego was unfolding in South Texas, a much different Huerta plot was under consideration in Europe. In February German intelligence officer Captain Franz von Rintelen contacted Huerta in Barcelona and offered German financial and military aid in restoring him to the presidency of Mexico. The Germans presumed that the restoration of Huerta would lead to severely strained relations between the United States and Mexico and might possibly provoke the desired intervention. Although contemplating a return to power and in need of financial support, Huerta did not immediately agree to the German offer.[3] Instead, a final piece needed to be added to the revolutionary exile puzzle before the real "Huerta conspiracy" of 1915 would be set in motion; this final piece was to be provided by revolutionary exiles operating in San Antonio, Texas.

While German intelligence was making its overture to Huerta, a group of prominent—and mostly conservative—Mexican exiles met in San Antonio to form what became known as the Mexican Peace Assembly, whose ostensible goal was to bring peace to Mexico and an end to the excesses of Revolution. In reality the Assembly became the vehicle for another exile plot directed against the Constitutionalist government. In March the Assembly dispatched Enrique Creel, former governor of Chihuahua and member of the wealthy Terrazas family, to recruit Huerta for the burgeoning conspiracy. Creel brought several informational items of interest for the general about developments in Mexico along the border. Creel told Huerta that Pascual Orozco had already joined the conspirators and was prepared to play a prominent military role. There was also a report that Carranza had formulated a proscription list composed primarily of Huerta's supporters. Creel drew a connection between the new conspiracy and the already discovered Plan of San Diego, indicating that the Mexican American population of South Texas was prepared to aid in a new rebellion. Huerta for his part had an interesting bit of news for Creel: the German offer of aid for Huerta's return to power.[4]

In late March, Huerta and Creel left Spain for New York City; there was no effort to conceal either the departure or the destination. Word of the exiles' travels provoked considerable interest in the United States even before their April 12th arrival in New York. Agents for both Carranza and Villa protested Huerta's trip and asked the State Department to block his entry into the United States, citing revolutionary plotting by exiles along the border. The State Department refused the requests, and Huerta arrived in New York amid considerable speculation and apprehension about the purpose of his visit. The general ingenuously informed reporters that he was on a "pleasure trip," a statement partially belied by the fact that one of his traveling companions was New York businessman Abraham Ratner who had been an important arms purchaser for Huerta while he was president.[5]

Huerta's actions soon indicated the more serious purpose behind his journey. In statements to the press, Huerta decried the chaotic conditions that existed in Mexico and predicted that a strong leader would appear to restore order, modestly declining to offer any insight as to who that leader might be. He also publicly criticized President Wilson's Mexican policy and warned against American intervention in Mexico's internal affairs. More ominously, Huerta was in frequent contact with Mexican exiles—many of them former army officers—and with German agents. The general received several hundred "courtesy calls" from Mexican officers. He held discussions with Captain von Rintelen, Huerta's German contact in Spain who had arrived in New York City shortly before Huerta. Moreover, Huerta was in contact with German Naval Attaché Karl Boy-Ed and Military Attaché Franz von Papen, who both had recently returned from the border where they had conferred with other leaders of the growing Huerta conspiracy.[6]

The offered financial assistance soon became a central feature of Huerta's plans to return to power. German officials deposited $800,000 to Huerta's account in a Havana bank and placed another $95,000 for his use in a Mexican account. German agents acquired first eight million rounds of ammunition and then another three million rounds for the group. There was even a promise to supply ten thousand rifles which were to be landed on the Mexican coast by German U-boats. Von Papen made trips to Brownsville, San Antonio, and El Paso to distribute funds for the plot. Germany's financial commitment to the huertista conspiracy totaled approximately $12,000,000.[7]

Huerta and Orozco

In addition to accepting financial aid from the Germans, Huerta in effect had also taken over the leadership of other revolutionary exile movements in Texas, principally that of his former ally Pascual Orozco. Following the overthrow of Huerta in July 1914, Orozco immediately rebelled against the new government. Lacking supplies, financing, and popular support, the effort faltered, and Orozco fled to Texas where he was the target for extradition proceedings. He avoided arrest and was soon involved in new revolutionary plotting with fellow Mexican exiles, loosely described as the "El Paso group." Several former *orozquista* generals were involved with this group, most notably Emilio Campa and José Inés Salazar. Campa and Salazar started a minor insurrection in Chihuahua in December 1914 as a prelude to a major rebellion to be led by Orozco, who busied himself traveling around the United States arranging for arms purchases. Before the revolt under Orozco could take place, however, it merged into the broader based Huerta conspiracy. In early May 1915, Orozco visited Huerta in New York City, where the final plans were laid for the revolution. The date set for the uprising was June 28. Orozco was to precede Huerta to El Paso to notify the various revolutionary organizations and to make final arrangements for Huerta's arrival.[8]

Suspecting some sort of plot, U.S. officials had been monitoring the activities of Huerta and his associates from the very beginning. As soon as Huerta arrived in New York, Secretary of State Bryan observed to the United States Customs Collector at El Paso, Zachary Cobb, that his appearance "indicated some kind of scheme."[9] Weekly intelligence reports from U.S. Army units along the Mexican border revealed increased traffic in arms, presumably in connection with a huertista uprising. Large numbers of Huerta sympathizers gravitated to the Texas-Mexican border, especially to El Paso, in anticipation of the rebellion. Assistant Attorney General Charles Warren ordered the United States attorney in El Paso, J. J. Camp, to be especially vigilant if Huerta appeared in San Antonio. He directed Camp to watch for any possible violations of the neutrality laws and to prosecute Huerta if possible. In response, Camp recommended that the most effective way of dealing with the conspiracy was to try to deport Huerta. This view reflected the fact that he could post bail if charged with violation of the neutrality laws and would be at liberty to continue his conspiratorial activities. Cobb, a veteran border watcher who often had better intelligence information than the State and War Departments, warned Secretary of State Bryan that the huertistas were about to launch an attack on Ciudad Juárez.[10]

The Unraveling of the Conspiracy

The conspiracy began simultaneously to unfold and unravel on June 24 when Huerta left New York City by train, ostensibly for San Francisco. With the June 28 date for the revolution fast approaching, Huerta was actually enroute to the vicinity of El Paso, where Orozco was already making final arrangements for the rebellion. Because of the large number of U.S. federal agents operating in El Paso, Orozco and Huerta had arranged to meet in Newman, New Mexico, approximately twenty miles away. After the rendezvous, Orozco and Huerta would cross into Mexico near Sierra Blanca, Texas, to lead the revolt. At the same time, several huertista generals were to leave San Antonio for El Paso to participate in the revolution.[11]

At Kansas City, Huerta left the train for San Francisco and boarded one destined for El Paso. Keeping surveillance, railroad officials notified federal authorities of this change in itinerary. Huerta arrived at Newman early on the morning of Sunday, June 27. Awaiting Huerta's arrival were Orozco and Huerta's son-in-law, Luis Fuentes, who had a car prepared to carry Huerta to the border. Also waiting to welcome the generals were Justice Department officials, federal marshals, a cavalry detachment, and local law enforcement officers who had received advance information from Cobb that Huerta would leave the train at Newman. As soon as Huerta alighted, federal officials appeared and "requested" that the two generals accompany them to El Paso. None of the conspirators offered any resistance.[12]

Department of Justice officials escorted Huerta and Orozco to the federal building in El Paso where already assembled was a crowd of exiles and pro-Huerta Mexican Americans. The federal government charged both Huerta and Orozco with violation of the neutrality laws, although the evidence accumulated to that point was limited. On the same day, federal agents raided a warehouse in El Paso which had been rented by Mexican exiles; the raid disclosed an arms cache consisting of 14 machine guns, 500 rifles, and 100,000 rounds of ammunition.[13] While the confiscation was a serious blow to the conspiracy, it was not crucial since large quantities of arms and ammunition also had been smuggled across the border and hidden at strategic points in the northern Mexican states. What was a potentially fatal blow was the arrest and detention of Huerta and Orozco. Both men personified the political and military leadership of the movement; were they to remain in federal custody for an extended period of time, months of revolutionary planning would be undone.

Of concern to El Paso Mayor Tom Lea was the large crowd of Huerta sympathizers gathered outside the federal building, which presented the possibility of a violent demonstration or even an attempt to liberate the prisoners. To guard against such action, Lea asked that federal authorities transfer the prisoners to Fort Bliss outside the city. Although suspicious of the mayor's motives since Lea already had quickly agreed to serve as Huerta's lawyer, they approved the movement of both Huerta and Orozco to the more secure confines of the fort, where the two revolutionary leaders were treated more like visiting celebrities than prisoners. Huerta was even invited to dinner at the home of the commander of Fort Bliss. Other federal authorities, however, were less gracious. Representatives of the Department of Justice attempted to have the bonds of Huerta and Orozco set so high that they would not be able to meet them, but Lea outmaneuvered government lawyers, keeping them at only $15,000 and $7,500 respectively, which both easily posted. Huerta, for his part, continued to deny publicly that any conspiracy existed, maintaining that he had merely stopped in El Paso to visit his daughter while traveling to San Francisco.[14]

From the beginning of their investigation, federal officials had worried that arresting the conspirators would have a minimal effect on the revolutionary movement since they would be able to post bond. With the border close by, government agents especially feared that Huerta and Orozco might jump bail and cross into Mexico. To prevent such a move, Department of Justice agents and U.S. Army personnel kept Orozco and Huerta under constant surveillance while other federal agencies worked to achieve a more permanent solution to the problem. Immigration authorities investigated Huerta's entrance into the United States hoping to find some irregularity that would permit his deportation, but found none.

President Wilson followed the case of his old antagonist closely. He was particularly concerned that Huerta and Orozco might elude their surveillance and cross into Mexico. The Department of Justice did little to allay the President's apprehension when it reported that Huerta could not be legally prevented from crossing the border once released on bail. There was further discouraging news from the legal department; the assistant attorney general at El Paso who had the primary responsibility of prosecuting the case reported that evidence of a conspiracy was "meager." Meanwhile, Huerta continued to meet regularly with the revolutionary exile leadership, and there were frequent public displays of support for the general. Even more distressing for federal officials was the arrival in El Paso on June 30 of General Félix Díaz who had long been prominent in revolutionary exile activity and whose supporters had often been linked to the Huerta conspiracy in recent months.[15]

Huerta's legal difficulties, however, were far from finished. The hearing on the general's case was scheduled for July 12. While Huerta awaited his federal adversaries, a new threat appeared: a request by the villista governor of Chihuahua, General Fidel Avila, that Governor Ferguson arrest Huerta to await extradition proceedings on a charge of murder. Although governors of border states had the authority to grant extradition without referring the matter to Washington, Ferguson was reluctant to take action without first consulting with federal authorities because of the unsettled conditions in Mexico and especially because of the prominence of the individual involved. On June 30 the Governor wrote to Secretary of State Lansing that "I have no intention or disposition to do anything in this matter until I have the advice and suggestions of your Department."[16]

While the State Department delayed its response, there were further legal and diplomatic developments. The Constitutionalist government of Venustiano Carranza also requested the extradition of Huerta on charges of murder. This request added to a confusing situation because the United States recognized neither the villista nor the Constitutionalist factions. After a second request by Ferguson for guidance on July 7, Secretary of State Lansing replied that the department considered the extradition of Huerta to either of the two factions to be "unwise." Lansing cited the unsettled political conditions in Mexico (that is, nonrecognition), concerns about the "political character of the crime," the difficulty of assuring a fair trial, and the possibility of an effort to free Huerta. Having shown little inclination to extradite Huerta in the first place, Ferguson used the State Department's recommendation as a basis for refusing the request.[17] The threat of extradition, however, would continue to influence Huerta's legal situation.

On July 3 Pascual Orozco successfully eluded the federal agents and army personnel assigned to watch him and disappeared. Federal authorities responded by cancelling Huerta's bond and rearresting him. This second arrest left Huerta visibly shaken and bitter. There was none of the deferential treatment accorded Huerta after his first arrest; he found himself in a cramped cell in the El Paso jail like anyone else. After almost a week's delay, Huerta's bond was once again set at $15,000. Although sufficient funds were available to post bond, Huerta declined after reaching an agreement with government authorities that he would be transferred to Fort Bliss. The general's explanation for this turn of events was that he had been under such surveillance after posting bond the first time that he saw no advantage in repeating the process. A Department of Justice lawyer assigned to the case, R. E. Crawford, speculated that Huerta was remaining in jail for the "political effect" on the Mexican people. A more likely explanation is that federal attorneys intimated to Huerta that they might honor requests for his extradition if he posted bail.[18] Federal officials were determined to put an end to Huerta's revolutionary activities, a goal which could be achieved only if Huerta remained in custody.

The United States government transferred Huerta to Fort Bliss where he was placed under guard in the officer's quarters. Huerta's wife and children had moved from New York City to El Paso, and the general received special permission to visit them. Huerta's first encounter with his family following his arrest proved upsetting rather than encouraging. The family had settled in a house in El Paso only to have it searched almost immediately by agents from the Department of Justice. Huerta protested the action to federal authorities but received no reply. He then turned for help to his earlier benefactors, the Germans. On July 27 he telegraphed the German ambassador in Washington, Count Johann von Bernstorff, asking the German government to intervene with U.S. authorities on behalf of his family. The Germans, however, had already written off the Huerta conspiracy as a failure and were fearful that American agents had intercepted Huerta's telegram, which might prove embarrassing to the German government. Bernstorff turned a copy of the telegram over to the State Department without action and without any reply to Huerta.[19]

Further indications suggested that the Huerta conspiracy was coming to an unsuccessful conclusion for the general and his supporters. For example, Orozco had remained in the vicinity of El Paso following his escape. On the morning of August 30, Orozco and four of his men had stopped at a ranch near Sierra Blanca, Texas, for food and water. Orozco soon found himself pursued by a motley posse composed of ranch personnel, local law enforcement officials, federal marshals, Texas Rangers, and U.S. Army cavalry. The posse caught up with the fleeing Mexicans in Green River Canyon, approximately twenty-five miles from Sierra Blanca; in the ensuing shoot-out, the pursuing force killed Orozco and his four companions while suffering no casualties of its own. The one-sided nature of the casualties gave rise to accusations that Orozco had been "assassinated" by the posse. Mexican exiles in San Antonio and El Paso protested the slayings, and Anglo residents of the Big Bend feared that the incident might lead to reprisals along the border, leading cattlemen in the area to ask Governor Ferguson for special protection that he would be unable to provide. Even the Carranza administration—the target of the Huerta-Orozco plotting—asked for an investigation into the killings. The official position of the United States government was that Orozco had been killed in a "fair fight" by members of the posse who were acting in "self-defense."[20]

With Orozco dead and Huerta in federal custody, one of the best planned and most heavily financed of the border conspiracies was at an end. Despondent over his situation, Huerta resumed his heavy drinking, and his health rapidly declined. Huerta's deteriorating medical condition prompted federal officials to let him return to his home in November 1915, but in December he was returned to Fort Bliss after federal officials feared he might try to escape. After two operations Huerta died on January 13, 1916, from a combination of gall bladder and liver problems. The day before, a federal grand jury in San Antonio had indicted Huerta for "conspiracy to begin and set on foot a military expedition" against the government of Mexico in violation of federal neutrality laws. Huerta's trial was supposed to have begun in May.[21]

The German Threat on the Border

While the Orozco-Huerta Plan represented the last major revolutionary conspiracy formulated in Texas during the period from 1910 to 1920, it did not bring an end to German activities on the border. The failure to reinstall the pro-German Huerta in the presidency only led to new efforts by Germany to manipulate revolutionary activity to realize its global aims. The Germans attempted to win over the most prominent surviving Mexican exile, General Félix Díaz, who had earlier indicated that he was interested in reaching an arrangement with them. After the failure of the Huerta conspiracy, however, Díaz abstained from further negotiations with the Germans.[22]

German attention then shifted to Pancho Villa as the most likely prospect for provoking American intervention along the border. Even before the failure of the Huerta conspiracy, the Germans had been cultivating ties with Villa. The key figure in their efforts to manipulate Villa was Felix A. Sommerfeld, a German-born international adventurer who had close connections with the German secret service and who was also a major arms purchaser for Villa. These two roles merged in April 1915, when the Germans began funneling money through Sommerfeld to purchase arms and ammunition for Villa. Using accounts in a St. Louis bank, Sommerfeld continued to acquire arms for Villa through December 1915. There is no direct evidence linking the Germans with Villa's attack on Columbus, New Mexico, in March 1916; nevertheless, Sommerfeld had been in contact with the Austrian-German Dr. Lyman Rauschbaum who served as Villa's personal physician and trusted advisor. After the Columbus attack, which did induce the desired American intervention, the Germans continued to supply Villa with arms and equipment.[23]

When American intervention did not produce a major military confrontation between the Carranza government and the United States, the Germans then encouraged Villa to attack the oil fields at Tampico, a major source of oil for the British. The German consul at Torreón, temporarily under *villista* control, promised that German ships would be waiting with arms and money for him if he captured Tampico. Villa briefly considered the offer but ultimately decided to move in the opposite direction against Chihuahua.[24] The motives affecting Villa's decision are not precisely known, but fear of further American intervention and his own familiarity with Chihuahua must have figured strongly in his thinking. Had Villa decided to move against Tampico, it would have caused substantial turmoil in the Mexican border states along the Rio Grande and further complicated border policy.

This series of failures with forces opposed to the Carranza regime led to German efforts to cultivate closer relations with Carranza himself. Germany's connection with Huerta before and after his fall from power understandably had produced a mutual antagonism between Carranza and Germany. By 1916, however, it was in the political interests of both parties to seek a rapprochement. The Germans needed Carranza if they were to realize their goals of interrupting the flow of American arms to the Allies and of occupying American forces on the border or in Mexico itself. Carranza, for his part, following an increasingly nationalistic policy likely to produce friction with the United States, could use Germany as a force to counterbalance the always strong influence of his northern neighbor. Both sides had an interest in seeing the freedom of action of the United States restricted, so Germany and the Carranza administration drew more closely together in the face of this common problem. The realignment started slowly, first with a more pro-German attitude in the Carranza-controlled press and then accelerating rapidly with the entrance of the Pershing expedition into Mexico in March 1916. By late 1916 Mexico was suggesting closer commercial relations as well as German assistance in improving its army and navy. Germany, however, was unwilling to engage in any overt challenge to the dominant American position in Mexico as long as the United States remained neutral.[25]

In this context of increasing ties between Mexico and Germany, the so-called Zimmermann telegram seems much less shocking than it did at the time of its revelation to American authorities in February 1917. Germany had made the decision in January to renew unrestricted submarine warfare, a move which the German high command assumed would lead to the entrance of the United States into the war on the side of the Allies. The German foreign secretary, Arthur Zimmermann, decided to offer a formal military alliance to Carranza if America did indeed enter the war. In a soon-to-be-famous telegram on January 16, Zimmermann instructed the German ambassador in Mexico City to offer an alliance to Carranza in the event Germany found itself at war with the United States. Germany proposed "generous financial assistance" in a carrancista war to "reconquer the lost territories of Texas, New Mexico, and Arizona." The German ambassador was also to attempt to recruit Carranza as an intermediary in bringing the Japanese into an anti-American alliance. British intelligence intercepted and decoded the telegram and later passed it on to American authorities.[26]

The publication of the Zimmermann telegram on March 1 created a sensation throughout the United States, but nowhere more so than on the border. Earlier rumors linking the Germans with the Plan of San Diego and the Huerta conspiracy now seemed verified. The jumbled image of Mexican bandits, the dreaded "Huns," and the "yellow peril" provoked considerable alarm along the Rio Grande. Heightening the alarm was the fact that this latest incident had occurred at a time when the United States was reducing its military strength on the border. Since May and June 1916, the entire

National Guard of the United States had been mobilized and sent to the U.S.-Mexican border. In early March 1917, the War Department had ordered a demobilization of all National Guard units remaining on the border – approximately 30,000 troops – and directed that they be returned to their home states by the end of the month. During the last week in March, however, the department halted this action and began calling back units that had been released earlier. The Texas Guard was one of several units mobilized on March 31. On April 6, the United States declared war on Germany, at least partially motivated by German activities in Mexico.[27]

Carranza and Neutrality

Carranza's repeated protestations of Mexican neutrality during the war did little to relieve American fears about his pro-German inclinations or German intelligence activities in Mexico. Frequent reports claimed that the Mexicans, urged on by the Germans, were planning attacks along the Rio Grande. One report had Germans invading both Texas and British Honduras from Mexican bases. There was also talk of secret German submarine bases in the Gulf of Mexico. Federal authorities arrested four German nationals in El Paso on charges that they attempted to induce Mexican military commanders to invade Texas. Carrancista officials at Juárez created further confusion and unrest by claiming that Pancho Villa had reached an agreement with the Germans and was leading his troops toward the border to attack American towns; the officials heroically added that they had stationed an additional 4,000 troops at Juárez to protect the border against the ravages of Villa. In spite of the Zimmermann telegram, the War Department publicly dismissed such reports.[28]

While the War Department officially discounted any German threat to the border region, high-ranking army officers privately were worried about security along the international boundary. After an inspection tour from Brownsville, Texas, to Yuma, Arizona, General Pershing, commander of the Southern Department, wrote from San Antonio to Army Chief of Staff Scott: "As to the operations of the Germans in Mexico, there is little doubt that they are active, and I think it certain that those in Mexico intend to give us all the trouble possible." Pershing was not afraid that the Mexican government would take official action against the United States but was worried that individual Mexican military leaders, "led by German influence and perhaps by German money," might instigate raids along the lines of those carried out earlier under the Plan of San Diego. The inability of federal authorities to stop the traffic in arms across the border especially disturbed Pershing.[29] Scott – a veteran of service on the border himself – urged Pershing not to be discouraged by the arms-smuggling problem but rather to "keep everlastingly hammering at it." Scott concurred with Pershing's views on

German activities in northern Mexico: "I think the Germans are going to stir up the Mexicans to do all the petty damage to us they can."[30]

Other major disagreements concerning U.S.-Mexican relations further encouraged suspicions about Carranza's neutrality. The Mexican minister of foreign affairs, General Cándido Aguilar, informed U.S. Ambassador Henry P. Fletcher in Mexico City that the Carranza administration might indemnify Europeans for losses suffered during the Revolution but not Americans, since the United States was "directly or indirectly responsible for much that happened during the revolution."[31] The Mexican government had issued a new constitution in February 1917, which had several provisions that would disturb U.S.-Mexican relations for years to come. Also by 1917 a considerable personal animosity had developed between Carranza and Wilson; Carranza's increasingly nationalistic policies frequently clashed with Wilson's determination to "guide" the Mexican Revolution. In a letter to Secretary of State Lansing shortly after American entry into the war, Wilson dismissed Carranza as "that pedantic ass" and characterized his administration in these terms: "All that Carranza has said and done shows his intense resentment towards this administration."[32]

Many U.S. officials, including Wilson, incorrectly equated being anti-American with being pro-German, an attitude which encouraged an exaggerated concept of German activity along the Rio Grande. Typical of this group was Mayor Lea of El Paso, who believed that Mexico was to be used as a base of operations against the United States and that "German influence was being brought to bear all over Mexico." Lea advocated a policy of supporting anti-Carranza factions so that "the brains of Mexico could gain control of the northern border." The mayor offered no evidence to support his convictions.[33] While there were reports linking German agents with anti-American activities by Mexicans, convincing evidence of such a connection was elusive. George Carothers, veteran border-watcher and special agent for the State Department, summarized the situation: "I have been making every effort to connect the Germans with the Mexicans, but I must say that, outside of general rumors, I can find nothing."[34]

Anti-Carranza forces in Texas were eager to exploit this confusion. Revolutionary conspirators attempted to depict themselves as being not only anti-Carranza but also anti-German and pro-American. Some of the plotters promised to close Mexican newspapers that supported the German position and to expel all Germans from Mexico; there was even talk of executing all Germans in Mexico "who were anti-American," a category which presumably included most of the German residents in that country. The exiles often linked high-ranking carrancista military officers with the Germans; one name often mentioned in this connection was that of General Emiliano Nafarrate, the former commander at Matamoros who had also been linked with the Plan of San Diego raids which were believed by many to be German-inspired.[35] Since there was no effective revolutionary organization operating in Texas during the 1917-1918 period, the exiles never had the opportunity to carry out their pro-American rhetoric.

While federal authorities assumed much of the responsibility for greater security along the border during the war, state officials also increased their activities as well. William P. Hobby—who succeeded to the governorship upon the impeachment of Ferguson in August 1917—suggested to the War Department that a special border guard of 16,000 men between the ages of thirty-one and forty-five be organized in the Texas National Guard with federal military and financial support. Later he recommended that a cavalry division of some 30,000 men be authorized to serve along the Rio Grande as "the situation in Mexico would be improved by such a guard and it would be one of the wisest steps of protection our country could make at this time." When the War Department balked at such a move and authorized only six cavalry regiments, Hobby asked the Department to change three infantry

Governor William P. Hobby.
Photograph courtesy of the Barker
Texas History Center.

regiments already approved to cavalry regiments since "most Texans are good horsemen." Hobby later found it difficult to raise even the three regiments of infantry, much less the six of cavalry designated for the Texas National Guard.[36]

In the absence of large-scale reinforcements for the border, Governor Hobby had to depend upon a more traditional response for strengthening security along the Rio Grande: an increase in the Ranger force. Such a move was not without controversy since the Rangers were under growing criticism for their rough tactics, particularly in regard to the Mexican American population. There was a major expansion in the regular Ranger force, aimed primarily at protecting the border.[37] The state adjutant general also established a special investigation bureau to improve intelligence collection along the border. In charge of this new operation was W. M. Hanson, a well-known figure along the Rio Grande. Hanson had extensive law enforcement experience in South Texas, including service as a federal marshal for the Southern District of Texas; he also had considerable knowledge of northern Mexico where he had engaged in oil and land operations between 1906 and 1914. In 1914, however, carrancista officials had expelled Hanson for his support of the Huerta regime, and there was even an effort to link Hanson with the Plan of San Diego, which he allegedly had hoped to use as a device to embarrass the Carranza administration. Hanson filled his reports with praise for the Rangers and information from Mexican exiles, but there is little evidence that they had a major effect on state activity along the Rio Grande.[38]

In spite of fears about border security, the war years brought no renewal of large-scale raiding along the lines of earlier raids under the Plan of San Diego. Germany continued to use Mexico City as the headquarters for its espionage activities in Latin America and to have as one of its main goals destabilizing the border region in order to occupy large numbers of U.S. troops. American uneasiness over the situation on the border, however, far exceeded the capability of the Germans or the willingness of the Mexicans to create trouble in the area. In fact, during the war years it was not Mexican raiders but the U.S. Army that was involved in most of the major border crossings.[39]

6 World War I and Its Aftermath

The entrance of the United States into World War I in April 1917 required a major change in military emphasis. Starting with the formation of the Maneuver Division in 1911, the U.S. government had concentrated a growing amount of its military resources on the U.S.-Mexican boundary, especially along the Rio Grande. This had reached its peak in late 1916 when most of the regular army and the entire National Guard were either in northern Mexico or on the border. With the advent of the European war, of course, the army experienced a major redeployment, with most forces destined for war-related service. The War Department viewed those forces that remained on the border as in a training situation for the larger war against Germany.[1]

Although wartime demands for personnel were great, the Wilson administration still left approximately 30,000 troops on the border. While the war brought many military changes to the border, one important prewar policy remained in force; the army would continue its policy of "hot pursuit" of Mexican raiders who crossed into U.S. territory. There were, however, important operational limitations imposed on such crossings. Troops were not to remain in Mexico for more than three days nor to penetrate more than sixty miles beyond the border. Army commanders must initiate the pursuit within one week after the attack occurred. If their forces encountered carrancista troops, they were to turn over all information that they had about the raiders and return immediately to American soil.[2]

Bandit raids followed by hot pursuit on the part of American forces continued throughout the war years of 1917-1918. As had been the case in the past, most of the raids and subsequent crossings took place along the Rio Grande. While the raids were not as serious as those of 1915-1916 and usually involved relatively small numbers of both raiders and U.S. troopers, casualties often occurred on both sides. On December 3, 1917, a group of bandits on the Mexican side of the river fired on an army patrol near Indio, Texas, wounding one soldier. Troops immediately crossed the river and subsequently killed twelve of the bandits. One of the bloodier incursions took place in March 1918 as the result of a raid on a ranch near Van Horn, Texas. Approximately thirty bandits attacked and looted the ranch, killing the rancher's son and a Mexican worker. Army forces crossed into Mexico and caught up with the raiders at a ranch near Pilares which U.S. authorities considered a center of bandit activity. A running battle ensued with the raiders, who had been reinforced by additional bandits from Pilares. U.S. troopers killed thirty-three Mexicans, recovered part of the stolen loot, and capped their foray by burning the ranch where the bandits had been found. The local carrancista commander notified the force that he was dispatching troops—not to pursue the remaining bandits but to intercept the Americans. The U.S. force subsequently withdrew without incident, having suffered only one trooper killed. On April 21, 1918, a group of Mexicans raided a ranch near Bosque Bonito, Texas, stealing six horses and other provisions. With no loss of life on either side and with only a limited response by U.S. cavalry, it would have been considered a minor incident except for the fact that the raiders were carrancista soldiers. The local carrancista commander later compensated the rancher for his losses.[3]

These incursions brought frequent complaints from the Carranza government about violations of national territory; carrancista officials also accused U.S. soldiers of firing across the Rio Grande without provocation. In an effort to answer these grievances and still maintain border security, the U.S. secretary of war in May 1918 issued new instructions to military commanders along the international boundary: U.S. troops were not to fire upon persons on the Mexican side of the boundary unless fired upon first and the return of fire was necessary for self-defense. Military commanders were to implement the hot-pursuit policy only to rescue American captives and only then if it appeared that Mexican forces would be unable to recapture them. If there was pursuit, U.S. forces were to penetrate no more than twenty miles, and the officers in charge were to notify promptly the nearest Mexican commander. The War Department authorized U.S. commanders to enter into "special agreements" for cooperation with local carrancista officials on the border.[4] When the Carranza administration continued to complain, Secretary of State Lansing wrote to Secretary of War Baker that he was "embarrassed by and found it difficult to answer" Mexican charges about the firing and pursuit across the border by U.S. troops. Lansing recommended that a policy be implemented prohibiting such actions "without specific orders in each case from the War Department."[5] Baker rejected such a policy, saying that it would be "most undesirable from a military standpoint."[6] Thus, U.S. forces were still free to cross the border and return fire under the existing limitations without prior consultation with authorities in Washington.

Disagreements over border policy were only part of a broader range of problems between the United States and the Carranza regime. Although the United States had extended full recognition to the Carranza government in August 1917, this did little to improve actual relations between the two countries. The recently promulgated Mexican Constitution of 1917 conferred constitutional legitimacy on the Carranza administration but had several articles disturbing to the United States, particularly the provisions relating to property rights in Article 27. Carranza's tax policies, especially in regard to the U.S.-dominated oil industry, also provoked criticism. Further, the

U.S. government perceived a pro-German bias in his widely advertised neutrality and objected to German intelligence activities in Mexico, especially along the border. On the Mexican side, the Carranza administration heatedly denounced American violations of Mexican territory, restrictions on American exports to Mexico, and the use of American territory by anti-Carranza rebels.[7] This array of problems created an environment for a new "war crisis," more incidents at Juárez, and another occasion for American intervention on the border in 1919.

The end of the war in Europe in November 1918 was significant for the future of border relations along the Rio Grande for two reasons. First, Wilson continued to concentrate on European affairs, especially the peace conference at Versailles and the creation of a League of Nations; this preoccupation left the formulation of Mexican policy increasingly in the hands of other members of the administration. Second, the conclusion of European hostilities allowed the border once again to become the principal focus of U.S. military interest; the return of troops from Europe meant a strengthening of forces along the international boundary and permitted the United States to adopt a tougher stance in its dealings with the Carranza administration.

Besides border security, other problems continued to disturb relations between the two countries: the petroleum question, tax and trade policies, and American claims arising out of the Revolution. There were growing pressures on the Wilson administration from Republicans in Congress and U.S. business interests to take a harder line with Carranza, even to the extent of military intervention. Senator Albert B. Fall of New Mexico continued his campaign for military action in Mexico while important business leaders with interests in Mexico formed the "National Association for the Protection of American Rights in Mexico" to propagandize the public about the "true conditions" in Mexico.[8]

On March 1, 1919, United States Ambassador to Mexico Fletcher wrote a confidential memorandum to President Wilson in which he painted a pessimistic picture of conditions in Mexico under the Carranza regime. Fletcher reported that Carranza was channeling more than eighty percent of government revenue into "pacification" efforts but with little effect. Article 27 of the Constitution of 1917 "practically closes the door to future foreign investments and threatens those already made in the country." The ambassador stated that Mexico had no foreign or domestic credit, that the government had paid no bond interest since 1914, and that the national debt had reached an estimated 350 million dollars. Fletcher believed there were only two courses of action available to the Wilson administration: 1) let matters continue to drift, amidst growing domestic and foreign criticism; 2) call upon the Mexican government to perform its duties or confess its inability to do so. If the Carranza administration admitted its inability to meet its responsibilities, it should be prepared to accept "disinterested assistance" from the United States.[9] The deteriorating position of the Carranza administration and the growing disenchantment of the U.S. government with his regime would soon lead to another intervention crisis.

Final Act at Juárez

The developing situation along the border involved a familiar figure — Pancho Villa — and a familiar place — Juárez. Although long since eliminated as a national political contender, Villa retained his status as a regional military leader and periodically emerged to bedevil the Carranza regime. Villa's strength in northern Mexico had been increasing since late 1917; by June 1919 he had regained control of most of the state of Chihuahua. The major prize of Juárez, however, still remained under carrancista control.

Since Juárez had changed hands seven times since the beginning of the Revolution in 1910, U.S. civil and military officials considered it a likely target for the villistas, who had effectively isolated the town by June. Given his past record, Villa was not likely to be concerned that an attack on Juárez might lead to intervention. U.S. War Department officials, however, were planning for just such an eventuality. This time the United States was prepared to respond in a much different manner than it had in May 1911 when the first Juárez crisis ushered in a decade of turmoil along the border. This latest villista threat prompted Secretary of War Newton Baker to issue new orders concerning border crossings; forces could enter Mexico in defense of U.S. lives and property but could not engage in any "invasion or occupation" of Mexican territory. Baker did not explain how U.S. troops could "enter" Mexico without "invading" it, but the orders continued a distinction that the Wilson administration had made since the Pershing expedition. The War Department also issued specific orders concerning an attack on Juárez. If the villistas took Juárez, then military authorities were to close the border. In the event that Villa's troops fired into El Paso, then American forces were to cross the border and disperse his troops. Again the orders contained seemingly contradictory provisions; American commanders had the authority to lead their forces across the border but not "to undertake an expedition into Mexico." In addition, the State Department arranged for the exportation of 150,000 rounds of ammunition to the carrancista commander at Juárez.[10]

When the expected attack began early on the morning of June 15, shells fell in El Paso almost immediately, causing several casualties. Operating under the recently received orders, General James B. Erwin, commander of the El Paso military district, informed the carrancista commander at Juárez, General Federico González, that troops would be crossing the border to halt the shooting into El Paso. General González promptly removed his forces to

Fort Hidalgo in the hills overlooking Juárez where he would have a good view of the coming struggle between the villistas and the U.S. Army. On the evening of the fifteenth, a force of approximately 3,600 – including cavalry, infantry, and artillery – crossed into Juárez. The U.S. soldiers quickly dispersed the villistas, inflicting casualties estimated at 100, and returned to the American side by the evening of June 16. Unexpectedly light casualties for the U.S. Army included two killed and ten wounded, with only one soldier actually being killed on the Mexican side; civilian casualties in El Paso were two killed and four wounded.[11]

The carrancista response to the incursion was surprisingly restrained. General González, safely ensconced at Fort Hidalgo, characterized the intervention as unnecesssary since his forces had "defended the town most bravely." González showed little disposition to make a major issue of the incident, however, observing, "This is a matter for my superior officers and for my president to consider. I am not in a position to impose my own views upon the situation."[12] Carranza himself made no effort to prolong the affair, declaring the incident officially closed three days after the withdrawal of the U.S. force. Carranza promptly promoted González for his defense of the national sovereignty despite reports that the general was "exceedingly friendly" toward the invaders. The U.S. consul at Juárez even reported that there was "no important ill feeling against Americans" as a result of the intervention.[13]

Actions by other carrancista officials, however, indicated the growing friction between the United States and Mexico. Governors of the Mexican states bordering the Rio Grande declined to attend formal meetings with Governor Hobby. The Mexican War Department sent out an extensive questionnaire to Mexican consulates in the Southwest, asking for information concerning roads, railways, and the number of foreigners; such information would be useful in the event that the United States decided to intervene in northern Mexico again on a large scale. The Carranza administration even sent agents into South Texas to organize protests by the Mexican American population and to distribute handbills which urged Mexican Americans to engage in strikes and acts of sabotage as a means of regaining the territory lost during the Mexican War.[14] With no military support for these activities, Carranza's efforts produced little in the way of tangible results.

U.S. border policy increasingly carried with it the threat of intervention. The War Department dispatched additional army units to the border, including eighteen aircraft for patrol duty. This new border air patrol had as its nucleus a group of veterans of combat flying in Europe. Officially American aircraft were not supposed to cross the international boundary, but there were frequent violations of this restriction.[15] There was also a major effort to increase fortifications along the border. By the summer of 1919, there were twenty-four Army posts in Texas alone; El Paso and Brownsville were the sites of the two largest U.S. Army ordnance depots in the United States. The army also dispatched additional tanks to San Antonio and El Paso in response to worsening conditions along the Rio Grande.[16]

The harsher policy had diplomatic as well as military aspects. Unlike the period from 1913 to 1915 when the Wilson administration would not even inform state authorities about possible military options, War and State Department officials were no longer guarded in their comments about intervention. After the action in Juárez, Secretary of War Baker made it clear that the operation was not an isolated incident but part of a new approach: "If Villa or Carranza cut any capers along the border, our troops will go after them into Mexico. The War Department has adopted and will carry out a firm and decisive policy hereafter regarding border affairs."[17] The State Department talked sternly of the possibility of adopting "a radical change in policy with regard to Mexico," clearly implying that American patience was being exhausted and that intervention was a possibility.[18] To indicate further its displeasure over lack of border security, the government imposed a total embargo on the shipment of arms to Mexico on July 12.[19] This action put the Wilson administration in the rather inconsistent position of criticizing the Mexican government for its failure to restore order while simultaneously restricting Mexican access to the arms needed to do so. With fears of a villista reprisal for the intervention at Juárez, the border region was suffering its worst case of war nerves since the summer of 1916.

The Last Punitive Expedition

The last of the "punitive expeditions" was to take place as a result of the newly instituted border air patrol. On August 10, 1919, one of the border patrol aircraft with two crew members disappeared while on a reconnaissance from Marfa to El Paso. A land and air search for the missing plane on the American side produced no results. On August 12 American aviators extended the air phase of the search to the Mexican side of the Rio Grande, continuing until August 17 without finding either aircraft or crew. Then Jesús Rentería—notorious border bandit and sometime villista officer—informed American officials that he had the two flyers and demanded a $15,000 ransom for their return.[20]

The Rentería gang was holding the aviators near San Antonio, Chihuahua, a well-known center of bandit and villista activity, across the Rio Grande from Candelaria, Texas, which was about forty miles upriver from Presidio. Although the State Department protested the incident to the Carranza administration, the War Department decided to pay the ransom. Military officials on the border were instructed to pay the amount, but lacked the cash to do so. When area ranchers attending a Baptist revival meeting near Marfa heard of the problem, they immediately subscribed the money, and the Marfa National Bank provided the necessary cash based on the ranchers' pledges. The person selected to handle the exchange was Captain Leonard F. Matlack, commander of the cavalry unit at Candelaria and a colorful border veteran who always wore two Colt revolvers. When problems developed over the mechanics of the exchange, Matlack announced that he was personally holding every Mexican in the towns of San Antonio and Boquillas responsible for the safety of the aviators and that he would rescue the captives by force if they were not promptly returned. Rentería quickly agreed to an exchange.[21]

Early in the morning of August 19, Matlack alone crossed the river, paid half of the ransom money, and obtained the release of one of the aviators whom he escorted back to Candelaria. The captain then returned to the Mexican side of the river to secure the release of the remaining captive. Fearing a trap, Matlack had decided not to pay the remainder of the ransom but rather to make a run for the border as soon as the hostage was surrendered. Two bandits soon appeared with the second American who was turned over to Matlack. Instead of transferring the remaining $7,500, he drew his pistol and ordered the two bandits to return to Rentería and tell him to "go to hell." The two Mexicans withdrew without resistance while the captain and the flyer made a daring and successful dash across the border. After arriving safely back at Candelaria with the second airman, Matlack displayed the unpaid ransom and announced that "I'm going back tomorrow and get the rest."[22]

The army had already formulated plans to help Matlack carry out his promise. Even before the safe return of the missing flyers, Colonel Langhorne had alerted air and cavalry units to be prepared to cross the river in pursuit of the bandits as soon as the aviators were safely on the American side. Within a few hours after Matlack's return with the second airman, cavalry units crossed into Mexico at three points along the Rio Grande; the border air patrol—armed with machine guns and bombs—also joined in the chase. The carrancista response to this latest incursion was confused and contradictory. The Mexican ambassador in Washington officially protested the pursuit and demanded the immediate recall of all U.S. forces. When part of the expeditionary force encountered a column of some 200 carrancista troops, the carrancista leader asked the U.S. commander where the force was going. When informed that the force was pursuing Rentería's gang, the officer told the U.S. troops to "go ahead." General Manuel Diéguez, commander of carrancista forces in Chihuahua, directed his officers not to resist the incursion since the U.S. force had the right to enter Mexico under the terms of the Treaty of 1882 on reciprocal crossing; Diéguez was either ignorant of, or found it convenient to ignore, the fact that the Treaty of 1882 had not been in effect since the 1890s and did not apply to bandit raids in any case. The War Department ordered the pursuit to continue as long as the expeditionary force was on a "hot trail." After six days below the border, the expedition returned on August 25. A rainstorm had washed out the trail, and carrancista forces had assumed the pursuit of the bandits. The expedition had killed five bandits and had captured six others; Rentería, however, eluded his pursuers although he had originally been reported killed by aircraft fire. Captain Matlack made his promised return to Mexico but was not successful in recovering the rest of the ransom money.[23]

The air and cavalry punitive expedition of 1919 highlighted the connection between the world war and the border conflict. Just as the Pershing expedition had served as a training ground for World War I, in turn the war provided cavalry and aviation veterans for the latest phase of the border conflict. The aftermath of World War I also influenced border policy in another important way. Although the Wilson administration was pursuing a more belligerent policy in regard to Mexico, it was also rapidly dismantling the instrument which it would need to enforce such a policy: large-scale armed forces. The U.S. Army continued to assign a high priority to the border, but postwar demobilization precluded any major military intervention in Mexico.

State officials welcomed—and, in fact, as had previous administrations lobbied for—a tougher border policy. Governor Hobby had already ordered state officials to crack down on the smuggling of arms and liquor across the border although such enforcement was basically a federal responsibility. The continued deterioration of the situation on the Rio Grande had also led Hobby to suggest to Secretary of War Baker that two brigades of Texas National Guard cavalry be federalized for service on the border, but Baker declined because of the expense involved.[24] After the incident involving the ransom of the two aviators, the governor wrote to Secretary of State Lansing to urge intervention as "justifiable and the only hope to relieve a bad condition on this continent." Hobby maintained that "intervention of the friendliest kind" would be welcomed by the "better element of the people of Mexico." The governor concluded by saying that intervention would be "an act of wisdom, of justice, and of humanity on the part of our government."[25] The state adjutant general, James Harley, also pushed for an interventionist policy, offering the entire Texas National Guard for service in Mexico.[26]

The Retreat from Intervention

Leading the agitation for intervention at the national level was Senator Fall. With personal financial interests in Mexico and close ties to American oil companies operating there, Fall had started his campaign for intervention as early as the Madero presidency. As chairman of the Senate Foreign Relations sub-committee to investigate Mexican affairs, Fall conducted widely publicized hearings between August 1919 and May 1920. Examining the entire revolutionary decade, Fall's committee developed testimony outlining a long series of outrages against Americans in Mexico and along the border: murder, rape, theft, destruction and confiscation of property, Mexican propaganda activities in the United States, and German intelligence activities in Mexico. Fall accused the Wilson administration of withholding information about the true situation in Mexico and attempted to use the hearings to arouse public support for intervention. Carranza considered the establishment of the Fall committee an affront to Mexican sovereignty and ordered Mexicans residing in the United States not to testify before it.[27]

The pressure for intervention continued through 1919, culminating in a memorable confrontation on November 28 between Secretary of State Lansing and the Mexican ambassador, Ignacio Bonillas. In the course of a heated exchange, Lansing proclaimed that he was "hoping against hope that sense and decency would finally penetrate the thick skull of President Carranza. He seems as obstinate, as impervious to reason, and as hostile to Americans as he has ever been." The secretary of state warned that U.S. public opinion might force a break in diplomatic relations that "would almost inevitably mean war." Lansing then dismissed Bonillas, who left "manifestly offended."[28]

Lansing continued to push for a policy which, if implemented, would almost certainly have led to a break in relations between the United States and Mexico and quite possibly intervention. In a proposal to President Wilson in January 1920, Lansing outlined a three-point plan of action: 1) the Mexican government would take more effective action to protect American lives and property; 2) a joint commission would be established to mediate claims against both countries; 3) the Mexican government would sign a treaty agreeing to submit the question of American property rights under the Constitution of 1917 to the Hague Tribunal, with all decrees, regulations, and laws based on the Constitution of 1917 to be suspended until the Tribunal reached a decision which would be binding on both countries. Unless the Mexican government agreed to this plan within a "reasonable time" (approximately five weeks), the United States would break diplomatic relations with Mexico. Lansing emphasized that the severance of relations would not automatically mean intervention, but it might lead to the overthrow of Carranza.[29]

Lansing's proposal would have almost guaranteed a break in relations, which in turn would have increased substantially the likelihood of intervention. While the Mexican government could have agreed to a stronger program of protecting Americans and to the establishment of a joint commission to settle claims, it would have been politically impossible for Carranza to have turned over to the Hague Tribunal the disposition of the Constitution of 1917, even if Carranza had been personally willing to do so, which his nationalistic sensibilities would not have permitted. With Mexican presidential elections scheduled for 1920, it would have been political suicide for Carranza to propose such international arbitration on the Constitution that was already considered an integral part of the revolution.

Lansing's growing militancy was misleading. The situation in late 1919 and early 1920 was reminiscent of the summer of 1916. As events seemed to be moving toward a major military confrontation between Mexico and the United States, the diplomatic storm clouds quickly disappeared. In February 1920 two of the strongest advocates in the Wilson administration for a more forceful policy toward Mexico—Secretary of State Lansing and Secretary of the Interior Franklin Lane—resigned their positions. Their resignations followed shortly after that of U.S. Ambassador to Mexico Fletcher, whose views on the Mexican situation increasingly coincided with those of Lansing.[30] While Lansing, Fletcher, and Lane had been steadily evolving in the direction of a harsher policy toward Mexico, with implications of intervention, Wilson—entering the latter stages of his administration—was reverting in effect to his old policy of "watchful waiting." Carranza, for his part, made some concessions on the oil issue, one of the matters causing a great deal of interventionist pressure. Faced with a crisis over presidential succession in 1920, Carranza was in no position to risk U.S. intervention.

Carranza's efforts to impose his choice as president in the elections of 1920, Ambassador to the United States Bonillas, in the face of the military and political support for General Alvaro Obregón, turned a succession crisis into revolution in April 1920. There were brief fears of renewed fighting along the U.S.-Mexican border since the center of revolutionary opposition was in Sonora. There were, however, no major confrontations along the border as had occurred in earlier revolutions; even the oft-traded Juárez went over to the revolutionaries in May without a fight. The fact that the revolution had its origins on the border gave rise to speculation that U.S. interests—perhaps even the Wilson administration itself—had promoted the insurrection; in reality the revolt led by General Adolfo de la Huerta, governor of Sonora, on behalf of Obregón had caught Wilson and his advisors unprepared. This revolt did accomplish something that years of negotiation and confrontation had failed to do; it brought an end to the antagonism between Carranza and Wilson. A group of rebels overtook Carranza while he was attempting to flee from Mexico City to Veracruz and assassinated him on May 21.

The new leaders of Mexico, Interim President de la Huerta and President-elect Obregón, had extensive border experience and were interested in improving relations between the United States and Mexico. Business and political leaders along the Rio Grande responded favorably to the overthrow of Carranza. The chambers of commerce in Laredo, San Antonio, and El Paso urged rapid recognition for the new Mexican government while the

Texas Senate unanimously passed a resolution commending the new regime for "its efforts to establish a stable government and its demonstrated desire to protect lives and property of foreigners."[31] Governor Hobby also came out in favor of the new administration, urging President Wilson to "grant recognition at once."[32]

In October 1920, President-elect Obregón visited Texas. Arriving in El Paso on October 6, he was welcomed by a crowd of about 10,000 people. At a banquet the following day, Governor Hobby called for recognition of Obregón's new government; in the same room in the same hotel approximately a year earlier, the governor had called for U.S. military intervention in Mexico. During the course of the proceedings, Hobby enthusiastically if inappropriately observed, "I want Mexico and Texas to be pals. In fact, I want them to be the Mutt and Jeff of the Western Hemisphere."[33] A decade of bitter conflict on the Texas-Mexican border came to an ironic and improbable conclusion when Obregón traveled to the State Fair of Texas in Dallas where Mexico was sponsoring an exhibit featuring the theme of closer relations between Texas and Mexico. In December, Hobby returned the visit, attending Obregón's inauguration as an honored guest, much to the discomfiture of the U.S. Department of State. During his visit to Mexico City, Hobby even placed a memorial wreath at the monument to the *niños héroes*, the military cadets who had died in the defense of Chapultepec against the American invaders during the Mexican War.[34]

While the government of the State of Texas was willing to assume that a new era in border relations was beginning, the federal government proved less receptive to the overtures of the Mexican administration. President Wilson left office with U.S.-Mexican relations in the same condition that he had inherited—with an unrecognized revolutionary regime in Mexico seeking improved relations with the United States. One of the bloodiest and most controversial periods in border history, however, had come to a close.

Notes

List of Abbreviations

CPD – La colección General Porfirio Díaz
CP: UT – Colquitt Papers: University of Texas at Austin
EPMT – El Paso Morning Times
FBI – United States, National Archives, Federal Bureau of Investigation, Record Group 65
FR – Papers Relating to the Foreign Relations of the United States
FRC-FW – Federal Records Center, Fort Worth, Texas
HLS – Hugh Lennox Scott Papers, Library of Congress
IMA – United States, Senate, Investigation of Mexican Affairs
POWW – The Papers of Woodrow Wilson
RDS-IA – Records of the Department of State Relating to the Internal Affairs of Mexico, 1910-1929
RDS-PR – Records of the Department of State Relating to Political Relations Between the United States and Mexico, 1910-1929
SAE – San Antonio Express
TSA, AG: GC: – Texas State Archives, Adjutant General: General Correspondence
TSA, GP: JEF – Texas State Archives, Governors' Papers: James E. Ferguson
TSA, GP: OBC – Texas State Archives, Governors' Papers: Oscar Branch Colquitt
TSA, GP: WPH – Texas State Archives, Governors' Papers: William P. Hobby
WP – Washington Post

Chapter 1: The Border Background

1. For a detailed examination of Texas-Mexican relations during this period, see Joseph W. Schmitz, *Texan Statecraft, 1836-1845* (San Antonio: Naylor Company, 1941).

2. There is some disagreement over Texas' claim to the last battle of the Civil War – Palmito Ranch on May 13, 1865 – on the grounds that it took place after Lee's surrender to Grant at Appomattox on April 9.

3. The "Reconstruction" period came to an end in 1874 when Democrat Richard Coke replaced radical Republican Edmund J. Davis as governor. The military phase had ended even earlier in 1870.

4. William Ray Lewis, "The Hayes Administration and Mexico," *Southwestern Historical Quarterly*, 24 (October 1920), 140-53.

5. The U.S. government had a lengthy list of lesser demands upon which it was seeking concessions before extending recognition. See Luis G. Zorrilla, *Historia de las relaciones entre México y los Estados Unidos de América, 1800-1958*, 2 vols. (México: Editorial Porrua, 1965-1966), 1:547.

6. Robert D. Gregg, *The Influence of Border Troubles on Relations between the United States and Mexico, 1876-1910* (Baltimore: Johns Hopkins Press, 1937), 58-80. César Sepúlveda, *La frontera norte de México* (México: Editorial Porrua, 1976), 81-84. Daniel Cosío Villegas, ed., *Historia moderna de México*, 9 vols. (México: Editorial Hermes, 1955-1972), VI:34-37.

7. Gregg, *Border Troubles*, 87-89.

8. La colección General Porfirio Díaz, LegajoV, Documents, 3166-68, 3188. Hereafter cited as CPD, followed by legajo number and document number.

9. Don M. Coerver, The Porfirian Interregnum: The Presidency of Manuel González of Mexico, 1880-1884 (Fort Worth: Texas Christian University Press, 1979), 135-36.

10. Ibid., 137-38.

11. Davis to Morgan, August 18, 1882, in United States, Department of State, Papers Relating to the Foreign Relations of the United States, 1882, 396-97. Hereafter cited as FR, followed by year.

12. Don M. Coerver, "From Morteritos to Chamizal: The U.S.-Mexican Boundary Treaty of 1884," Red River Valley Historical Review, 2 (Winter 1975), 531-34. The secretary of war said he had only a "vague recollection" of having issued the occupation order; the army chief-of-staff confessed that he "knew nothing" about the issuance of the order.

13. Ibid., 534-38. The Treaty of 1884 also applied to that limited portion of the Colorado River (twenty miles) that served as the international boundary.

14. See Coerver, Porfirian Interregnum, chapters 1 and 7. Díaz discredited González by linking him to large-scale government corruption. González' long-term political prospects were further circumscribed by deteriorating health due to serious combat injuries suffered in the 1870s.

15. México, Ministerio de Fomento, Colonización, Industria y Comercio, Memoria, enero, 1883-junio, 1885, 5 vols. (México: Officina Tip. de la Secretaría de Fomento, 1887), V:551. There was considerable opposition in Mexico to such north-south railroads on the grounds that they would facilitate American economic penetration of Mexico, a fear that was soon realized.

16. Oscar J. Martínez, Border Boom Town: Ciudad Juárez since 1848 (Austin: University of Texas Press, 1978), 32-35. Mario T. García, Desert Immigrants: The Mexicans of El Paso, 1880-1920 (New Haven: Yale University Press, 1981), 18-20, 107-08.

17. Jorge Espinosa de los Reyes, Relaciones económicas entre México y Estados Unidos, 1870-1910 (México: Nacional Financiera, 1951), 50-65. Cosío, ed., Historia moderna de México, VII:637-38,688-711.

18. Raymond Vernon, The Dilemma of Mexico's Development (Cambridge: Harvard University Press, 1963), 42-43. Zorrilla, Historia, II:89-90, 127-31. British and French investment also increased substantially during this period.

19. Vernon, Dilemma, 50.

20. Friedrich Katz, "Labor Conditions on Haciendas in Porfirian Mexico: Some Trends and Tendencies," Hispanic American Historical Review, 54 (February 1974), 1-47.

21. Cosío, ed., Historia moderna de México, VI:321-52. Zorrilla, Historia, II:178-94. Alberto María Carreño, La diplomacia extraordinaria entre México y Estado Unidos, 1789-1947, 2 vols., 2d ed. (México: Editorial Jus, 1961), II:232-33.

Chapter 2: Colquitt, Taft, and Border Revolution

1. The only biography of Colquitt is George P. Huckaby's "Oscar Branch Colquitt: A Political Biography" (Ph.D. diss., University of Texas at Austin, 1946). Colquitt furnishes a brief autobiography in Governor O. B. Colquitt Tells of Early Life and of his Newspaper and Political Experiences (Pittsburg, Texas: Pittsburg Gazette, 1934). Colquitt started his career as a newspaper publisher, owning the Pittsburg Gazette and the Terrell Times-Star. Serving as a state senator from 1895 to 1899, Colquitt earned a reputation as an expert on taxation. A lobbyist and a lawyer, he was on the

No

state railroad commission from 1903 until his assumption of the governorship in 1911.

2. For Díaz' maneuvering on the reelection issue, see Don M. Coerver, *The Porfirian Interregnum: The Presidency of Manuel González of Mexico, 1880-1884* (Fort Worth: Texas Christian University Press, 1979). Ramón Corral, former governor of Sonora and vice-president from 1904-1910, had sparked widespread criticism for his role in the deportation of Yaqui Indians from Sonora into virtual slavery in southern Mexico.

3. William Dirk Raat, "The Diplomacy of Suppression: *Los Revoltosos*, Mexico, and the United States, 1906-1911," *Hispanic American Historical Review*, 56 (November 1976), 529-33.

4. *Ibid.*, 547-50. Charles C. Cumberland, "Mexican Revolutionary Movements from Texas, 1906-1912," *Southwestern Historical Quarterly*, 52 (January 1949), 306-07.

5. Charles C. Cumberland, *Mexican Revolution: Genesis under Madero* (Austin: University of Texas Press, 1974), 121-23. Cumberland, "Mexican Revolutionary Movements," 308-09.

6. Michael Dennis Carman, *United States Customs and the Madero Revolution* (El Paso: Texas Western Press, 1976), 19-23, 40-44. Dorothy Pierson Kerig, *Luther T. Ellsworth: U.S. Consul on the Border during the Mexican Revolution* (El Paso: Texas Western Press, 1975), 35-45.

7. Cumberland, *Mexican Revolution: Genesis*, 124-28; "Mexican Revolutionary Movements," 309-12.

8. Texas, Adjutant General, *Biennial Report of the Adjutant General of Texas from January 23, 1911 to December 31, 1912* (Austin: Von Boeckmann-Jones Co., 1913), 3-8. Adjutant General Hutchings to C. W. Dawson, March 8, 1911, Texas State Archives, Adjutant General: General Correspondence. Hereafter cited as TSA, AG: GC. Hutchings served as adjutant general throughout Colquitt's two terms as governor.

9. *El Paso Morning Times*, February 2, 3, and 5, 1911. Hereafter cited as *EPMT*. *San Antonio Express*, February 3, 4, and 10, 1911. Hereafter cited as *SAE*. Edwards to Hutchings, February 2, 1911, TSA, AG: GC. It was "ladies' day" at the Juárez race tracks the same day that the *Morning Times* was running headlines saying "Orozco at Gates of Juárez." See *EPMT*, February 7, 1911.

10. Governor Colquitt to President Taft, February 7, 1911, Texas State Archives, Governors' Papers: Oscar Branch Colquitt, Letter Press Books. Hereafter cited as TSA, GP: OBC. Governor Colquitt to President Taft, February 23, 1911, *Records of the Department of State Relating to the Internal Affairs of Mexico, 1910-1929*, National Archives Microfilm Publication, Microcopy No. 274, File No. 812.00/854. Hereafter cited as RDS-IA, followed by the file number. Pierce was closely connected both politically and financially with Texas Senator Joseph Bailey, political ally of Governor Colquitt.

11. A copy of the proclamation is in Texas Secretary of State to U.S. Secretary of State, February 14, 1911, RDS-IA, 812.00/809.

12. Colquitt to Hughes, February 23, 1911, and March 8, 1911, TSA, GP: OBC. Letter Press Books. *United States v. Francisco I. Madero et al.*, U.S. Commissioner, El Paso, no. 771, Federal Records Center-Fort Worth, Texas. Hereafter cited as FRC-FW. Madero had already crossed into Mexico on February 14.

13. *Ibid.* Office of the Solicitor, Department of State, to Latin American Division, Department of State, March 4, 1911, RDS-IA, 812.00/854. Colquitt to Taft, February 23, 1911, TSA, GP: OBC, Letter Press Books.

14. See U.S. Army Adjutant General to Commanding Officer, Department of

Texas, November 19, 1910, and February 2, 1911, RDS-IA, 812.00/436½ and 812.00/715.

15. *SAE*, March 8-18, 1911. *EPMT*, March 8-18, 1911. *Washington Post*, March 8-18, 1911; hereafter cited as *WP*.

16. P. Edward Haley, *Revolution and Intervention: The Diplomacy of Taft and Wilson with Mexico, 1910-1917* (Cambridge: MIT Press, 1970), 26-27.

17. Texas, Adjutant General, *Biennial Report, 1911-1912*, 3-8.

18. Colquitt to Taft, March 20, 1911, TSA, GP: OBC, Letter Press Books.

19. *EPMT*, February 6, 1911. One enterprising woman in Presidio, Texas, hosted a "battle tea" when rebels attacked the town of Ojinaga across the Rio Grande. The hostess entertained guests on her roof so that all could get a better view of the fighting. See *WP*, March 15, 1911.

20. *EPMT*, May 6, 1911. In a more responsible vein, the *Morning Times* had earlier published an extra edition warning El Paso residents to take cover if shooting started in Juárez.

21. Sloan to Taft, April 17, 1911, and Taft to Sloan, April 18, 1911, *FR, 1911*, 459-61.

22. *WP*, April 22, 1911.

23. Michael C. Meyer, *Mexican Rebel: Pascual Orozco and the Mexican Revolution, 1910-1915* (Lincoln: University of Nebraska Press, 1967), 25-28.

24. *Ibid.*, 28-37. *EPMT*, May 8, 1911.

25. *WP*, May 9, 1911. Army troops did have authorization to fire across the border to protect lives and property on the U.S. side.

26. City Clerk of El Paso to Colonel E. Z. Steever, May 12, 1911, in Acting Secretary of War to Secretary of State, May 22, 1911, RDS-IA, 812.00/1916.

27. United States, Congress, *Congressional Record*, 62nd Congress, 1st Session, vol. 47, part 2, 1135. Even while the battle for Juárez was raging, Colquitt said he was planning a trip to Mexico for late summer or fall. See *SAE*, May 10, 1911.

28. *WP*, May 8, 1911. Díaz went into a comfortable exile in France, dying in Paris on July 2, 1915. The Mexican government still refuses to permit Díaz' remains to be returned to Mexico.

29. *SAE*, July 2 and 30, August 8, 1911. *WP*, August 8, 1911. Despite the mobilization, the number of troops actually patrolling the border was only about 3,000. See Carman, *United States Customs*, 48-50.

30. The Democrats completely dominated the state legislature; Colquitt's problems with the legislature to a great extent resulted from the prohibition question.

31. *WP*, September 16, 1911. Colquitt to Taft, November 17, 1911, Colquitt Papers: University of Texas at Austin. Hereafter cited as CP: UT.

32. Assistant Attorney General of Texas to State Adjutant General, November 19, 1911, TSA, AG: GC.

33. For an early example of the political and military maneuverings of Reyes in northern Mexico, see Don M. Coerver, "Federal-State Relations during the Porfiriato: The Case of Sonora, 1879-1884," *The Americas*, 33 (April 1977), 567-84.

34. Elections were scheduled for October 1911 with the new president to take office in November. Francisco León de la Barra, a Díaz holdover, served as interim president from May to November 1911. The best account of the role played by Reyes in the closing years of the Díaz era is Anthony T. Bryan, "Mexican Politics in Transition, 1900-1913: The Role of General Bernardo Reyes" (Ph.D. diss., University of Nebraska, 1969).

35. Vic Niemeyer, "Frustrated Invasion: The Revolutionary Attempt of General

Bernardo Reyes from San Antonio in 1911," *Southwestern Historical Quarterly*, 67 (October 1963), 213-14.

36. *Ibid.*, 214-15. Cumberland, "Mexican Revolutionary Movements," 316-17. Charles H. Harris III and Louis R. Sadler, "The 1911 Reyes Conspiracy: The Texas Side," *Southwestern Historical Quarterly*, 83 (April 1980), 332.

37. Niemeyer, "Frustrated Invasion," 214-15. Harris and Sadler, "The 1911 Reyes Conspiracy," 332.

38. Adjutant General to Colquitt, December 1, 1911, TSA, AG: GC. Harris and Sadler, "The 1911 Reyes Conspiracy," 332-33. The expanded Ranger force consisted of three companies with each company having one captain, one sergeant, and twelve privates. Even after this expansion, the force was still only up to approximately one-half of its authorized strength. The entire force was deployed along the Rio Grande.

39. Niemeyer, "Frustrated Invasion," 216-17. Harris and Sadler, "The 1911 Reyes Conspiracy," 331-32.

40. Mexican Ambassador to Secretary of State, November 10, 1911, *FR, 1911*. Wilson to Secretary of State, November 15, 1911, RDS-IA, 812.00/2495. Wilson later played a central role in the overthrow of the Madero administration in 1913.

41. *SAE*, November 16, 1911. Adjutant General to Colquitt, December 1, 1911, TSA, AG: GC. Harris and Sadler, "The 1911 Reyes Conspiracy," 333.

42. Assistant Attorney General to Secretary of State, November 14 and 22, 1911, RDS-IA, 812.00/2504 and 812.00/2538.

43. Chief of Staff to Commander, Southern Department, November 17, 1911, RDS-IA, 812.00/2511.

44. Colquitt to Hutchings, November 19, 1911, TSA, GP: OBC, Telegrams.

45. Colquitt to Hutchings, November 21, 1911, TSA, GP: OBC, Telegrams.

46. Niemeyer, "Frustrated Invasion," 221-22.

47. Colquitt to Taft, November 21, 1911, TSA, GP: OBC, Telegrams.

48. Colquitt to Taft, November 27, 1911, in President's Secretary to Secretary of State, December 1, 1911, RDS-IA, 812.00/2581.

49. *SAE*, November 24, 1911.

50. Harris and Sadler, "The 1911 Reyes Conspiracy," 333-34.

51. Hutchings to Colquitt, November 19, 1911, TSA, GP: OBC, Adjutant General's Department.

52. Adjutant General to Duncan, November 12, 1911, RDS-IA, 812.00/2533. In reality, Colquitt was not asking for federal assistance to enforce state laws but rather federal assistance in helping state officials enforce federal legislation—the immigration laws.

53. Colquitt to Taft, November 22, 1911, TSA, GP: OBC, Telegrams.

54. Colquitt to Hutchings, November 22, 1911, TSA, AG: GC.

55. Colquitt to Taft, November 27, 1911, CP: UT.

56. *SAE*, November 19, 1911.

57. Harris and Sadler, "The 1911 Reyes Conspiracy," 334-35.

58. State Department Memorandum to Acting Secretary of State, December 2, 1911, RDS-IA, 812.00/2540.

59. Niemeyer, "Frustrated Invasion," 222. Harris and Sadler, "The 1911 Reyes Conspiracy," 335.

60. Hutchings to Colquitt, December 1, 1911, TSA, AG: GC.

61. Niemeyer, "Frustrated Invasion," 222-24. Mexican authorities captured Reyes on December 25. Reyes did finally lead a successful revolt against Madero but never achieved his goal of the presidency. He was killed in the early stages of the revolt of

February 1913 that would ultimately lead to the death of Madero and the establishment of the regime of Victoriano Huerta.

62. Harris and Sadler, "The 1911 Reyes Conspiracy," 335. A prohibition amendment to the state constitution was narrowly defeated in a referendum held in 1911. Colquitt and Wolters were two of the most prominent antiprohibition leaders.

63. *Ibid.*, 335-36. SAE, December 12 and 31, 1911, and January 9, 1912. Sánchez, while under indictment and still serving as sheriff of Webb County, had confiscated 160 rifles offered for sale to reyistas. See *SAE*, December 25, 1911.

64. SAE, January 10-11 and February 3, 1912. Harris and Sadler, "The 1911 Reyes Conspiracy," 338-39.

65. SAE, April 15, 1912. Harris and Sadler, "The 1911 Reyes Conspiracy," 339-47. According to Judge Burns, Chapa and Sánchez were not convicted "felons." Burns had erroneously interpreted violations of the neutrality laws as misdemeanors when in reality they were felonies.

66. Colquitt to Taft and Colquitt to Hutchings, January 26, 1912, TSA, GP: OBC, Letter Press Books. SAE, January 13, 1912. Hutchings had earlier expressed his concerns in even stronger terms, accurately predicting that "Mexico will have another revolution which will make the Madero revolution seem insignificant." See Hutchings to Colquitt, December 1, 1911, TSA. AG: GC.

67. EPMT, February 1, 1912, Extra Editions. Emilio Vásquez Gómez was the brother of Francisco Vásquez Gómez who was Madero's unsuccessful vice-presidential running mate in the 1910 elections. The Vásquez Gómez brothers turned against Madero when he dropped Francisco from the ticket in the successful presidential campaign of 1911.

68. Colquitt to Hughes, February 2, 1912, TSA, GP: OBC, Telegrams.

69. Colquitt to Taft, February 2, 1912, TSA, GP: OBC, Telegrams.

70. EPMT, February 3, 1912.

71. RDS-IA, 812.00/2733 and 812.00/2857. EPMT and WP, February 4, 1912.

72. Colquitt to Taft, February 25, 1912, TSA, GP: OBC, Telegrams.

73. See Secretary of War to Secretary of State, February 5, 1912, RDS-IA, 812.00/2738.

74. WP, February 4, 1912.

75. EPMT, February 4, 1912.

76. *Ibid.* Meyer, *Mexican Rebel*, 50-52.

77. SAE, February 9, 1912. WP, February 9, 1912.

78. EPMT, February 9, 1912. In the same article, the *Morning Times* observed that such a movement had taken place twice before without incident.

79. Colquitt to Hutchings, February 9, 1912, TSA, GP: OBC, Letter Press Books.

80. Adjutant General to Hughes, February 9, 1912, TSA, AG: GC.

81. SAE, February 11, 1912. WP, February 11 and 14, 1912.

82. EPMT, February 10, 1912.

83. Colquitt to Hutchings, February 14, 1912, TSA, AG: GC. In addition to the embarrassing connection between state officials and the Reyes conspiracy, there had been frequent charges that the Texas Rangers were involved in Mexican political affairs. Colquitt made similar charges against federal officials.

84. Secretary of War to Secretary of State, February 16, 1912, RDS-IA, 812.00/2807. SAE, February 16 and 17, 1912.

85. EPMT, February 16, 1912.

86. SAE, February 17, 1912. EPMT, February 16, 1912.

87. Acting Secretary of State to Mexican Ambassador, February 26, 1912, FR,

1912, 726-27.

88. *SAE*, February 17, 1912. *WP*, February 24 and March 26, 1912.

89. *SAE*, February 24 and 25, 1912. *WP*, February 24, 1912.

90. Colquitt to Taft, February 24, 1912, RDS-IA, 812.00/2986. At the time Colquitt wrote his letter, three different men were claiming to be mayor of Juárez.

91. Colquitt to Hutchings, February 16, 1912, TSA, GP: OBC, Letter Press Books. Colquitt to Duncan, February 19, 1912, TSA, GP: OBC, Letter Press Books.

92. Duncan to Colquitt, February 17, 1912, CP: UT.

93. Colquitt to Duncan, February 19, 1912, TSA, GP: OBC, Letter Press Books.

94. Duncan to Colquitt, February 20, 1912, CP: UT.

95. *SAE*, February 2, 3, 7, and 18, 1912.

96. *SAE*, February 24-27, 1912.

97. *SAE*, February 27, 1912.

98. *SAE*, February 25, 1912. *EPMT*, February 25 and 27, 1912.

99. *EPMT*, February 27, 1912.

100. See telegram from Colquitt to Taft, February 25, 1912 in *EPMT*, February 26, 1912.

101. *SAE*, February 24, 1912. *EPMT*, February 25, 1912.

102. *WP*, February 27, 1912.

103. Meyer, *Mexican Rebel*, 67. *SAE*, February 28, 1912. Even though there was no resistance to the rebel takeover, there was still firing of weapons; three bullets fell on the American side during the transfer of control. See *EPMT*, February 28, 1912.

104. Kelly to Taft, March 11, 1912, TSA, GP: OBC, Adjutant General's Department.

105. Wilson to Kelly, March 20, 1912, RDS-IA, 812.00/3357.

106. Kelly to Secretary of State, March 26, 1912, RDS-IA, 812.00/3474. The Constitution provides that a state may not wage war on a foreign country "unless actually invaded or in such imminent danger as will not admit of delay." There was, of course, virtually no danger of an "invasion" of El Paso from Juárez.

107. Meyer, *Mexican Rebel*, 57-60.

108. Colquitt to Hutchings, May 20, 1912, TSA, GP: OBC, Telegrams. *WP*, May 20, 1912.

109. Colquitt to Hutchings, May 23, 1912, TSA, GP: OBC, Telegrams. Colquitt to Secretary of War, May 21, 1912, RDS-IA, 812.00/4014.

110. Hutchings to Colquitt, May 21 and 22, 1912, TSA, GP: OBC, Telegrams.

111. *Ibid.*, May 23, 1912.

112. Hughes to Hutchings, June 25, 1912, TSA, AG: GC.

113. *EPMT*, June 16, 1912. The rebel reference to U.S. aid was the American policy of permitting the Madero regime to import arms.

114. Colquitt to Secretary of War, June 18, 1912, RDS-IA, 812.00/4311.

115. Colquitt to Hutchings, June 18, 1912, TSA, AG: GC. By the following day, Colquitt had become more restrained, at least fiscally. He wired Hutchings: "Do nothing that incurs expense until you fully investigate and report to me." See AG: GC.

116. Taft to Secretary of State, June 19, 1912, RDS-IA, 812.00/4310.

117. Wilson to Taft, June 22, 1912, RDS-IA, 812.00/4308.

118. Quoted in Colquitt to Taft, June 24, 1912, CP: UT.

119. Colquitt to Taft, June 28, 1912, TSA, AG: GC.

120. Taft to Colquitt, June 29, 1912, TSA, AG: GC.

121. Texas, Adjutant General, *Biennial Report, 1911-1912*, 192.

122. EPMT, July 2, 1912.

123. Logan to Hutchings, July 1, 1912, TSA, GP: OBC, Adjutant General's Department.

124. Hutchings to Colquitt, July 7, 1912, TSA, GP: OBC, Adjutant General's Department.

125. Meyer, Mexican Rebel, 80-87. Huerta would later overthrow Madero, rule as president, flee into exile, and end his career in alliance with Orozco. U.S. Army officers served as advisors to Huerta in his campaign against Orozco.

126. Hughes to Hutchings, July 13, 1912, TSA, AG: GC.

127. Texas, Adjutant General, Biennial Report, 1911-1912, 194.

128. Colquitt to Madero, August 6, 1912, CP: UT.

Chapter 3: Watchful Waiting on the Rio Grande

1. Huckaby, "Colquitt," 296-324. A religious journal described Colquitt as the "whiskey man's candidate. His picture hangs in all the saloons in Texas."

2. Arthur S. Link, Woodrow Wilson and the Progressive Era, 1910-1917 (New York: Harper & Row, 1963), 3-23. In the electoral voting, Wilson received 435, Roosevelt 88, and Taft 8.

3. Wilson rewarded his southern organizers well. Page became Minister to Great Britain, McCombs National Chairman of the Democratic Party, and McAdoo Secretary of the Treasury. Colonel Edward M. House of San Antonio joined the Wilson movement in late 1911 and emerged as Wilson's chief advisor.

4. Arthur S. Link, "The Wilson Movement in Texas, 1910-1912," Southwestern Historical Quarterly, 48 (October 1944), 179.

5. Love to Wilson, December 27, 1912, in Arthur S. Link, ed., The Papers of Woodrow Wilson, 29 vols. (Princeton: Princeton University Press, 1966-1979), XXV: 624-26. Hereafter cited as POWW.

6. Link, "Wilson Movement," 183. Bailey resigned his senate seat in January 1913 and was replaced by Morris Sheppard, an early supporter of Wilson and a political foe of Governor Colquitt.

7. Ibid., 175. Thomas M. Campbell, Colquitt's immediate predecessor in the governorship, had endorsed Wilson even earlier.

8. Colquitt to McAdoo, September 23 and 28, 1912, CP:UT.

9. Colquitt to Collins, September 27, 1912, CP:UT.

10. Colquitt to Haven, September 25, 1912, CP:UT.

11. Colquitt to Wilson, December 27, 1912, CP:UT. Colquitt wrote the same day to Senator Culberson on a question of federal patronage. See Colquitt to Culberson, December 27, 1912, CP:UT.

12. Wilson to Colquitt, January 3, 1913, CP:UT.

13. Colquitt to Wilson, January 7, 1913, CP:UT.

14. Wilson to Secretary of State, January 7 and February 4, 1913, FR, 1913, 692-93, 696-99.

15. Colquitt to Taft, January 30, 1913, TSA, GP:OBC, Telegrams.

16. Colquitt to Hughes, January 30, 1913, TSA, GP:OBC, Telegrams. Hutchings to Colquitt, January 30, 1913, TSA, AG:GC.

17. Wilson to Secretary of State, February 9, 1913, FR, 1913, 699-700.

18. The period from February 9 to 18 is known in Mexico as the decena trágica, "the tragic ten days." For the central role played by Ambassador Wilson, see FR, 1913.

19. Colquitt to Taft, February 12, 1913, TSA, GP:OBC, Telegrams. Secretary of

State to Colquitt, February 12, 1913, RDS-IA, 812.00/6119. The "precautionary naval dispositions" consisted of sending additional U.S. naval vessels to Mexican ports.

20. Colquitt to Taft, February 15, 1913, TSA, GP:OBC, Telegrams.

21. *WP*, February 17, 1913. *SAE*, February 20, 1913.

22. *WP*, February 20 and 21, 1913. *EPMT*, February 25 and 27, 1913. The troops dispatched were "additional" in only a limited sense. They had originally been on the Texas-Mexican border but were reassigned to Galveston after the latest crisis in Mexico City.

23. Colquitt to Head, February 24, 1913, CP:UT. Commander, Southern Department, to Adjutant General, February 24, 1913, in Secretary of War to Secretary of State, February 25, 1913, RDS-IA, 812.00/6354.

24. Colquitt to Ryan, February 24, 1913, CP:UT. Secretary of War to Steever, February 25, 1913, RDS-IA, 812.00/6354. Steever to Colquitt, March 17, 1913, TSA, AG:GC.

25. Colquitt to Steever, February 25, 1913, TSA, GP:OBC, Telegrams.

26. Colquitt to Steever, February 25, 1913, TSA, GP:OBC, Telegrams.

27. Steever to Colquitt in Secretary of War to Secretary of State, February 26, 1913, RDS-IA, 812.00/6382.

28. *SAE*, February 25, 1913. *WP*, February 26, 1913.

29. Colquitt to Hutchings, February 27, 1913, TSA, GP:OBC, Telegrams.

30. *EPMT*, March 2, 1913. The *Morning Times* had earlier featured headlines on what it called the threatened "Texan Invasion" of Matamoros. See February 25 and 26, 1913.

31. Colquitt to Secretary of State, March 6, 1913, RDS-IA, 812.00/6629. The Matamoros incident started in the last days of the Taft administration and carried over into the Wilson administration.

32. Johnson to Secretary of State, February 26, 1913, RDS-IA, 812.00/6393. Captain Head, commander of the National Guard unit at Brownsville, had informed Colquitt of a threat to the American consulate and of demands for money from Americans. Sheriff C. T. Ryan and County Judge E. H. Goodrich at Brownsville had referred only to the demand for money and the threat by the Mexican commander to withdraw his troops. See Colquitt to Secretary of State, March 6, 1913, RDS-IA, 812.00/6629.

33. *EPMT*, March 3, 1913.

34. Ambassador Wilson to Secretary of State, February 23, 1913, *FR*, *1913*, 731-32. *WP*, February 24, 1913. Ambassador Wilson admitted that he played a central role in Huerta's rise to the presidency and defended his actions in his *Diplomatic Episodes in Mexico, Belgium, and Chile* (Garden City, N. Y.: Doubleday, Page and Company, 1927). For Huerta's role in the death of Madero, see Michael C. Meyer, *Huerta: A Political Portrait* (Lincoln: University of Nebraska Press, 1972), 70-82.

35. Arthur S. Link, *Wilson the Diplomatist* (Chicago: Quadrangle Press, 1963), 5.

36. *SAE*, April 4, 1913. Colquitt also complained to Secretary of State Bryan about neutrality violations. See Colquitt to Secretary of State, April 7, 1913, TSA, GP:OBC, Letter Press Books and May 19, 1913, RDS-IA, 812.00/7578.

37. Colquitt to Hughes, April 25, 1913, TSA, GP:OBC, Telegrams.

38. Colquitt to Wilson, April 29, 1913, TSA, GP:OBC, Telegrams.

39. Colquitt to Secretary of State, April 28, 1913, GP:OBC, Letter Press Books.

40. Colquitt to Secretary of War, April 28, 1913, TSA, GP:OBC, Letter Press Books.

41. *EPMT*, August 5, 1913.

42. *EPMT*, August 20, 1913.

43. See *FR, 1913*, 820-27.

44. Secretary of State to Chargé, August 4, 1913, *FR, 1913*, 817-18.

45. P. Edward Haley, *Revolution and Intervention: The Diplomacy of Taft and Wilson with Mexico, 1910-17* (Cambridge: MIT Press, 1970), 101-11. Mark T. Gilderhus, *Diplomacy and Revolution: U.S.-Mexican Relations under Wilson and Carranza* (Tucson: University of Arizona Press, 1977), 2-7. Philander C. Knox, Taft's Secretary of State, later said that he would have extended recognition to Huerta if he had known that Wilson would never do so.

46. Colquitt to Wilson, July 16, 1913, TSA, GP:OBC, Telegrams.

47. Colquitt to Wilson, July 21, 1913, TSA, GP:OBC, Letter Press Books.

48. Secretary of State to Colquitt, July 18, 1913, RDS-IA, 812.00/8065.

49. Bryan to Wilson, July 20, 1913, in *POWW*, 28:51-52.

50. From the Diary of Colonel House in *POWW*, 27:383.

51. The letter from Bliss is in Secretary of War to Secretary of State, August 14, 1913, RDS-IA, 812.00/9122. American planning for large-scale intervention in Mexico called for a landing at Veracruz, followed by a march to Mexico City; such a movement would require most of the regular army, leaving few troops to protect the border.

52. Secretary of War to Secretary of State, August 18, 1913, in President to Secretary of State, August 20, 1913, RDS-IA, 812.00/8679. Garrison euphemistically referred to intervention as "the efforts of our government to bring about an improvement in the national affairs of the Republic of Mexico." The Secretary of War wryly observed that the New York City Police Department was about three times the size of the American force on the border.

53. Texas, Adjutant General, *Biennial Report of the Adjutant General of Texas, 1913-1914* (Austin: Von Boeckmann-Jones Co., 1915), 5-10. The authorized Ranger force consisted of four companies with each company having a captain, a sergeant, and twenty privates; total actual strength was three captains and thirteen enlisted personnel.

54. *Ibid.*, 6-7. The four occasions involved Laredo three times and Brownsville once. Under state law the authority to call out the local Guard company resided not only in the governor but also in all district judges, sheriffs, and mayors. Only the governor could call out a Guard unit for service in another location as Colquitt had done during the Brownsville-Matamoros incident. Colquitt preferred shifting the Rangers to calling out the Guard because it involved less expense.

55. *EPMT*, November 18, 1913. Forces under the rebel leader Pancho Villa had captured Juárez on November 15 without incident on the American side.

56. *SAE*, February 26, 1914. The status of islands in the Rio Grande was a longstanding problem between Mexico and the United States. See Don M. Coerver, "From Morteritos to Chamizal: The U.S.-Mexican Boundary Treaty of 1884," *Red River Valley Historical Review*, 2 (Winter 1975), 531-38.

57. Walter Prescott Webb, *The Texas Rangers*, 2d ed. (Austin: University of Texas Press, 1965), 489-91. Harris and Sadler, "The 1911 Reyes Conspiracy," 344-45.

58. *SAE* and *WP*, February 27, 1914.

59. *WP*, February 28, 1914.

60. *Ibid. SAE*, February 28, 1914.

61. *SAE*, March 1, 1914. Under a treaty signed in 1899, governors of American states on the U.S.-Mexican border could make direct requests for extradition to governors of Mexican border states without going through the central governments of

either country.

62. *Ibid.* While Colquitt raged, President Wilson remarked at a press conference on March 2 that "a country of the size and power of the United States can afford to wait just as long as it pleases." See *POWW*, 29:302.

63. *SAE*, March 4, 1914.

64. *SAE*, March 4-6, 1914. *WP*, March 5 and 6, 1914.

65. *SAE*, March 4, 1914.

66. Sanders to Colquitt, March 8, 1914, CP:UT.

67. *WP*, March 9, 1914.

68. *SAE*, March 9, 1914.

69. *WP*, March 9, 1914.

70. *Congressional Record*, Sixty-third Congress, Second Session, March 9, 1914, vol. 51, part 5, 4532-33. Sheppard was a leader of the prohibition movement at the state and national levels, introducing the Eighteenth Amendment in Congress and helping to write the Volstead Act. He served continuously in the U.S. Senate from 1913 until his death in 1941.

71. Hutchings to Colquitt, March 13, 1914, CP:UT. Webb, *Texas Rangers*, 491-94. *EPMT*, March 9, 1914.

72. Sanders to Hutchings, March 9, 1914, CP:UT.

73. Cook to Colquitt, March 11, 1914, CP:UT.

74. *SAE*, March 10, 1914. *WP*, March 10, 1914.

75. Huckaby, "Oscar Branch Colquitt," 391. *SAE*, March 13, 1914.

76. Colquitt's March 9 statement is in *SAE* and *WP*, March 10, 1914.

77. *SAE*, March 11, 1914.

78. *Ibid.*

79. *SAE* and *WP*, March 11, 1914.

80. *WP*, March 12, 1914. *SAE*, March 14, 1914. *EPMT*, March 12, 1914. The nature of the reinforcements dispatched was further evidence of the political motivation behind the troop movement. Infantry forces were of limited use in patrolling the border; if the War Department had been moved primarily by military factors, it would have dispatched cavalry units.

81. *SAE*, March 13, 1914. Colquitt's baiting of federal authorities did reflect an important legal consideration. Texas Rangers were law enforcement officials and could make arrests whereas U.S. Army troops could not.

82. *EPMT*, March 16 and 21, 1914.

83. *WP*, March 25 and 26, 1914.

84. *SAE*, March 16, 1914.

85. Colquitt to Huerta, March 12, 1914, and Huerta to Colquitt, March 17, 1914, CP:UT.

86. *WP*, March 11, 1914. The only political casualty apparently was Sheriff Amador Sánchez. After a Ranger investigation revealed his role in the Vergara affair, Sánchez withdrew as a candidate for reelection in 1914. See Harris and Sadler, "The 1911 Reyes Conspiracy," 345.

87. Sir Cecil Spring Rice to Sir Edward Grey, January 23, 1914, *POWW*, 29:168-69. The British government had recognized the Huerta regime in May 1913 and often found itself at odds with the Wilson administration over Mexican policy. With the Royal Navy's conversion from coal to oil, Britain was much concerned with maintaining access to the Mexican oil fields.

88. Secretary of State to Consular Officers in Mexico, August 27, 1913, *FR, 1913*, 895-96.

89. Diary of Colonel House, October 30, 1913, *POWW*, 28:477-78.

90. President Taft had imposed an embargo in March 1912 in an effort to limit fighting in the wake of the Orozco rebellion against the Madero administration; shortly after the imposition of the embargo, Taft exempted the Madero government from its provisions. After the overthrow of Madero, no Mexican faction could legally import arms from the United States. See Meyer, *Mexican Rebel*, 70-88.

91. *WP*, February 4, 1914. Villa's warm feelings about Wilson and the Americans would eventually dissipate, leading to the Columbus Raid and the Pershing Expedition in 1916. See Chapter 6.

92. The basic work on the Tampico incident and the subsequent occupation of Veracruz is Robert E. Quirk's *An Affair of Honor: Woodrow Wilson and the Occupation of Veracruz* (New York: W. W. Norton and Company, 1962).

93. Lind to Bryan, February 24, 1914, *POWW*, 29:286-87.

94. See Sir Cecil Spring Rice to Sir Edward Grey, February 14, 1914, *POWW*, 29:248-50.

95. *FR, 1914*, 456-71.

96. Kenneth J. Grieb, *The United States and Huerta* (Lincoln: University of Nebraska Press, 1969), 66, 142-45. Link, *Woodrow Wilson*, 122-23. *FR, 1914*, 479-80. The occupation failed to block the arms shipment to Huerta; the *Ypiranga* simply unloaded its cargo at another Huerta-controlled port.

97. See footnote 51. Bliss to Adjutant General, April 20, 1914, RDS-IA, 812.00/11798. Bliss to Wood, April 20, 1914, in Secretary of War to Secretary of State, April 20, 1914, RDS-IA, 812.00/11577.

98. *FR, 1914*, 483-94. Link, *Woodrow Wilson*, 123-26. Villa's response to the American occupation of Veracruz did a great deal to shape the Wilson administration's initially favorable attitude toward him.

99. *SAE*, April 19 and 21, 1914.

100. *SAE* and *EPMT*, April 24, 1914.

101. Blackshear to Colquitt, April 20, 1914, and Howard to Colquitt, April 22, 1914, CP:UT. See also TSA, AG:GC for the same period.

102. Colquitt to Bliss, April 22, 1914, TSA, GP:OBC, Letter Press Books. *SAE*, April 24, 1914.

103. Bliss to Secretary of War, May 2, 1914, RDS-IA, 812.00/11883. Bliss reported that "not a single incident has occurred to produce such fears."

104. Hughes to Hutchings, April 14, 1914, CP:UT.

105. Bliss, as commander of the Southern Department, had the authority to deploy all forces under his command as he saw fit. Ironically, that same day Colquitt had praised Bliss as the only federal official from whom he had received cooperation. See *SAE*, April 24, 1914.

106. Garrison to Colquitt, April 24 and 25, May 2, 1914, CP:UT. Colquitt to Garrison, April 25 and May 2, 1914, CP:UT. Colquitt to Hutchings, May 6, 7, and 8, 1914, TSA, GP:OBC, Adjutant General's Department.

107. *SAE*, April 25 and 26, 1914.

108. *SAE*, April 24, 1914. Sheppard had no military experience prior to 1914; indeed his only official connection with the military was as chairman of the powerful military affairs committee of the Senate. Although he had no military record, he later had a military installation named after him—Sheppard Air Force Base at Wichita Falls, Texas.

109. *Congressional Record*, Sixty-third Congress, Second Session, May 6, 1914, vol. 51, part 8, 8152-53.

110. *WP*, April 27, 1914. Efforts at mediation were unsuccessful. See Haley, *Revolution and Intervention*, Chapter 8.

111. *SAE*, December 10, 1914.

112. *SAE*, December 27, 1914.

113. *EPMT*, January 3, 1915.

114. Huckaby, "Oscar Branch Colquitt," 420-21. Colquitt ran unsuccessfully for the U.S. Senate in 1916, his last attempt at elected office. He later became active in the oil industry and supported the Republican Herbert Hoover for the presidency in 1928.

115. Sir Cecil Spring Rice to Sir Edward Grey, March 30, 1914, *POWW*, 29:216.

116. J. R. Clark, State Department Solicitor under Taft, summarized the test for intervention when he said that "the time to intervene will be when we can save more lives by going into Mexico than by staying out of Mexico." See Haley, *Revolution and Intervention*, 49-50.

117. *EPMT*, June 29, 1914.

118. *SAE*, March 11, 1914.

119. *Congressional Record*, Sixty-third Congress, Third Session, December 29, 1914, vol. 52, part 1, 664-65.

120. See, for example, President Wilson's letter to Senator Sheppard, March 28, 1914, in Ray S. Baker's *Woodrow Wilson: Life and Letters*, 8 vols. (Garden City, N. Y.: Doubleday, Page & Co., 1927-1939), 4:309. Wilson told Sheppard that two more Army regiments were being sent to the border "for the peace of mind of the people there, not because I thought it really necessary." The following month still more units were sent to placate Governor Colquitt, not because of any military emergency.

121. Senator Henry Cabot Lodge in *Congressional Record*, Sixty-third Congress, Third Session, January 6, 1915, vol. 52, part 1, 1017.

Chapter 4: Border Raiding and the Plan of San Diego

1. Official reports and Anglo custom rarely distinguished between "Mexican American" and "Mexican," usually lumping the two together as simply "Mexican." For the background to the Plan of San Diego, see Douglas W. Richmond, "La guerra de Texas se renova: Mexican Insurrection and Carrancista Ambitions, 1900-1920," *Aztlán*, 11 (Spring 1980), 1-32.

2. U.S. v. Basilio Ramos, Jr., et al., District Court, Brownsville, no. 2152 and U.S. v. Basilio Ramos, Jr., et al., U.S. Commissioner, Brownsville, no. 249, Federal Records Center, Fort Worth, Texas. Hereafter cited as FRC-FW. United States, National Archives, Federal Bureau of Investigation Record Group 65, Mexican File No. 232-144. Hereafter cited as FBI.

3. *Ibid*. Charles H. Harris III and Louis R. Sadler, "The Plan of San Diego and the Mexican-United States War Crisis of 1916: A Reexamination," *Hispanic American Historical Review*, 58 (August 1978), 384-85.

4. Harris and Sadler, "Plan of San Diego," 384-85.

5. *Ibid*. RDS-IA, January 31, 1916, 812.00/17245. James A. Sandos, "The Plan of San Diego: War and Diplomacy on the Texas Border, 1915-1916," *Arizona and the West*, 14 (Spring 1972), 9-10.

6. U.S. v. Basilio Ramos, Jr., et al., no. 2152, FRC-FW.

7. Harris and Sadler, "Plan of San Diego," 385. The judge at Ramos' bond hearing had observed that the accused "ought to be tried for lunacy, not for conspiracy against the United States." See Sandos, "Plan of San Diego," 11.

8. Harris and Sadler, "Plan of San Diego," 386. Sandos, "Plan of San Diego," 9-11.

9. Texas, House of Representatives, *Texas House Journal*, Thirty-fourth Legislature, Regular Session, January 12, 1915, 48-49. Ferguson to Funston, July 7, 1915, Texas State Archives, Governors' Papers: James E. Ferguson, Letter Press books. Hereafter cited as TSA, GP: JEF.

10. *EPMT*, June 29, 1915. Sandos, "Plan of San Diego," 13-14.

11. Breckinridge to Funston, July 24, 1915, RDS-IA, 812.00/15547.

12. Funston to McCain, August 10, 1915, RDS-IA, 812.00/15887. Charles C. Cumberland, "Border Raids in the Lower Rio Grande Valley-1915," *Southwestern Historical Quarterly*, 57 (January 1954), 287-89.

13. *EPMT*, August 13, 1915.

14. *SAE*, August 8 and 10, 1915.

15. Bliss to Garrison, August 12, 1915, in Garrison to Secretary of State, August 12, 1915, RDS-IA, 812.00/15745. *SAE*, August 13 and 27, 1915. The *San Antonio Express* reported that workers at the main headquarters of the King Ranch were prepared to use two muzzle-loading cannons from the Civil War, previously used for decoration, to defend the ranch house. See August 27, 1915.

16. Funston to McCain, August 30, 1915, RDS-IA, 812.00/16002. American soldiers were also involved in some of the cross-border provocations. One U.S. Army corporal was fined and demoted to private after he initiated fire across the Rio Grande; the corporal explained that he had "a good shot and couldn't resist the opportunity." See *SAE*, August 27, 1915.

17. *EPMT*, August 12, 1915.

18. U.S. v. Basilio Ramos, Jr., et al., no. 2152, FRC-FW.

19. *SAE*, September 25 and 26, 1915.

20. *WP*, August 15, 1915. *SAE*, September 26, 1915. Funston to McCain, September 28, 1915, RDS-IA, 812.00/16326.

21. *SAE*, August 13 and September 7 and 27, 1915. *WP*, September 7 and October 6, 1915. Funston to McCain, October 21, 1915, in Secretary of War to Secretary of State, October 22, 1915, RDS-IA, 812.00/16545.

22. Harris and Sadler, "Plan of San Diego," 389-90. Sandos, "Plan of San Diego," 18-19. Douglas Richmond has suggested that Carranza's involvement in the Plan of San Diego was an effort on his part to assist Mexican Americans in Texas. See Douglas W. Richmond, "La guerra se renova."

23. Sheppard to Lansing, October 23, 1915, RDS-IA, 812.00/16563. Bryan had resigned as secretary of state in June over President Wilson's handling of the *Lusitania* incident. Robert Lansing, State Department counselor, replaced him.

24. *SAE*, October 28, 1915.

25. *Ibid.* Colquitt had made similar complaints to federal officials. See Chapter 2.

26. *SAE*, October 30, 1915.

27. See chapter 3, note 70.

28. *SAE*, October 31, 1915.

29. Ferguson to Wilson, October 27, 1915, in Wilson to Lansing, October 29, 1915, RDS-IA, 812.00/16666. Lansing to Ferguson, November 3, 1915, RDS-IA, 812.00/16665.

30. *SAE*, October 28 and November 24, 1915. *EPMT*, November 24, 1915. Ferguson to Secretary of War, November 26, 1915, TSA, GP:JEF, Letter Press Books. Governor Ferguson's familiarity with Venustiano Carranza was apparently of recent origin. On October 20, 1915, Ferguson had mistakenly addressed a letter to "General Victoriano Carranza."

31. *SAE* and *WP*, October 23, 1915.

32. *WP*, October 4, 1915. For Captain Head's earlier involvement in border affairs during the Colquitt administration, see chapter 3, note 23.

33. *SAE*, December 4, 9, and 21, 1915. Ferguson's trip to Washington was only partially motivated by border policy; he also was trying to promote Dallas as the site for the Democratic National Convention in 1916. After visiting Washington, Ferguson went to New York where he described Carranza as "an educated man, not brilliant, not a fighter, of the McKinley type." On the same occasion, the Governor described Woodrow Wilson as the "greatest president since Lincoln." Curiously the Democrat Ferguson chose two Republican presidents for purposes of comparison.

34. Numerous similar reports are in Special Agent Barnes to Department of Justice, November 12, 1915, FBI, file number 232-84. The same file, however, contained reports that Luis de la Rosa and Aniceto Pizana were openly recruiting around Monterrey with the support of carrancista officers and German nationals.

35. *SAE*, December 2, 1915. Carrancista officials later took Pizana into custody at Matamoros but did not execute him. See RDS-IA, 812.00/17358.

36. In December 1915 Governor Ferguson had permitted large-scale movements of carrancista forces through Texas in order to attack villista forces at various border points. The governor authorized the movements over the objections of El Paso officials and businessmen. See Wroe to Secretary of State, December 9, 13, and 15, 1915, TSA, GP:JEF, Letter Press Books; *EPMT*, December 18, 1915.

37. The account of the sole American survivor of the incident, Thomas B. Holmes, is in Cobb to Secretary of State, January 12, 1916, *FR, 1916*, 652. Cobb, customs collector at El Paso, had earlier warned the State Department of possible villista reprisals due to recognition of the Carranza regime.

38. Lansing's message to Carranza is in Lansing to Silliman, January 13, 1916, *FR, 1916*, 656.

39. *SAE*, January 14, 1916. *WP*, January 14 and 16, 1916. *EPMT*, January 14, 1916.

40. Ferguson to Garrison, January 21, 1916, TSA, GP:JEF, Letter Press Books.

41. Ferguson to Garrison, February 7, 1916, TSA, GP:JEF, Letter Press Books. The appropriations for the Adjutant General's office for the fiscal year ending August 31, 1916, totaled $102,230. See Texas, Adjutant General *Biennial Report*, 1915-1916, 8-11.

42. Ferguson to Garner, February 8, 1916, TSA, GP:JEF, Letter Press Books. The argument over federal financing was rendered moot by the federalizing of the Texas National Guard in May 1916 for border service and again in 1917 for service in World War I.

43. Report of the Secretary of State to the President, February 17, 1916, *FR, 1916*, 471. The Secretary of State did not indicate what he considered "normal" conditions after five years of revolution on the border.

44. Carothers to Secretary of State, March 8, 1916, *FR, 1916*, 480.

45. Weekly Report in RDS-IA, 812.00/17513. Columbus, on the railroad line west of El Paso, had a civilian population of about 400; there were approximately 350 army troops stationed there.

46. Villa's presence at Columbus and his motives in making the attack have sparked a lengthy historical debate. E. Bruce White provides a good review of the arguments but few conclusive answers in "The Muddied Waters of Columbus, New Mexico," *The Americas*, 32 (July 1975), 72-98.

47. Carranza to Arredondo, March 11, 1916, *FR, 1916*, 486. Carranza to Millán, March 11, 1916, *Diplomatic Dealings of the Constitutionalist Revolution of Mexico* (México: Imprenta Nacional, 1919), 142.

48. The Pershing Expedition initially consisted of 5,000 troops, reaching a peak of 11,000; it penetrated more than 300 miles into Mexico.

49. Special Agent Barkey to Department of Justice, November 13, 1915, FBI, File No. 232-84.

50. Commander, Southern Department, to Secretary of War, April 18 and 25, 1916, RDS-IA, 812.00/17908 and 812.00/17981. Weekly Report for February 26, 1916, RDS-IA, 812.00/17358.

51. WP, March 19, 1916. Weekly Reports for April 13 and 20, 1916, RDS-IA, 812.00/17908 and 812.00/17981.

52. Pershing to Scott, undated [late March or early April 1916], Hugh Lennox Scott Papers, Library of Congress. Hereafter cited as HLS.

53. Funston to Scott, April 5, 1916, HLS.

54. Clarence C. Clendenen, *Blood on the Border: the United States Army and the Mexican Irregulars* (New York: MacMillan Company, 1969), 260-66. Frank E. Vandiver, *Black Jack: The Life and Times of John J. Pershing*, 2 vols. (College Station: Texas A&M University Press, 1977), II:627-36.

55. Scott and Funston to Secretaries of War and State, April 29, 1916, HLS. Carranza to Obregón, May 7, 1916, *Diplomatic Dealings*, 181-82. Ronnie C. Tyler, "The Little Punitive Expedition in the Big Bend," *Southwestern Historical Quarterly*, 78 (January 1975), 277-82. Calvin W. Hines, "The Mexican Punitive Expedition of 1916" (Master's thesis, Trinity University, 1961), 186-95.

56. Texas, Adjutant General, *Biennial Report*, 1915-1916, 4-11, 118. RDS-IA, 812.00/18144^1/$_2$. Available funds could only sustain a force of thirty, causing a deficit of $25,000.

57. WP, May 9, 1916. Funston to Secretary of War, May 7 and 17, 1916, FR, 1916, 542, 549. Tyler, "Little Punitive Expedition," 283-84. Sibley spent most of his time pursuing Langhorne's force which in turn was pursuing the raiders.

58. WP, May 23, 1916. Tyler, "Little Punitive Expedition," 285-87.

59. Generals Scott and Funston to Secretary of War, May 8, 1916, FR, 1916, 543-44. Funston to Pershing, May 19, 1916, in Funston to McCain, May 19, 1916, RDS-IA, 812.00/18270.

60. Funston to McCain, May 22, 1916, RDS-IA 812.00/18313. Funston pointed out to Adjutant General McCain that he had only one squadron of cavalry in the Laredo military district which had a 144-mile front on the Rio Grande and one regiment in the Big Bend district which had a 390-mile front.

61. McCain to Funston, May 5, 1916, RDS-IA, 812.00/18068. Sandos, "Plan of San Diego," 21-22.

62. Sandos, "Plan of San Diego," 22. Harris and Sadler, "Plan of San Diego," 394. Ferguson to Secretary of State, May 10, 1916, TSA, GP:JEF, Letter Press Books.

63. Garrett to Secretary of State, June 1, 1916, RDS-IA, 812.00/18296.

64. Aguilar to Lansing, May 22, 1916, FR, 1916, 552-63. See also México, Ministerio de Relaciones Exteriores, *Nota enviada por el gobierno constitucional al de la casa blanca* (México: Compañía Editora Mexicana, 1916).

65. Harris and Sadler, "The Plan of San Diego," 395-97.

66. *Ibid.*, 398. See RDS-IA, 812.00/18318 and 812.00/18355.

67. IMA,vol. 1, 1247-48. Johnson to Secretary of State, June 17, 1916, FR, 1916, 577-78. WP, June 18, 1916.

68. IMA, vol. 1, 1248. WP, June 16 and 17, 1916.

69. Scott to Chief, War College Division, June 16, 1916, HLS.

70. United States, War Department, *Annual Report*, 1916, vol. I, 193.

71. WP, June 17 and 19, 1916. At the same time Governor Ferguson was at the Democratic National Convention urging an amendment to the platform which would eliminate the provision that the United States would intervene in Mexico "only as a last resort." Citing the size of the Pershing Expedition, Ferguson observed: "Hell, that isn't hunting a bandit—that's intervention." SAE, June 17, 1916.

72. Treviño to Pershing and Pershing to Treviño, June 16, 1916, in Funston to Secretary of War, June 17, 1916, FR, 1916, 577. Pershing also had a warning for Treviño; if carrancista forces attacked the expedition, "the responsibility for the consequences will lie with the Mexican government." Pershing had orders to destroy any carrancista forces attacking the expedition. See note 59.

73. Clendenen, Blood, 303-11. Vandiver, Pershing, II:650-52.

74. McCain to Funston, June 22, 1916, RDS-IA, 812.00/18590. Scott to Funston, June 22, 1916, HLS.

75. WP, June 24, 1916.

76. The Veracruz operation turned into the Veracruz occupation, lasting from April to November 1914. The Pershing expedition was in Mexico from March 1916 to February 1917.

77. Haley, Revolution and Intervention, 219-23.

78. Harris and Sadler, "The Plan of San Diego," 401-02. Sporadic bandit activity continued in the Rio Grande Valley after July 1916 without official support and protection from the Carranza regime. During his detention, de la Rosa was comfortably situated in a Monterrey hotel with General Fierros paying the bill.

79. WP, August 12, 1915.

80. Secretary of War to Secretary of State, September 11, 1916, RDS-IA, 812.00/19142.

81. SAE, August 15, 1915.

82. WP, August 14, 1915.

83. SAE, August 15, 1915.

84. SAE, October 20, 1915.

85. Cumberland, "Border Raids," 300-02. SAE, September 9, 1915.

86. SAE and WP, November 1, 1915.

87. Ferguson to Secretary of State, October 25, 1915, TSA, GP:JEF, Letter Press Books.

88. Funston to Adjutant General, June 7, 1916, RDS-IA, 812.00/18364. Funston used the high death rate to argue for a tougher border policy to preclude the possibility that Texans would "cross the river in large numbers and take drastic action."

89. SAE, September 11, 1915.

Chapter 5: Huertistas and "Huns" on the Border

1. Friedrich Katz, The Secret War in Mexico: Europe, the United States and the Mexican Revolution (Chicago: University of Chicago Press, 1981), 210-18, 243-48.

2. Ibid., 328-48.

3. Michael C. Meyer, "The Mexican-German Conspiracy of 1915," The Americas, 23 (July 1966), 81-82.

4. Ibid., 80-81. SAE, February 6-10, 1915. Meyer, Huerta, 213-16.

5. Meyer, "Mexican-German Conspiracy," 82-83. Grieb, The United States and Huerta, 180-81.

6. Meyer, "Mexican-German Conspiracy," 83. Grieb, The United States and Huerta, 181-82.

7. George J. Rausch, Jr., "The Exile and Death of Victoriano Huerta," *Hispanic American Historical Review*, 42 (May 1962), 136-37. Allen Gerlach, "Conditions along the Border—1915: The Plan de San Diego," *New Mexico Historical Review*, 43 (July 1968), 196-97.

8. Ralph H. Vigil, "Revolution and Confusion: The Peculiar Case of José Inés Salazar," *New Mexico Historical Review*, 53 (April 1978), 152-56. Michael C. Meyer, *Mexican Rebel: Pascual Orozco and the Mexican Revolution* (Lincoln: University of Nebraska Press, 1967), 115-27.

9. Bryan to Cobb, April 26, 1915, RDS-IA, 812.00/14928.

10. Weekly Report, April 21 and May 5, 1915, RDS-IA, 812.00/14899 and 812.00/14971. Cobb to Bryan, June 7, 1915, RDS-IA, 812.00/15155. Grieb, *The United States and Huerta*, 186.

11. Meyer, *Huerta*, 220. Grieb, *The United States and Huerta*, 187.

12. Rausch, "Exile," 139. Cobb to Bryan, June 27, 1915, FR, *1915*, 828-29.

13. The United States v. Victoriano Huerta et al., District Court, Western District of Texas, No. 2185, FRC-FW. FBI, file number 232-162. Weekly Report, September 11, 1915, RDS-IA, 812.00/16125.

14. Cobb to Secretary of State, June 30, 1915, FR, *1915*, 830. Meyer, "Mexican-German Conspiracy," 86. Meyer, *Huerta*, 221-22. SAE, June 29, 1915.

15. SAE, June 29 and 30, 1915. Grieb, *The United States and Huerta*, 188-89.

16. Ferguson to Lansing, June 30, 1915, TSA, GP:JEF, Letter Press Books.

17. Confidential Agent of the Constitutionalist Government of Mexico to Lansing, July 1, 1915, FR, *1915*, 830-32. Ferguson to Lansing, July 7, 1915, TSA, GP: JEF, Letter Press Books. Lansing to Ferguson, July 7, 1915, FR, *1915*, 834. Lansing to Confidential Agent of the Constitutionalist Government of Mexico, July 10, 1915, FR, *1915*, 835. The phrase, "political character of the crime," was a reference to the long-standing policy of extraditing only on legitimate criminal charges, not merely for political activity unacceptable to the current Mexican government.

18. Grieb, *The United States and Huerta*, 189-90. Meyer, *Huerta*, 223-25.

19. Meyer, *Huerta*, 225-26. Meyer, "Mexican-German Conspiracy," 87.

20. Cobb to Secretary of State, August 30 and 31, September 2 and 4, 1915, RDS-IA, 812.00/15971, 15982, 16008, and 16016. EPMT, September 1 and 2, 1915. Meyer, *Mexican Rebel*, 131-33. Stone to Bureau of Investigation, August 31, 1915, FBI, file number 232-162.

21. The United States v. Victoriano Huerta et al., District Court, Western District of Texas, No. 2185, FRC-FW. Rausch, "Exile," 149-51. Huerta most likely died from cirrhosis of the liver which would be in keeping with his reputation as a heavy drinker. Although the Department of Justice charged that Huerta was trying to overthrow "the government of Mexico," the Department of State maintained that there was no "government of Mexico" at the time of Huerta's first and second arrests.

22. Katz, *The Secret War*, 330-31.

23. James A. Sandos, "German Involvement in Northern Mexico, 1915-1916: A New Look at the Columbus Raid," *Hispanic American Historical Review*, 50 (February 1970), 70-88. Friedrich Katz, "Alemania y Francisco Villa," *Historia Mexicana*, 12 (julio-septiembre 1961), 88-108. Michael C. Meyer, "Villa, Sommerfeld, Columbus y los Alemanes," *Historia Mexicana*, 28 (abril-junio 1979), 546-66. Sandos makes no definitive statement on German involvement in the Columbus raid but leaves the distinct impression that there was one. Katz maintains that there is no direct evidence linking the Germans to the attack, while Meyer makes a strong circumstantial case for German involvement.

24. Katz, *The Secret War*, 339. U.S. Army intelligence reports confirmed that German interests were attempting to persuade Villa to attack Tampico. See Funston to McCain, December 27, 1916, RDS-IA, 812.00/20199.

25. *Ibid.*, 346-50.

26. The text of the Zimmermann Telegram is in James B. Scott, ed. *Diplomatic Correspondence between the United States and Germany, August 1, 1914-April 6, 1917* (New York: Oxford University Press, 1918), iv. The basic work on the incident, although from an essentially European viewpoint, is Barbara Tuchman, *The Zimmermann Telegram* (New York: Viking Press, 1958).

27. *SAE*, March 8, 26, 27, 28 and April 1, 1917. Scott, ed., *Diplomatic Correspondence*, 323, 335. German involvement in the Plan of San Diego is disputed. Allan Gerlach and James Sandos see a definite German connection while Friedrich Katz and especially Charles Harris and Louis Sadler maintain that German involvement is unproven.

28. México, Presidente, *Un siglo de relaciones internacionales de México a través de los mensajes presidenciales*, 2d ed. (México: Editorial Porrua, 1970), 270, 276-77, 308-09. EPMT,April 3 and 6, 1917. WP, April 4 and 14, 1917.

29. Pershing to Scott, April 7, 1917, HLS.

30. Scott to Pershing, April 11, 1917, HLS.

31. Fletcher to Secretary of State, March 30, 1917. *Records of the Department of State Relating to Political Relations between the United States and Mexico*, 711.12/36. Hereafter cited as RDS-PR.

32. Wilson to Lansing, April 19, 1917, RDS-PR, 711.12/36$^{1}/_{2}$. The most controversial aspect of the new constitution related to property rights, especially to foreign activities in the oil industry which was dominated by American and British companies.

33. Lea to A. A. Jones, U.S. Senator from New Mexico, March 19, 1917 in Jones to Secretary of State, April 12, 1917, RDS-IA, 812.00/20788.

34. Carothers to Secretary of State, April 5, 1917, RDS-IA, 812.00/20780.

35. Hanson to Adjutant General, February 20, 26, 27, and 28, March 5 and 7, 1918, TSA, AG:GC. U.S. officials believed that there was a "military party" within the Carranza administration which was "intensely pro-German or at least anti-American." See Secretary of State to President Wilson, April 18, 1917, RDS-PR, 711.12/43A. Nafarrate—who had a controversial career along the border during the Revolution—was assassinated at Tampico in April 1918. At the time he was acting governor of Tamaulipas and had refused to back the "official" candidate in an election for the governorship.

36. Hobby to Secretary of War, December 8, 1917, January 14, April 19, and September 7, 1918, Texas State Archives, Governors' Papers: William P. Hobby, Letter Press Books. Hobby had succeeded to the governorship in August 1917 after Governor James E. Ferguson had been impeached, convicted, and removed from office over charges brought against him after a controversy over funding for the University of Texas.

37. Texas, Adjutant General, *Biennial Report of the Adjutant General of Texas from January 1, 1917 to December 31, 1918* (Austin: Von Boeckmann-Jones Co., 1919), 63-70. Walter Prescott Webb, *The Texas Rangers*, 2d ed. (Austin: University of Texas Press, 1965), 496-516. Ranger misconduct led to a postwar investigation of the organization in 1919 by the state legislature.

38. Hanson to State Adjutant General, February 1, 11, 13, 15, 20, 26, 27, and 28, and March 5, 7, 15, and 22, 1918, TSA, AG: GC. Hanson anticipated that his

appointment might provoke controversy; in his February 1 letter, he included a detailed account of his activities in case "some 'hidebound' political enemy of your administration may so far forget himself as to criticize you for my appointment." Harris and Sadler, "Plan of San Diego," 382.

39. State Department Counselor to Secretary of State, June 4, 1918, RDS-IA, 812.00/22199. Katz, *The Secret War*, Chapter 10. Secretary of State to Fletcher, June 15, 1918, *FR, 1918*, 568-71.

Chapter 6: World War I and Its Aftermath

1. See testimony of Colonel George T. Langhorne of "little punitive expedition" fame in U.S., Senate, *Investigation of Mexican Affairs*, Senate document 285, 66th Congress, 2d Session, vol. 1, 1634. Hereafter cited as *IMA*.

2. Clendenen, *Blood*, 343-44. Gilderhus, *Diplomacy and Revolution*, 76. By way of comparing the new limitations on crossings, the Pershing expedition had remained almost eleven months in Mexico and had penetrated more than 300 miles; Langhorne's "little punitive expedition" had operated in Mexican territory for ten days, penetrating more than 100 miles.

3. Weekly Report for December 8, 1917, RDS-IA, 812.00/21592. *IMA*, vol. 1, 1634-35. Secretary of State to Fletcher, June 15, 1918, *FR, 1918*, 569-70.

4. Secretary of War to Secretary of State, May 11, 1918, RDS-IA, 812.00/21981. Secretary of State to Secretary of War, May 14, 1918, RDS-IA, 812.00/21981. Secretary of War Baker specifically rejected any "international agreement relating to pursuit of raiding parties." Of the new operating restrictions, the State Department informed the Mexican government only of the one relating to firing on the Mexican side.

5. Secretary of State to Secretary of War, July 10, 1918, *FR, 1918*, 571.

6. Secretary of War to Secretary of State, July 15, 1918, *FR, 1918*, 572.

7. Lansing to Wilson, June 27, 1918; Fletcher to Lansing, June 28, 1918 in United States, Department of State, *Records of the Department of State Relating to Political Relations between the United States and Mexico, 1910-1929*, 711.12/104 and 711.12/108. Hereafter cited as RDS-PR. Article 27 said that only Mexican citizens had the "right" to acquire land and established the principle of the "social function" of property which held out the possibility of extensive government regulation. Americans with investments in mining and petroleum felt particularly threatened by Article 27.

8. Gilderhus, *Diplomacy and Revolution*, 87-91. Manuel A. Machado, Jr. and James T. Judge, "Tempest in a Teapot?: The Mexican-United States Intervention Crisis of 1919," *Southwestern Historical Quarterly*, 74 (July 1970), 1-5. Senator Fall had investments in Mexico and had close connections with oilman Edward L. Doheny; both were later involved in the Teapot Dome scandal.

9. Fletcher to Wilson, March 1, 1919, RDS-PR, 711.12/187. Fletcher at the time was not among those lobbying for intervention.

10. Clendenen, *Blood*, 351-52. Gilderhus, *Diplomacy and Revolution*, 94. Machado and Judge, "Tempest," 9. Governor Hobby refused to let carrancista troops travel through Texas to reinforce Juárez. See *SAE*, June 11, 1919 and *EPMT*, June 14, 1919.

11. RDS-IA, 812.00/22572, 22817, 22822, and 22826.

12. *EPMT*, June 16, 1919.

13. Clendenen, *Blood*, 355. Machado and Judge, "Tempest," 10. Consul Dow to Secretary of State, June 17, 1919, RDS-IA, 812.00/22826. See also RDS-IA, 812.00/22830.

14. Richmond, "La guerra de Texas se renova," 29-32.

15. For an autobiographical account of flying with the border air patrol, see Stacy C. Hinkle, *Wings over the Border* (El Paso: Texas Western Press, 1970).

16. *SAE*, June 26, 1919. *EPMT*, August 17, 1919.

17. *SAE*, June 27, 1919.

18. Phillips to Summerlin, July 21, 1919, RDS-PR, 711.12/216.

19. Machado and Judge, "Tempest," 12.

20. Stacy C. Hinkle, *Wings and Saddles: The Air and Cavalry Punitive Expedition of 1919* (El Paso: Texas Western Press, 1967), 8-11.

21. *Ibid.*, 12-16.

22. *Ibid.*, 16-18.

23. Weekly Reports for August 23 and 30, 1919, RDS-IA, 812.00/72844. *SAE*, August 20-25, 1919. *EPMT*, August 18-25, 1919.

24. Hobby to Commander of Southern Department, May 29, 1919, TSA, GP: WPH, Letter Press Books. *SAE*, June 8, 1919.

25. Hobby to Lansing, August 25, 1919, RDS-PR, 711.12/210. When Colquitt had recommended intervention under much worse conditions in the 1913-1915 period, the Wilson administration had dismissed him as a political crank. In the summers of 1916 and 1919, Wilson was much more receptive to the idea of intervention.

26. *EPMT*, August 22, 1919.

27. Fall to Lansing, November 13, 1919, RDS-PR, 711.12/227. Senate Concurrent Resolution, December 3, 1919, RDS-PR, 711.12/225½. Machado and Judge, "Tempest," 12-13. Michael C. Meyer, "Albert Bacon Fall's Mexican Papers: A Preliminary Investigation," *New Mexico Historical Review*, 40 (April 1965), 165-74.

28. Lansing memorandum, November 28, 1919, RDS-PR, 711.12/229¾.

29. Lansing to Wilson, January 23, 1920, RDS-PR, 711.12/263a.

30. Gilderhus, *Diplomacy and Revolution*, 104. Fletcher had resigned on January 20, 1920. Lane had served on the joint commission of 1916 which had tried unsuccessfully to settle the differences between Carranza and Wilson.

31. RDS-IA, 812.00/24371, 24512, 24513, and 24622.

32. Hobby to Wilson, October 20, 1920, RDS-IA, 812.00/24705.

33. *SAE*, October 7 and 8, 1920.

34. *SAE*, October 10 and 17, 1920; November 19 and 28, 1920; December 1 and 3, 1920. RDS-IA, 812.00/24776. Accompanying Hobby to Obregón's inauguration was Francisco Chapa of San Antonio, still a "colonel" on the governor's personal staff. The State Department did not openly oppose attendance at Obregón's inauguration but did "clearly perceive the possibility of misconstruction and other regrettable results as the sequel of such a visit."

Bibliography

Archival Sources and Government Publications

La colección General Porfirio Díaz. University of the Americas. Puebla, Mexico.

México. Ministerio de Fomento, Colonización Industria y Comercio. *Memoria presentada al Congreso de la Unión por el Secretario de Fomento, Colonización Industria y Comercio, enero, 1883-junio 1885*. 5 vols. México: Oficina Tip. de la Secretaría de Fomento, 1887.

México. Ministerio de Relaciones Exteriores. *Nota enviada por el gobierno constitutional al de la casa blanca*. México: Compañía Editora Mexicana, 1916.

México. Secretaría de Relaciones Exteriores. *Diplomatic Dealings of the Constitutionalist Revolution of Mexico*. México: Imprenta Nacional, 1919.

México. Presidente. *Un siglo de relaciones internacionales de México*. 2d ed. México: Editorial Porrua, 1970.

Texas. Adjutant General. *Biennial Reports of the Adjutant General of Texas, 1911-1918*. Austin: Von Boeckmann-Jones Co., 1913-1919.

_____. *Annual Report of the Adjutant General of Texas for the Year Ending December 31, 1918*. Austin: Von Boeckmann-Jones Co., 1919.

_____. *Biennial Report of the Adjutant General of Texas from January 1, 1919 to December 31, 1920*. Austin: Knape Printing Co., 1921.

Texas. House of Representatives. *Texas House Journal*, Thirty-fourth Legislature, Regular Session.

Texas State Archives. Austin, Texas.
    Adjutant General: General Correspondence, 1910-1920
    Governors' Papers: James E. Ferguson
    Governors' Papers: William P. Hobby
    Governors' Papers: Oscar Branch Colquitt

United States. Congress. *Congressional Record*, 62nd, 63rd, 64th, and 65th Congresses.

United States. Department of State. *Papers Relating to the Foreign Relations of the United States, 1910-1920*.

United States. Department of State. *Records of the Department of State Relating to the Internal Affairs of Mexico, 1910-1929*.

United States. Department of State. *Records of the Department of State Relating to Political Relations between the United States and Mexico, 1910-1929*.

United States. Department of the Treasury. United States Secret Service. Daily Reports of Agents, 1875 thru 1936, Record Group 87.

United States. Library of Congress. Hugh Lenox Scott Papers.

United States. National Archives. Federal Bureau of Investigation. Record Group 65, Mexican File.

United States. Senate. *Investigation of Mexican Affairs*, Senate Document 285, 66th Congress, 2nd Session, Volumes I and II.

United States, War Department. *Annual Reports, 1910-1920* (Washington: Government Printing Office, 1910-1921).

Books, Monographs, and Theses

Acheson, Sam Hanna. *Joe Bailey: The Last Democrat*. New York: MacMillan Company, 1932.

Baker, Ray S. *Woodrow Wilson: Life and Letters*. 8 vols. Garden City, N.Y.: Doubleday, Page & Co., 1927-1939.

Beezley, William H. *Insurgent Governor: Abraham González and the Mexican Revolution in Chihuahua*. Lincoln: University of Nebraska Press, 1973.

Bryan, Anthony T. "Mexican Politics in Transition." Ph.D. diss., University of Nebraska, 1969.

Carman, Michael Dennis. *United States Customs and the Madero Revolution*. El Paso: Texas Western Press, 1976.

Carreño, Alberto María. *La diplomacia extraordinaria entre México y Estados Unidos, 1789-1947*. 2 vols. México: Editorial Jus, 1951.

Clendenen, Clarence C. *Blood on the Border: The United States Army and the Mexican Irregulars*. New York: MacMillan Company, 1969.

Coerver, Don M. *The Porfirian Interregnum: The Presidency of Manuel González of Mexico, 1880-1884*. Fort Worth: Texas Christian University Press, 1979.

Coerver, Don M. and Linda B. Hall. *Revolution on the Rio Grande: Governor Colquitt of Texas and the Mexican Revolution, 1911-1915*. San Antonio: Trinity Border Research Institute, 1981.

Cosío Villegas, Daniel, ed. *Historia Moderna de México*. 9 vols. México: Editorial Hermes, 1955-1972.

Cumberland, Charles C. *Mexican Revolution: Genesis under Madero*. Austin: University of Texas Press, 1974.

Espinosa de los Reyes, Jorge. *Relaciones económicas entre México y Estados Unidos, 1870-1910*. México: Nacional Financiera, 1951.

García, Mario T. *Desert Immigrants: The Mexicans of El Paso, 1880-1920*. New Haven: Yale University Press, 1981.

Gilderhus, Mark T. *Diplomacy and Revolution: U.S.-Mexican Relations under Wilson and Carranza*. Tucson: University of Arizona Press, 1977.

Gregg, Robert D. *The Influence of Border Troubles on Relations between the United States and Mexico, 1876-1910*. Baltimore: Johns Hopkins Press, 1937.

Grieb, Kenneth J. *The United States and Huerta*. Lincoln: University of Nebraska Press, 1969.

Haley, P. Edward. *Revolution and Intervention: The Diplomacy of Taft and Wilson with Mexico, 1910-1917.* Cambridge: MIT Press, 1970.

Hall, Linda B. *Alvaro Obregón: Power and Revolution in Mexico, 1911-1920.* College Station: Texas A & M University Press, 1981.

Hines, Calvin W. "The Mexican Punitive Expedition of 1916." Master's thesis, Trinity University, 1961.

Hinkle, Stacy C. *Wings and Saddles: The Air and Cavalry Punitive Expedition of 1919.* El Paso: Texas Western Press, 1967.

_____. *Wings over the Border: The Army Air Service Armed Patrol of the United States-Mexican Border, 1919-1921.* El Paso: Texas Western Press, 1970.

Huckaby, George P. "Oscar Branch Colquitt: A Political Biography." Master's thesis, University of Texas at Austin, 1946.

Katz, Friedrich. *The Secret War in Mexico: Europe, the United States, and the Mexican Revolution.* Chicago: University of Chicago Press, 1981.

Kerig, Dorothy Pierson. *Luther T. Ellsworth: U.S. Consul on the Border during the Mexican Revolution.* El Paso: Texas Western Press, 1975.

Link, Arthur S., ed. *The Papers of Woodrow Wilson.* 29 vols. Princeton: Princeton University Press, 1966-1979.

Link, Arthur S. *Wilson the Diplomatist.* Chicago: Quadrangle Press, 1963.

_____. *Woodrow Wilson and the Progressive Era, 1910-1917.* New York: Harper & Row, 1963.

Martínez, Oscar J. *Border Boom Town: Ciudad Juárez since 1848.* Austin: University of Texas Press, 1978.

Meyer, Michael C. *Huerta: A Political Portrait.* Lincoln: Univesity of Nebraska Press, 1972.

_____. *Mexican Rebel: Pascual Orozco and the Mexican Revolution, 1910-1915.* Lincoln: University of Nebraska Press, 1967.

Morison, Elting E., ed. *The Letters of Theodore Roosevelt.* 8 vols. Cambridge: Harvard University Press, 1951-1954.

Perkins, Clifford Alan. *Border Patrol: With the U.S. Immigration Service on the Mexican Boundary, 1910-1954.* El Paso: Texas Western Press, 1978.

Quirk, Robert E. *An Affair of Honor: Woodrow Wilson and the Occupation of Veracruz.* New York: W. W. Norton & Company, 1962.

Schmitt, Karl M. *Mexico and the United States, 1821-1973.* New York: John Wiley & Sons, 1974.

Schmitz, Joseph W. *Texan Statecraft, 1836-1845.* San Antonio: Naylor Company, 1941.

Scott, James B., ed. *Diplomatic Correspondence between the United States and Germany, August 1, 1914-April 6, 1917.* New York: Oxford University Press, 1918.

Sepúlveda, César. *La frontera norte de México.* México. Editorial Porrua, 1976.

Tuchman, Barbara. *The Zimmermann Telegram*. New York: Viking Press, 1958.

Vandiver, Frank E. *Black Jack: The Life and Times of John J. Pershing*. 2 vols. College Station: Texas A & M University Press, 1977.

Vernon, Raymond. *The Dilemma of Mexico's Development*. Cambridge: Harvard University Press, 1963.

Webb, Walter Prescott. *The Texas Rangers*. 2d ed. Austin: University of Texas Press, 1965.

Wilson, Henry Lane. *Diplomatic Episodes in Mexico, Belgium, and Chile*. Garden City, N.Y.: Doubleday, Page and Company, 1927.

Zorrilla, Luis G. *Historia de las relaciones entre México y los Estados Unidos de América, 1800-1958*. 2 vols. México: Editorial Porrua, 1965-1966.

Articles

Coerver, Don M. "Federal-State Relations during the Porfiriato: The Case of Sonora, 1879-1884." *The Americas*, 33 (April 1977), 567-84.

————. "From Morteritos to Chamizal: The U.S.-Mexican Boundary Treaty of 1884." *Red River Valley Historical Review*, 2 (Winter 1975), 531-38.

Cumberland, Charles G. "Border Raids in the Lower Rio Grande Valley — 1915." *Southwestern Historical Quarterly*, 57 (January 1954), 285-311.

————. "Mexican Revolutionary Movements from Texas, 1906-1912." *Southwestern Historical Quarterly*, 52 (January 1949), 301-24.

Gerlach, Allen. "Conditions along the Border — 1915: The Plan de San Diego." *New Mexico Historical Review*, 43 (July 1968), 195-212.

Hall, Linda B. "The Mexican Revolution and the Crisis in Naco, 1914-1915." *Journal of the West*, 16 (October 1977), 26-35.

Harris, Charles H. III, and Louis R. Sadler. "The 1911 Reyes Conspiracy: The Texas Side." *Southwestern Historical Quarterly*, 83 (April 1980), 325-48.

————. "The Plan of San Diego and the Mexican-United States War Crisis of 1916: A Reexamination." *Hispanic American Historical Review*, 58 (August 1978), 381-408.

Hill, Larry D. "The Progressive Politician as Diplomat: The Case of John Lind in Mexico." *The Americas*, 27 (April 1971), 355-72.

Katz, Friedrich. "Alemania y Francisco Villa." *Historia Mexicana*, 12 (julio-septiembre 1962), 88-103.

————. "Labor Conditions on Haciendas in Porfirian Mexico: Some Trends and Tendencies." *Hispanic American Historical Review*, 54 (February 1974), 1-47.

Lewis, William Ray. "The Hayes Administration and Mexico." *Southwestern Historical Quarterly*, 24 (October 1920), 140-53.

Link, Arthur D. "The Wilson Movement in Texas, 1910-1912." *Southwestern Historical Quarterly*, 48 (October 1944), 169-85.

Machado, Manuel A., Jr., and James T. Judge. "Tempest in a Teapot?: The Mexican-United States Intervention Crisis of 1919." *Southwestern Historical Quarterly*, 74 (July 1970), 1-23.

Meyer, Michael C. "Albert Bacon Fall's Mexican Papers: A Preliminary Investigation." *New Mexico Historical Review*, 40 (April 1965), 165-74.

_____. "The Mexican-German Conspiracy of 1915." *The Americas*, 23 (July 1966), 76-89.

_____. "Villa, Sommerfeld, Columbus y los Alemanes," *Historia Mexicana*, 28 (abril-junio 1979), 546-66.

Munch, Francis J. "Villa's Columbus Raid: Practical Politics or German Design?" *New Mexico Historical Review*, 44 (July 1969), 189-214.

Niemeyer, Vic. "Frustrated Invasion: The Revolutionary Attempt of General Bernardo Reyes from San Antonio in 1911." *Southwestern Historical Quarterly*, 67 (October 1963), 213-25.

Prisco, Salvatore, III. "John Barrett's Plan to Mediate the Mexican Revolution." *The Americas*, 27 (April 1971) 413-25.

Raat, William Dirk. "The Diplomacy of Suppression: *Los Revoltosos*, Mexico, and the United States, 1906-1911." *Hispanic American Historical Review*, 56 (November 1976), 529-50.

Rausch, George J., Jr. "The Exile and Death of Victoriano Huerta." *Hispanic American Historical Review*, 42 (May 1962), 133-51.

_____. "Poison Pen Diplomacy: Mexico, 1913." *The Americas*, 24 (January 1968), 272-80.

Richmond, Douglas W. "La guerra de Texas se renova: Mexican Insurrection and Carrancista Ambitions, 1900-1920." *Aztlan*, 11 (Spring 1980), 1-32.

Rippy, J. Fred. "Some Precedents of the Pershing Expedition into Mexico." *Southwestern Historical Quarterly*, 24 (April 1921), 292-316.

Sandos, James A. "German Involvement in Northern Mexico, 1915-1916: A New Look at the Columbus Raid." *Hispanic American Historical Review*, 50 (February 1970), 70-88.

_____. "The Plan of San Diego: War and Diplomacy on the Texas Border." *Arizona and the West*, 14 (Spring 1972), 5-24.

Tate, Michael L. "Pershing's Punitive Expedition: Pursuer of Bandits or Presidential Panacea?" *The Americas*, 32 (July 1975), 46-71.

Tyler, Ronnie C. "The Little Punitive Expedition in the Big Bend." *Southwestern Historical Quarterly*, 78 (January 1975), 271-91.

Vigil, Ralph H. "Revolution and Confusion: The Peculiar Case of José Inés Salazar." *New Mexico Historical Review*, 53 (April 1978), 145-70.

White, E. Bruce. "The Muddied Waters of Columbus, New Mexico." *The Americas*, 32 (July 1975), 72-98.

Index

166 · *Texas and the Mexican Revolution*

Don M. Coerver received his B.A. and M.A. degrees from Southern Methodist University and his Ph.D. in Latin American history from Tulane University. Active in a number of professional associations, he is former president of the Southwestern Historical Association. His articles have appeared in a variety of publications, including *The Americas*, *The American Jewish Historical Quarterly*, *Inter-American Economic Affairs*, and *Historia Mexicana*. Author of a monographic study of the early years of the Porfiriato, Professor Coerver is also a contributing editor to the Handbook of Latin American Studies and is a consultant to the Hispanic Division of the Library of Congress. He currently serves as chairman of the History Department and professor of Latin American and business history at Texas Christian University in Fort Worth, Texas.

Linda B. Hall received her M.Phil. and Ph.D. degrees in Latin American History from Columbia University. She lived for several years in Colombia, South America, where she taught at the Universidad de los Andes in Bogotá and at the Universidad del Valle in Cali. Her previous publications on Latin American history and literature include a book, *Alvaro Obregón: Power and Revolution in Mexico, 1911-1920*, and numerous articles in such journals as *The Hispanic American Historical Review*, *The Southwest Review*, *The Historian*, *The Journal of the West*, and *Historia Mexicana*. She is an associate professor in the Department of History at Trinity University, where she also serves as director of the Inter-American Studies Program.